FIGHT BACK

Also by G. Gordon Liddy

Will: The Autobiography of G. Gordon Liddy
Out of Control
The Monkey Handlers
When I Was a Kid, This Was a Free Country

FIGHT BACK!

TACKLING TERRORISM, LIDDY STYLE

G. Gordon Liddy

CDR James G. Liddy, US Navy SEAL (ret.)

J. Michael Barrett

Dr. Joel Selanikio, M.D.

ST. MARTIN'S GRIFFIN

NEW YORK

www.stmartins.com

Book design by Ellen Cipriano

Library of Congress Cataloging-in-Publication Data

Liddy, G. Gordon.
    Fight back : tackling terrorism, Liddy style / G. Gordon Liddy . . . [et al.].
        p. cm.
    ISBN-13: 978-0-312-36438-0
    ISBN-10: 0-312-36438-5
    1. Terrorism—United States. 2. Terrorism—United States—Prevention. 3. Security systems—United States. 4. Assistance in emergencies—United States. 5. Emergency management—United States.

HV6432.F535 2006
363.320973—dc22

2005044608

First St. Martin's Griffin Edition: January 2007

10 9 8 7 6 5 4 3 2 1

This book is dedicated to the passengers and crew of United Airlines flight 93, the fourth plane hijacked on September 11, 2001. With a target believed to have been the Capitol or the White House, they averted a national disaster by choosing to Fight Back. We salute you.

CONTENTS

PART III   Emergency Response Handbook   203

PREFACE
PERSONAL SECURITY
IN TROUBLED TIMES

Change is the only constant . . .

HERACLITES

We live in an era of ever-changing threats to our security, both collectively and individually. Security experts of all persuasions agree that radical Islamic terrorists continue to strive to carry out further and more spectacular terrorist attacks against the American homeland, to include assaults involving chemical, biological, or nuclear weapons. At the same time it is understood by terrorism experts that the nature of the threat will split, developing simultaneously along a parallel track that is marked by a greater number of smaller incidents such as the suicide bomber attacks on London's subway and bus systems, shooting sprees in well-populated areas, and heinous, nearly unimaginable hostage takings like the 2004 Chechen terrorists' takeover of an elementary school in Beslan, Russia. Your response to the terrorist threat will be dictated by your answer to a single question: Do you believe each new day brings you one day farther from September 11, 2001, or one day closer to the next terrorist event?

Threats to individual health and safety, however, extend well beyond those of radical Islamic terrorism. The ever-widening reach of globalization has seen the gulf between the modern democratic nations and the impoverished populations of the corrupt, undemocratic countries (the "haves" and "have nots") growing at an alarming rate. Coupled with increased travel between the rich and the poor countries, this societal upheaval is resulting in more and more incidents of theft, kidnapping, and murder, often with those from the more developed world falling prey to those left behind in society's transformation. Worse yet, threats to your safety can take place at work or at home, while traveling for business or for pleasure, and may be carried out by people you know well or those you've never met.

Nature offers its own share of threats, especially when the resultant damages are a lack of food, potable water, and the breakdown of civil order. At this writing the tragic effects of hurricane Katrina are just coming to light: rioting, looting, rape, and murder amid the devastation that has taken as yet uncounted lives. Armed gangs and narcotic traffickers firing upon rescue parties and helicopters while hundreds of police turn in their badges or desert their posts are just the begining of the negative effects of such calamitous events.

The cascading economic effects of Katrina will include disruption of oil production, refining, and distribution; natural gas production and distribution; destruction of critical road and rail overland transport; major reduction of water of waterborne transport; potable water and electric power infrastructure destruction; and a regional economic recession that will affect the national economy. Toxic pollution and the protective steps induced by fear of resultant disease will take their toll in slowing recovery operations. Add to this the oft-cited fear of another, near term, naturally occurring influenza pandemic and the causes of concern from natural disasters come into sharp focus.

The answer to these threats, as to the others discussed in this book, will become evident again and again. In this age of increased interdependency, occasioned by reduced redundancy and a mind-set that has substituted dependence upon government for self-reliance, our constant turning to government to solve all our problems has resulted in ever-increasing vulnerabilities. We the people, our elected officials, our private industries, and each individual citizen must understand these vulnerabilities and challenges and use our individual and collective talents and resources to fight back.

Preparedness and awareness are your best defenses, and this book will arm you with both pre-crisis planning solutions and aggressive crisis-response options. Learning to be aware of your environment and taking basic precautions can mean the difference between a close call and significant personal harm. There was a time when such precautions and planning were considered unnecessary. This is no longer the case. Risks of everything from petty thievery to kidnappings for ransom are prevalent, and in this new era Americans are likely to face homicide bombings, sabotage of our industries, and simultaneous attacks involving chemical, biological, or radiological materials. Each person must determine for himself the appropriate mix of individual fighting skills, kidnap response training, and escape-and-evasion planning. Given these threats, anything less than determined individual preparedness is woefully inadequate and could cost you your life or that of a loved one.

—G. Gordon Liddy
James G. Liddy
J. Michael Barrett
Dr. Joel Selanikio

September 2005,
Washington, D.C.

ACKNOWLEDGMENTS

The authors would like to thank each of the editors and publishers who allowed portions of their work and the authors' previous articles to be included in this text. In particular, this includes permission for reprinting sections describing domestic U.S. terrorist threats from the Memorial Institute for the Prevention of Terrorism's "Terrorism Knowledge Base" as well as an article published in the magazine of the American Legislative Exchange Council and several paragraphs of opinion editorials originally published in the *Baltimore Sun* and the *Journal of Commerce*. Last, but certainly not least, we acknowledge the courageous acts of those who quietly go about the business of defending democracy and providing for all Americans the security by which we remain able to live out our lives in freedom.

INTRODUCTION

On just another regular day in New York City, people woke up, kissed their husbands or wives good-bye, dropped their kids off at school, and went to their jobs. Then their lives were torn apart by an attack on their place of work: the World Trade Center. The date was February 26, 1993. Six people were killed and over one thousand injured.

In 1993 al Qaida–trained terrorists also participated in attacks against U.S. soldiers in Mogadishu, Somalia. As chronicled in the movie *Black Hawk Down,* 18 soldiers were killed and 73 wounded, with the body of an American soldier dragged through the streets by Islamic terrorists and local warlords. Two years later, in 1995, a massive plot to bomb twelve U.S.-bound airliners over the Pacific Ocean was disrupted when Khalid Sheik Mohammed's apartment in Manila caught fire and investigators uncovered his plans. Then, in 1998, U.S. Embassies in Kenya and Tanzania were attacked, leaving 224 killed and five thousand wounded. Then, on October of 2000, al Qaida struck the USS *Cole,* killing seventeen sailors and wounding thirty.

Consider that from the time of the first World Trade Center attack in 1993 until September 11, 2001, it took terrorists eight years to bring down the Towers. It took nineteen men from four countries aboard four hijacked airplanes to achieve that objective. It cost us over 3,000 lives and the terrorists' success seems only to have emboldened them.

Having survived more than four years since the last domestic attack, many Americans are beginning to wonder if future attacks will even affect them and whether they are something for which they need to prepare. If, as virtually all the national security experts have postulated, the terrorists have not relinquished their desire for mass-casualty attacks, then there will be more major attacks and you most certainly *will* be affected. *Your* place of work may not be attacked; *your* community may not be attacked; *your* industry may not be attacked; but *our* country and *our* economy will be, and the ripple effect will be felt by each and every one of us.

This is obvious when one considers the interrelatedness of the various systems of our modern world. The communications networks are the backbone of modern commerce. They rely heavily on the national power supply, which in turn relies on other critical nodes. The interstate commerce system relies on safe and open highways and on a dependable nationwide supply of fuel. Our economy and our food supply need controlled and safe borders and ports.

Consider maritime shipping. Every year millions upon millions of containers are moved globally, and only a small percentage of these containers are inspected at various countries' borders. The U.S. government has developed new initiatives to address this failure by inspecting cargo at the world's largest (and therefore most modern) ports. All well and good, but what about the smaller ports, those in underdeveloped nations, where smuggling is more of a way of life and where national controls over shipping are the least effective? The U.S. plan does not address the problems presented by those ports. Moreover, even today no more than 6 percent of maritime cargo is ever inspected by U.S. Customs. Accordingly, when the very real threat of terrorism presents itself again on the shores of the United States, it will affect our otherwise relatively free and open society, our economy, and all of our lives in profound ways.

Our enemies have observed the history of the past fifteen years and realize that they cannot go head-to-head with the United States and expect to win. The United States possesses the most powerful military in the history of the world. Period. So how will the weak challenge the strong? They will challenge us through adaptation, evolution, and attacks using weapons of mass destruction (WMD) or unconventional tools like airplanes and truck bombs. History has taught us this many times. In turn, we too must adapt, even evolve, and fight back in order to save our country and our way of life. Remember this: The terrorists' greatest asset is the ability to instill fear. If you follow the strategies in this book you can deny them that, and in the process deny it to anyone else who intends to do you, your family, or your community harm.

Think about it: What would happen post–9/11 if five people stood up in the aisle of an airplane and tried to take over the plane with box cutters? Half the passengers would stand up and beat them senseless, just as did the heroes of United Airlines flight 93 that crashed in Pennsylvania because the passengers refused to go quietly into the night. That is how you fight terrorism—you get prepared, you pay attention to what happens around you, and you deny the terrorists the ability to control you through fear. This book gives you a game plan to prepare yourself and those close to you to *fight back*.

If we are wise, let us prepare for the worst.

—GEORGE WASHINGTON

PART ONE

KNOW YOUR ENEMY

ONE

▼

Understanding the Terrorist Threat

It is not the strongest of the species
that survive, nor the most intelligent, but the one
most responsive to change.

CHARLES DARWIN

*T*en days ago a seemingly typical Asian family of four departed their recently adopted home of Southampton, England, for a six-day westbound transatlantic cruise aboard the famed Queen Mary II, docking in New York City. The forty-year-old Indonesian engineer, his thirty-five-year-old wife, and their twin sixteen-year-old daughters began exhibiting severe flulike symptoms halfway across the Atlantic.

The daughters were pale with temperatures of 103°F, but the shipboard medical facility's physical exam results were otherwise normal. The girls were presumed to have a viral infection and were instructed to drink fluids and take aspirin or ibuprofen for muscle aches. The father was also ill, suffering from severe lower backache, headache, shaking chills, and vomiting. He had a temperature of 102°F and a pale rash on his face. A preliminary diagnosis of dengue fever was made, and he was instructed to drink fluids and take ibuprofen.

Every effort was made to comfort them, including being seen by both the ship's medical officer and a half dozen doctors who happened to be vacationing aboard *themselves. Upon reaching New York City all three of the stricken family members were taken to a hospital and by the next day they were exhibiting red, vesicular rashes on their faces and arms and appeared acutely ill. Their temperatures ranged from 102° to 104°F, though their blood pressures remained normal. Another presumptive diagnosis was made, this time for adult chicken pox. Laboratory blood tests were run.* [1]

Unbeknownst to the family, now distraught with fear over what could be happening to them, the enemy had already accomplished their "mission." The family had been unwittingly infected by the father's brother, a medical doctor and member of Jemaah Islamiya, a known al Qaida affiliate and radical Islamic faction that had killed 202 westerners by carrying out the Bali bombings in 2002. The brother, who had helped pay for the family's vacation, had visited them in England just before their trip to America and had insisted on giving the family what he called "booster shots" to keep them healthy during their trip.

All told, the father, mother, and two daughters infected, in just under a week, nearly a fifth of the cruise ships' 3,251 passengers and crew, who themselves disembarked and boarded planes for dozens of cities in the United States and Canada, not to mention the practicing medical doctors who had been passing the disease on to some of their unsuspecting patients for the following several days. Word of the smallpox outbreak would spread when Americans turned on the evening news and learned about the beginning of the end of life as they knew it.

The government would respond the only way it could, by replacing the now seemingly benign Patriot Act with a new National Safety and Survival Act, which would include the lawfully imposed forcible quarantine of several major American cities and the immediate cessation of all interstate commerce. The Canadian and Mexican borders would be closed, and all air, sea, and international shipments and international travel options would be closed to Americans.

All this makes the abnormalities of the post–9/11 world seem downright genteel and leaves people wondering what more they could have done to prepare themselves for such events in the years that followed September 11, 2001, the wake-up call that all too few understood.

---

[1] Medical aspects of this scenario were derived from Dr. Tara O'Toole's article "Smallpox: An Attack Scenario" in *Emerging Infections Disease* 5, no. 4 (July–August 1999) at www.cdc.gov/ncided/EID/vol5no4/otoole.htm.

What is smallpox? Smallpox is a serious disease caused by a virus. It occurs naturally in animals and there is concern that smallpox virus could be obtained and used by terrorists.

How does it spread? Through coughs and sneezes, direct skin contact with an open wound or infected sores, and contaminated bed linens or clothing. People with smallpox are most contagious during the first week of illness, before symptoms appear.

What are the symptoms? Between seven and seventeen days after exposure, an infected person usually develops high fever, fatigue, headache, and backache. A rash usually appears on the mouth, face, and forearms and then spreads to the chest and stomach.

How is it prevented/treated? There is no known cure for smallpox. The immediate vaccination of people exposed to smallpox can prevent the disease or reduce its severity.

What are the government's response procedures? Patients are isolated, and persons who may have been exposed are quarantined to prevent spread of the disease. Although in most cases isolation and quarantine are voluntary, federal, state, and local governments have authority to compel isolation and quarantine to protect the general public.

*Adapted from *Public Health Emergencies: What You Can Do to Prepare* by the Rhode Island Department of Health.

FIGHT BACK

In the months and years since that fateful Tuesday morning in 2001, dozens of scenarios like the one above have been discussed in the public domain by experts both inside and outside of government, each frighteningly real and most of them shockingly plausible.[2] Hundreds more classified scenarios have been studied by intelligence and counterterrorism specialists at the Central Intelligence Agency (CIA); Department of Homeland Security (DHS); Federal Bureau of Investigation (FBI); the Pentagon; and elsewhere. Even Hollywood has gotten into the act with

[2]For additional detailed scenarios on the breadth of the threat we face, see *America the Vulnerable* by Stephen Flynn of the Council of Foreign Relations (NewYork: Harper Collins, 2004); "Smallpox: An Attack Scenario" by Dr. Tara O'Toole of Johns Hopkins, www.cdc.gov/ncidod/EID/vol5no4/otoole.htm; and "Ten Years Later," *The Atlantic Monthly* (January/February 2005), www.theatlantic.com/doc/prem/200501/clarke, "Infrastructure Protection," by Richard A. Clarke, former National Coordinator for Security and Counterterrorism.

television shows like Fox's *24,* scripting bioterrorism, kidnappings, and nuclear power plant attacks; and HBO films' excellent 2005 film *Dirty War,* which chronicles the events of a dirty bomb being set off in downtown London.

Many of the more severe of these threats—the chemical, biological, and nuclear attack scenarios—are also the ones we know al Qaida and others continue to work on, including variants of the "smallpox martyr" scenario above and the purchase of so-called "suitcase nukes" from the former Soviet Union. The nightmare scenarios of Hollywood have become our reality, and many of us believe the future of the "War on Terrorism" is increasingly dark, at least in the near term. Yet these simulations, war games, and screenplays all leave something to be desired, for none of them have had the effect to drive true, aggressive, and sufficient reform of our current security posture.

The Liddy Approach

Every American will continue to be affected by the scourge of international terrorism, as well as a whole host of lesser natural and man-made disasters, including such threats as mad cow disease, avian flu, earthquakes, and hurricanes. This fact is redefining life as we know it, affecting everything from airport security to the government's budget priorities and relations with other nations, both friend and foe alike. Fortunately the actions one takes in defeating the risks posed by terrorists are in many cases the same actions that reduce the risks of being affected by other threats. Absent the terrorist threat, some of the security measures outlined in this book may not be required; but given the reality of the terrorists' goals and intentions, these measures are nothing less than essential for protecting yourself and your loved ones.

Contrary to a popular but self-defeatist belief, individuals *do* have options when it comes to preparing for and dealing with terrorism, including mass-casualty events and attacks employing chemical, biological, or nuclear weapons. The Liddy approach is to FIGHT BACK, a strategy built on the core belief that what makes this country great is that individual Americans can and will act aggressively in defending themselves, their loved ones, and their way of life. Red Cell Associates, a specialized security-and-risk-mitigation solutions firm, has identified an approach to individual and collective homeland security that follows two distinct but related paths: *Deter, Defend* and *Respond, Recover.*™

> **Deter, Defend** encompasses the whole range of actions that deter terrorists—and, in the process, most other criminals—from targeting you, your company, or your community by improving your defenses to withstand and counter such an event should it occur. This includes improving exterior lighting or using defensive landscaping and design plans to reduce your risk at home or in the office.
>
> **Respond, Recover** describes the solutions that prepare you for absorbing, surviving, and recovering from those events that do inevitably take place, such as obtaining personal protective equipment; preparing a bag with food, water, and clothing; rehearsing emergency preparedness plans; and developing and testing rigorous business-continuity strategies.

This approach is derived from the process used to secure military and key private-sector critical infrastructures against terrorist threats. The same approach, with adjustments made for lesser threat conditions and more limited resources, applies to all individuals and businesses. It begins with assessing the threats that we all face and determining precisely how and why the threats are relevant to you. This requires understanding what the enemy is doing, how the U.S. government is responding, and how and why these factors affect you, your community, and your way of life. Next, the Liddy approach assesses certain protective measures you can take to reduce your risks at different relative costs in money and effort. Finally, it identifies and implements risk-reduction strategies to achieve one's optimal balance for accepting certain risks while lessening or eliminating others.

What the Enemy Is Doing

What we are witnessing through the growth of International Islamic Fundamentalist jihadi terrorism is a significant shift in the ability of a numerically insignificant number of people to challenge the established world order by harnessing the full potential of modernity and technology. The roots of terrorism and the specifics of some of the primary known groups are discussed more fully in chapter two, but two essential elements about the nature of the terrorist threat to America must be understood at the very outset:

- The threat to our collective well-being from newly empowered substate terrorist groups goes well beyond just al Qaida, and includes everything from other radical Islamic extremist groups to multinational gangs like MS-13, environmental extremists, and domestic hate groups.
- The nature of the attacks we experience will change into new and ever more challenging forms, including not only more mass-casualty chemical, biological, and nuclear attacks but also much more frequent but lower-level suicide and car and truck bombings aimed at the softest available targets.

It is clear that al Qaida is not the only threat to American interests. Prior to 9/11 the Iranian-sponsored Hizbollah had killed more Americans than al Qaida, and all of those deaths were overseas and none involved WMD (weapons of mass destruction) or using airplanes as missiles. Our greatest domestic threat was from American citizens like Timothy McVeigh and millennial and other apocalyptic cults operating right here at home. Today, with the justifiable concentration on the direct al Qaida threat, we have fewer resources to devote to monitoring these other threats.

Similarly, it is clear from enemy interrogations, media leaks of classified intelligence, and public pronouncements by the terrorists themselves that al Qaida and certain affiliates continue to plan to carry out "spectacular" attacks in the mold of 9/11. But historically terrorists have relied on much more modest—albeit more frequent—conventional attacks using explosive-laden cars, trucks, or even people. The weapons of choice for the hate groups and most other terrorist organizations are fully automatic rifles and truck bombs. As a result it is only sensible to conclude that our collective future will be shaped by two terrorist threats, not just one: the first will follow the scale, if not the specifics, of the mass casualty 9/11 attack or of the WMD scenario with which this book opens. If history is any guide, such attacks will be carried out every four to six years (and yes, that means that as of the writing of this book we are just about due for the next major attack!). At the same time a secondary method of attack will also migrate to America's shores—that of the suicide bomber or small group of gunmen, who could easily conceal themselves in the midst of the hundreds of thousands of illegal aliens overrunning our southern border annually.

This second branch of the terrorist threat, which is less sophisticated in its execution but still quite deadly and with potentially devastating economic and civil liberty repercussions, requires none of the college education, flight training, or ability to patiently assimilate displayed by Mohammed Atta and the rest of the 9/11 killers. Instead, its practitioners resemble the HAMAS and Hizbollah suicide bombers more familiar to Israel, Lebanon, and, more recently, Iraq. These attacks require only knowledge of the techniques being developed today in each of the above countries (and those that support them) and access to a cache of fully automatic rifles or to a cell-phone trigger device coupled with an explosives-laden vehicle. The government, much as it is trying to defeat this threat, simply will not be able to stop the waves of multiple, near-simultaneous, low-signature suicide attacks. It can't be prepared everywhere and all times, and therefore at least some of these smaller attacks are likely to succeed.

The July 7, 2005, suicide attacks on the London underground serve as a stark example that indeed there remains a significant threat to life as we used to know it, prior to this new chapter of Islamic Fundamentalist aggression. Three of the attackers were of Pakistani descent but had been born and raised in the United Kingdom, with the fourth having been born in Jamaica and a later convert to Islam. The explosions killed 56 and wounded 700 more. The bomber's backpacks were filled with explosives, nails, and ball bearings—the latter ingredients used to ensure that deadly projectiles claimed even more victims. Of particular note is the fact that all of the ingredients were apparently of common origin, versus consisting of specific military or specialized ingredients. The same was true of the four bombs used in the failed follow-on attacks two weeks later in which the bombs failed to detonate.

This trend of home-grown suicide bomber tactics should not come as a surprise, though at present our preparations for and defenses against it are woefully lacking. It is not surprising, therefore, that risk management has become an increasingly popular topic since the advent of the global war on terrorism, and all the more so since Michael Chertoff, the new secretary of the Department of Homeland Security, announced his intention to enforce a national policy of risk-based threat mitigation, declaring, "Everything is a tradeoff. . . . You will inevitably place money in different places . . . and we [DHS] have to judge, based on consequence, vulnerability, and threat, where to put those resources. . . . [T]he private sector will have to incorporate into its menu of responsibilities preparations for and an ability to respond to acts of violence and acts of terrorism."[3]

Consider that the Israel Defense Forces (IDF) estimate that they stop between 94 and 96 percent of the suicide bombers and gunmen attacking their country. This means the IDF, who have by far the most experience and the most surveillance and detention authority of the various Western governments fighting terrorism, is successful the vast majority of the time, a fairly astounding record in the high-ninety percentile of effectiveness. Similarly, the United Kingdom believes it was approximately 90 percent effective in disrupting Irish Republican Army (IRA) paramilitary attacks in the 1980s. But the effect of the few attacks that slip through can be truly devastating, literally altering the fabric of the democratic society within which the attacks take place.

How Is the U.S. Government Responding?

The U.S. government has reacted aggressively to the threat of international terrorism, although with mixed results. This especially is true overseas, where daring military policies led to stunning victories in Afghanistan and tactically, if not yet strategically, in Iraq. But the away game has gone more smoothly than the home game. Domestically the United States has responded to terrorism in a confused, conflicting, and inefficient manner. This

---

[3]Remarks by Secretary Chertoff, Department of Homeland Security, National Public Radio, "Challenges to Homeland Security," March 16, 2005, at www.npr.org/templates/story/story.php?storyId=4537004. See also "Chertoff Details Risk-Analysis Approach to Security, March 16, 2005, at www.npr.org/templates/story/story.php?storyId=4537007.

is perhaps not surprising given that the nature of the enemy and the threat are ill-defined, our laborious and multiagency bureaucracy is ill-equipped to deal with rapidly evolving threats, and the worthy prerogatives of states' rights and civil liberties are ill-suited to the realities of low-occurrence but high-severity events like mass-casualty terrorism. Nonetheless, the United States remains unprepared in dramatic ways and is unlikely to fix existing gaps in security absent further incidents.

The government's troubles in domestic preparedness partially stem from the failure to engage the U.S. private sector and the American public in becoming responsible for their own security. The government's course was a paternalistic one, characterized by the fear of imminent attack and re-markable for its "get-back-to-normal, we'll-handle-it" attitude. This was understandable in terms of the immediate need to get the economy moving, but it was predicated on a fatal flaw: the belief that government could organize itself and improve interagency cooperation before the inertia of the bureaucratic battles began to outweigh the overriding sense of urgency to accomplish the mission.

This was coupled with a "spend whatever's-necessary" approach to homeland security in which the usual special interests and the requirement to spread money evenly has resulted in higher-risk areas receiving signifi-cantly less money per capita than remote and unlikely targets. At the same time, the various private-sector lobbying groups have been quick to claim that the costs of security should not be borne by them alone, and that the government should provide the money to pay for the increased burdens of security in the post–9/11 world. Fair arguments can be made on both sides of this argument, depending on whether one feels the government is responsi-ble for the security of "common usage goods," like the free market flow of goods, or if various industries ought to have to bear the costs of increased safety alone. But at the end of the day, in most instances, we have been left with a thin veneer of industries engaging in "voluntary self-regulation" that is marginally effective and piecemeal in its implementation.

In addition, despite the purchase of much first-responder equipment and training, unfortunately the state and local governments have proven largely incapable of receiving, prioritizing, and spending the federally ap-propriated monies. Indeed, many news reports from CNN, *The Washington*

Post, and others have concluded that by early 2005 as much as 80 percent of the previous fiscal year's homeland security money remained unspent!

TYPES OF THREATS:

- International terrorists
- Domestic terrorists
- Disgruntled or former employees
- Criminals/computer hackers
- Activists/pressure groups
- Industrial espionage

It must be stated in the government's defense that those in power correctly acted on the reasonable premise that we were under imminent threat of additional attacks. Decisions and preparations were made at a breakneck pace, especially in the immediate aftermath of the WTC attacks; and though even President Bush declared this would be "a marathon, not a sprint," initial efforts were understandably being run at a sprinter's pace. Government officials therefore had to devise emergency funding plans and identify priorities in terms of achieving immediate results. To take a simple example, this meant making decisions, such as hiring many more security guards, rather than taking the time to assess overall needs, install or upgrade equipment, and rewrite security protocols. Even when effective, these measures were not efficient and therefore unsustainable in the long term. Extra guards provide additional security only once, during the specific hours they are present. Critical as this may be, in the long run it is always suboptimal compared to systemic security improvements because upgrading systems, rewriting protocols, and increasing training and drills have effects that last beyond the immediate guard shift.

In sum, the government's response to the terrorist menace has been acceptable, and even laudable, because the next event was believed to be imminent. Where the government has really stumbled is in the transition from the pace of the sprint to that of the marathon, from the reactionary immediate postattack activities to the more deliberate long-haul domestic security strategies.

How This Affects You

Understanding how the U.S. government has and has not prepared the nation for future attacks is critical in determining how and to what degree you will become responsible for your own security. The government is spending billions of dollars looking for clues and chasing down leads to prevent al Qaida terrorist attacks. However, the game is one of resources versus threats, and the reality is that the government has to accept risks in certain areas in order to focus on others. Also, the government has the mandate to save the most lives, without distinguishing between you and anyone else. As a result the federal government has to provide equal protection to all citizens in the nation, including those in less-threatened areas and smaller communities. Therefore, as the government is looking to prevent the next major attack, they are less focused on preventing a myriad of smaller events. This justifiably results in the government focusing more on chemical, biological, and nuclear threats than on car bombs or smaller-scale threats because the former will have a higher per-incident toll in terms of death and destruction.

CRITICAL INFRASTRUCTURE SECTORS

- Agriculture
- Banking and Finance
- Chemical Industry/HazMat
- Defense Industrial Base
- Emergency Services
- Energy
- Food
- Government
- Information/Telecommunications
- Postal and Shipping
- Public Health
- Transportation
- Water

The government is also hampered by the very nature of being a large bureaucracy wherein, almost by definition, it all too often finds itself reacting to previous events rather than anticipating future threats. This is what enables the terrorists to stay several steps ahead of our efforts and is in part why there continues to be an inordinate focus on airport security with relatively paltry attention paid to rail and port security, the disruption of which would have dire economic and international trade consequences. Sadly the government will not be able to get ahead of the emergent trends. Fortunately, when you understand and recognize the trends before they materialize, you can take extra measures in advance to protect yourself.

Critical Infrastructure Interdependencies

Perhaps the most significant shortfall in national preparedness efforts is in understanding, defining, and mitigating the interrelated failures of critical infrastructures when any single segment of the chain is affected. The term "critical infrastructure" refers to thirteen interrelated sectors of the economy that together make up its very lifeblood, including the telecommunications that enable global commerce, the defense systems we rely on for security, the energy we need to live (gas, electric, and nuclear), the food and water we consume, the industrial base that enables manufacturing, and the commercial transportation networks that deliver all of those goods, including ports, bridges, and tunnels. These sectors are deemed critical because they are essential to "the minimum operations of the economy and the government."[4] Yet their interoperability and interdependencies remain poorly understood, as do the cascading effects on various sectors that will accompany the incapacitation of any other sector.

Since 9/11 the government has begun more aggressively to explore these complex and interdependent infrastructures. Although DHS is still struggling to find solutions to the myriad problems, it worked with the Homeland Security Council in July 2004 to at least better describe the risks, concluding:

> The effect of disasters on national, state, and local transportation, communication, medical, and utility infrastructure will have a considerable effect on response strategies. As on 9/11, when the entire civilian air transportation system and much of the national telecommunications system were shut down or disabled, a terrorist incident may have repercussions that affect critical infrastructures necessary for coherent emergency response. These critical networks must be layered and properly coordinated across both civilian and military sectors to ensure the continuity of critical infrastructure support for responding jurisdictions.[5]

The initial recognition of the vulnerabilities inherent in our highly interdependent economic model first came to light at the federal level in the wake of the 1995 bombing of the Alfred P. Murrah Federal Building in Okla-

---

[4]Presidential Decision Directive 63 (PDD 63), May 1998 at www.fas.org/irp/offdocs/pdd-63.htm.
[5]"Planning Scenarios: Executive Summaries," The Homeland Security Council, by David Howe, senior director for Response and Planning, July 2004, at www.globalsecurity.org/security/library/report/2004/hsc-planning-scenarios-jul04.htm.

CASE STUDY: NORTHEAST BLACKOUT

On the afternoon of Thursday, August 14, 2003, twenty-one power plants shut down in just three minutes, causing trains, elevators, and the flow of traffic in eight American states and portions of Canada to come to a sudden stop. In New York City some forty thousand police officers and firefighters were called to duty, and a state of emergency was declared to mobilize additional state police. It took almost three hours to evacuate passengers from stalled subway trains. Water supplies in Michigan were affected by a failure in the electric-powered pumps. And while initial fears turned to terrorism, or to the "blaster" computer virus, which had that week been spreading across the Internet, in the end it turned out that the massive power outage had been caused by a series of unrelated and seemingly insignificant events, beginning with a brush fire that disabled a transmission line south of Columbus, Ohio. Total economic effect: an estimated $6 billion.

homa City. The attack demonstrated how the loss of a single strategically insignificant federal building created a ripple effect across multiple agencies by destroying a regional payroll center and an FBI field office (and all the specialized investigative files it held), among other government offices.[6] The vulnerability of our interconnectedness began to crystallize in the minds of people in both the public and private sectors and the concerns that were raised created a desire to examine the potentially catastrophic cascading effects of infrastructure failures. President Clinton responded to this need through Executive Order 13010, which created the President's Commission on Critical Infrastructure Protection (PCCIP) to explore the concept of critical infrastructures and national security.

The threat to critical infrastructure is analogous to what was feared would result from the Y2K computer concerns. When Y2K proved to be essentially a "nonevent," however, complacency set in about the risks to the nation's water, electrical, transportation, and key industries. Despite a decade of effort and the additional impetus of the terrorist threat to our nation, not only are security measures still broadly insufficient, but our understanding of the interdependencies among, for example, the railway, port, and energy industries, remains elementary. As a result the next significant event (be it nature, negligence, or terrorism) could potentially and

[6]Critical Infrastructure Protection Oral History Project, available at www.echo.gmu.edu/CIPP/essay.

needlessly affect many more thousands of Americans than would otherwise be the case.

Terrorism's Effect on Businesses

The 9/11 attacks affected all Americans in a myriad of ways, but one of the least understood is the way it affected businesses across the country, and indeed across the world. Direct effects were felt by at least fifteen thousand area businesses, and some 13.4 million square feet of real estate were damaged or otherwise affected. But there were other less direct costs that rippled throughout the economy as well, such as the five Ford Motor Company U.S.-based manufacturing plants left temporarily idle because in the immediate aftermath of the attacks and the enhanced border control and security protocols they prompted, parts suppliers in Canada could not get their goods across the border in a timely fashion.

Terrorism-related concerns for businesses range from outright destruction of production facilities or the death of key personnel to creating friction in supply-chain deliveries and slumps in sales cycles because of national grief. Without sounding cold or uncaring, businesses must find a means to put away the emotional and personal response to tragedy and focus on resuming operations as quickly as possible. This process is tremendously improved when pre-event planning and strategizing have been used to develop a coherent response plan. Even if the plan is not directly applicable or the catastrophe is beyond the scope of the plan, the value of having a guidebook and of having gone through the process to develop the plan will prove invaluable. Indeed, as the military saying goes: "No plan is worth much, but the planning process is invaluable."

For the most part businesses can take rational decisions at almost any cost about how to price their products and compete in the market. The uncertainty of the effect from terrorist events, however, causes incorrect pricing and over- or undersupply of goods and people, as well as suboptimal cash flow and investment decisions. This uncertainty is at the heart of the issues facing the business community.

Many critical questions arise in the case of terrorism. Who is the bill payer for the damages that occur? Will insurance companies cover the incident, and at what level will the catastrophic cap be met, such that the government will begin to compensate for losses? Will insurance be able to absorb the costs? Will travel or other affected economic sectors recover quickly? Will normative venues for commerce (shopping malls, public gatherings, public transport) be affected or impaired or unusable? Who will pay to cover costs in the meantime, until the government or insurance company funds begin to flow? Significantly, is the current approach stable, especially if there are many more attacks, or will the government or the insurance industry change the rules midstream?

Consider the other ambiguous facets of terrorism and the concerns it creates. The level of threat is ambiguous, even for companies outside of major cities, for as major cities become better prepared, the risk shifts to softer targets. There are little or no actuarial data for terrorism that are likely to be of relevance for the next event, and unlike nature there is neither a "high season" nor any clearly more likely locus for future attacks.

Small businesses, too, were hit quite hard by 9/11, and their resources were often insufficient to cover the cost of recovery and resumption of operations. By some accounts as many as six hundred small businesses in the World Trade Center complex, and as many as another thousand more in New York City and beyond, were driven out of business by the attack. This is in keeping with a Federal Emergency Management Agency (FEMA) assertion that almost half of all small businesses that experience a significant disaster are put out of business within two years.[7]

The issues get even more complicated when one examines the potential devastation that can be wrought by industry-wide or systemic failures and the cascading effects thereof. In our ever-more-interconnected world, other unforeseen but all-too-real risks are prevalent all along a business's value chain, which includes everything from the suppliers and transportation providers who deliver raw materials to your firm to the banking and finance houses that enable point-of-sale, credit-card transactions and the transportation nodes that foster online shopping with home delivery. For in-

[7]Mark Sauter, *Homeland Security* (New York: McGraw Hill, 2005), p. 332.

stance, a survey by Strategic Research Corporation found that a breakdown in the credit-card, sales-authorization system would cost some $2.6 million per hour, and the effect of a major service outage would cost brokerage operations up to $6.5 million per hour. Such issues could affect any industry, anywhere, and at any time.

As an additional concern, in the wake of the auditing and corporate scandals that rocked the business community in 2001 and 2002, congressional legislation like Sarbanes-Oxley now requires that firms certify compliance with "best practices" and understand and take responsibility for accounting for risk, which can be interpreted as implicitly including responsibility for business continuity in the face of adverse events, including terrorism. Businesses must therefore consider their vulnerabilities with respect to all manner of disruptive events, including not only how directly felt events may affect them but also how failures of peer competitors may trigger industry regulation or how sustained damage to the nation's infrastructure may alter their profit-and-loss equations.

THAT'S THE THREAT. SO NOW WHAT?

When one combines the enemy's declared intent to damage the American economy, their known willingness to inflict civilian casualties, various overseas attacks on Western interests, and the irrefutable evidence of al Qaida conducting WMD research, it becomes clear that all Americans, everywhere, remain at grave risk. Further, it is certain that future attacks will affect us all because of the interrelated nature of our critical infrastructure.

Fortunately, individuals and businesses alike can take an array of specific actions to improve their likelihood of surviving future attacks. This book begins by taking a deeper look at the enemy, their motivations, and their tactics. It then offers a methodology for understanding how to assess your own risks, explains personal-security preparedness alternatives, and offers practical guidance on actively addressing workplace emergency preparedness and making appropriate facility-design choices. Next, it offers specific advice for executives and others who may face a heightened risk of kidnapping, and offers overall conclusions and recommendations on where to look for further study. Finally, secure in the belief that during a crisis is no time to begin searching the Internet for answers to how to respond, the latter third of the book contains a detailed response guide for individual or institutional responses to chemical, biological, radiological, or nuclear attack.

TWO

▼

How Terrorists Attack the International Order

The ruling to kill the Americans and their allies—civilians and military—is an individual duty for every Muslim who can do it in any country in which it is possible to do it, in order to liberate the al-Aqsa Mosque and the holy mosque [Mecca] from their grip, and in order for their armies to move out of all the lands of Islam, defeated and unable to threaten any Muslim.

OSAMA BIN LADEN ET AL., IN THE WORLD ISLAMIC FRONT'S STATEMENT

"JIHAD AGAINST JEWS AND CRUSADERS," 1998

THE SCOPE OF THE THREAT

The threat of Islamic extremist terrorists striking the United States and its allies is real, acknowledged by experts from across the political spectrum and throughout the Western world. Police in a dozen European countries have arrested suspects from al Qaida or its affiliates. We know the enemy is actively recruiting "blue-eyed Islamists" and others who don't fit the profile of the 9/11 hijackers, and that the threat extends throughout the so-called arc of instability, an area that runs from the Caucasus and Western Africa across Southwest Asia and as far to the east as Malaysia. And while the many months without an attack on U.S. soil since 9/11 is laudable, it is but a blink of the eye in terms of the terrorists' timeline, where the struggle between Islam and the West is seen in terms of centuries, not months.

Somewhere in the world, right now, analysis of the history of terrorism tells us that a group of five to ten or more Islamic extremists are gathered in an apartment, a mosque, or a madrassa, and they are plotting a blow even more devastating than that of September 11, 2001. If particularly sophisticated, or lucky, they may possess one of the "suitcase nukes" missing from Russia's Cold War–era arsenal. Or perhaps they have learned to better employ their chemical or biological weapons, such as the deadly gas tested on a dog in footage discovered in Afghanistan and widely replayed on CNN and other news networks. More likely, this group is planning to hijack and destroy a shipment of toxic industrial chemicals moving by rail, sea, or truck or to carry out simultaneous dirty bomb attacks (explosives mixed with a low-yield radiological source like those discarded after use in medical or university laboratories) that could cripple our economy and our way of life. Such an attack might result in tens of thousands of deaths and untold economic devastation.

This threat assessment is openly acknowledged by the intelligence community to be accurate, and the United States should be working more effectively to deter "the next 9/11." This is all the more important as the world perceives that we are too distracted by Iraq to counter aggression elsewhere.

The next strike may come from al Qaida, or it may come from a Sunni copycat group inspired by bin Laden's perceived successes, or perhaps even a Shi'i group that is linked to a state sponsor such as Iran or Syria. Or it could come from one of the numerous sects in Asia, such as Indonesia's Jemaah Islamiyah. Let's examine these three scenarios and the United States's response options and effects in turn.

If a significant attack occurs and is linked to bin Laden, the United States will almost certainly cross into Pakistan militarily to capture or kill the senior leaders believed to be hiding in the northwestern provinces. The Pakistan military, to its credit, is conducting operations, albeit sporadically, but to date there have been all too few results. Meanwhile, press accounts detail how this area is now an al Qaida safe haven, a post–9/11 version of what Afghanistan once was. In the wake of a catastrophic attack, the United States would move decisively to eliminate the threat, accepting the potentially destabilizing effect this may have on President Musharraf's regime.

In the case of a Shi'i-sponsored attack, the most likely scenario is a Tehran-sponsored attack carried out by the terrorist wing of Hizbollah. Here, the United States would have to find proof, convince allies of the connections, and would still have few effective options. Even more complicated would be an attack by a Shi'i-based entity *not* supported by the leadership in Tehran. Not only would the United States be hard pressed to find suitable levers of influence with the mullahs, it would also be unable to violate Iran's sovereignty to strike the enemy hiding within (this scenario will be even more difficult after Iran develops nuclear weapons).

Finally, the next strike could emerge from an unexpected quarter, perhaps Indonesia's Jemaah Islamiyah or another of the small, secretive sects in growing Southeast Asian terrorist hotspots like Bangladesh or Cambodia. Effective, acceptable United States response options are limited because of the difficulty of convincing the world that we are certain of the sponsorship of the attack and the difficulty of tying the actions of the group to the support of the country's government. Nonetheless, if the event is severe enough, the United States will lash out in an attempt to remove the threat, wherever it may be. Though such action must be carried out, it will redouble the enemy's efforts to strike the United States, further increasing our risk here at home. This, sadly, is the backdrop to the insecure situation in which we find ourselves.

AN ATTACK ON THE WORLD ORDER

The very nature of the War on Terrorism presents a dramatic shock to the system of international relations that has dominated the past several centuries, the system that has shaped the development of all modern governments. This is, in part, the reason governments around the world, including the U.S. government, are having great difficulty dealing with this threat. Martin van Creveld, a prominent Israeli historian and military strategist, argued in the early 1990s that warfare was entering a postmodern phase, asserting, "As war between states exits through one side of history's revolving door, low intensity conflict among different organizations will enter through the other. . . . National sovereignties are being undermined by organizations [nonstate actors] that refuse to recognize the state's monopoly over armed violence."[1]

Bruce Hoffman, the noted terrorism scholar for the RAND Corporation, similarly observed that terrorism is, in essence, the rejection of the state's monopoly on the legitimate use of force.[2] This is the reason that terrorist groups, being less centralized and less cohesive than almost all prior significant threats to an established world order, are harder to target with traditional military tools and why the very nature of the conflict means it will spill over into the daily lives of the citizens of the countries whose policies and power are at issue.

This decentralization is why terrorism cannot be defeated by the nation-state alone; instead, its ultimate defeat lies in the collective power of ordinary citizens. The substate nature of terrorist groups dictates the form of their tactics, which will affect each of us much more directly and more often than was the case with a monolithic military threat such as that of the former Soviet Union. The same forces of globalization, innovation, and market segmentation that enabled small airlines like Southwest to displace more established airlines on select routes and have fostered the outsourcing of U.S. services like toll-free assistance telephone lines to India are enabling substate terrorists groups to coordinate their paramilitary actions even without significant state-based resources.

While terrorists could never compete with large, state-sponsored militaries on a traditional battlefield, they don't need to do so. Globalization and communications technologies have removed the time/distance barriers that in the past would have precluded viable global, substate operational coordination. The technology and resources required to pose such systemic international threats simply were not available until the communications and information revolutions altered the equation.

[1]Martin Van Creveld, *The Transformation of War* (New York: The Free Press, 1991).
[2]Bruce Hoffman, "Inside Terrorism" in *Terrorism and Counterterrorism: Understanding the New Security Environment,* Russell D. Howard et al. (McGraw Hill, 2004).

COUNTERTERRORISM CASE: AHMED RESSAM*

On December 14, 1999, Ahmed Ressam, a thirty-four-year-old Algerian, was arrested at Port Angeles, Washington, attempting to enter the United States with components used to manufacture improvised explosive devices. He subsequently admitted that he planned to bomb Los Angeles International Airport on the eve of the Millennium 2000 celebrations.

Forensic scientists from both the Royal Canadian Mounted Police (RCMP) and the FBI examined the evidence in this case. An FBI Laboratory Explosives Unit examiner compared evidence found in Ressam's motel room with items seized in Port Angeles. The RCMP laboratory identified the presence of explosives and developed a DNA profile from a pair of pants and shoes recovered in Ressam's apartment. They also observed several holes in the pants that were consistent with an acid spill. With this information, the FBI Seattle Field Office examined Ressam's legs and discovered a large burn. At the trial, a doctor specializing in burns testified that the burn on Ressam's leg was consistent with an acid burn.

In the FBI Laboratory, a piece of hair was observed on a piece of clear tape inside one of the four time-delay fusing systems. The questioned hair was examined by the Trace Evidence Unit and determined to have the same microscopic characteristics as Ahmed Ressam's hairs.

Latent prints developed on the four timing devices and a map of Los Angeles showing three airports circled were associated with Ressam. A date book, on which thirteen of Ressam's fingerprints were developed, included the addresses of two bin Laden collaborators. It also contained the addresses of the firms that Ressam used to obtain the electronic components and precursor chemicals for the manufacturing of the explosives.

Additionally, credit-card purchases at several electronics shops in Montreal, Canada, were discovered. An Explosives Unit examiner traveled to Canada and purchased the same items, demonstrating to the jury that Ressam could have purchased electronic components that were consistent with the components used in the construction of the time-delay fusing systems recovered in the trunk of the rental vehicle.

After reviewing the items recovered in Montreal and Vancouver, the Explosives Unit examiner obtained several rolls of tape and a small piece of wire insulation for comparison. Subsequently, a forensic chemist determined that the packaging tape and clear tape recovered in Ressam's Montreal apartment were consistent in physical characteristics and chemical composition to those removed from the time-delay fusing systems. Accordingly, the pieces of tape removed from the four time-delay fusing systems could have originated from the roll of packaging tape and clear tape recovered from Ressam's apartment. In addition, a small piece of wire insulation was recovered from the Vancouver motel room. The chemist determined that it was consistent in physical characteristics and chemical composition to the wires used in the time-delay fusing systems.

Ahmed Ressam was tried and convicted in federal court of Conspiring to Commit an Act of International Terrorism and eight related charges. Ressam was sentenced on July 27, 2005, to twenty-two years in prison.

*Adapted from the FBI Web site document "Counterterrorism Case: AHMED RESSAM," at www.fbi.gov/libref/factsfigure/counterterrorism.htm.

The decentralized, networklike characteristic of the enemy and their lack of a cohesive central command further make their actions much less predictable, in turn making their tactics, motivations, and thresholds for violence against civilians all the more malleable than those of traditional nation-states. This fluidity of action and decision thresholds makes deterrence, statesmanship, and preemptive action all the more complex. The international system consequently finds itself closer to a state of anarchy than at any time since the rise of the modern nation-state.

Consider that in dealing with the Soviet Union's nuclear threat during the Cold War, deterrence became the mainstay of U.S. policy. In essence, we knew where they lived, and they knew we knew, so no one wanted to take the first shot. There was, of course, the very real concern that a rogue actor might recklessly trigger a wider conflict, but in retrospect even that was perhaps an exaggerated threat, given the apparent restraint of both sides when it came to actually "pushing the button." Not so with today's terrorist groups.

Low-likelihood but high-consequence events such as chemical, biological, or nuclear attack become all the more plausible because the normative restraints of the established state-based system no longer apply. The only rational response is for individuals, businesses, and communities to prepare for the worst while the government and military work to eradicate the threat at its source.

ROOTS AND MOTIVATIONS OF TERRORISTS

Terrorism is the violent expression of a minority against the majority, the weak against the strong. This current version of the conflict also has come to be seen as East versus West, mostly a clash between the Islamic world, which once ruled the international system, and the Christian world, which has been dominating and expanding rapidly through the march of technological progress. But the basis of the conflict is broader than modern versus ancient or even competing religions. It is in many ways another round of the "haves" versus the "have nots," another external manifestation of the struggle for supremacy among those who profit from the current system and those who are unable to compete effectively in it.

There are myriad reasons for this state of affairs. On the one side, the Islamic militants claim that the United States is "stealing" their precious resources at bargain prices from corrupt rulers and that our cultural hegemony is corrupting their "pure" society. On the other hand, the region's lack of a sustainable approach to economic development has been a major factor in their failure to compete internationally in the global economy. This is especially true in two major areas: the importation of foreign labor, which has precluded development of a homegrown labor force, and the inability to promote economic diversity, resulting in economic overreliance on a single natural resource.

As an influential study by the United Nations, the "Arab Human Development Report 2002," concluded: "Although income poverty is low compared to other parts of the world, the Arab region is hobbled by a different kind of poverty—poverty of capabilities and poverty of opportunities. These have their roots in three deficits: freedom, women's empowerment, and knowledge."[3] In other words, the lack of regional progress can be traced, in large part, to the inability of the people to have a say in how they are ruled, the inability of half the population to have any say at all, and the lack of general knowledge of modern scientific and analytical thought and development.

So at its core the Islamic fundamentalist movement is about something deeper than surface issues of development and political structure or even just a replay of the centuries-old struggle between the Judeo-Christian West and the Islamic East. It is a violent manifestation of a part of the world that feels it is being subjugated by external forces and is now actively lashing out against them. While we reject the flawed thinking behind the militants' rage, the salient fact remains that these underlying factors are unlikely to change in the near term and therefore the enemy will continue to pursue its aims, and do so violently, for years to come.

[3]Executive Summary of the United Nations's "Arab Human Development Report 2002," pages 1–2, available at http://www.rbas.undp.org/ahdr/press_kits2002/PRExecSummary.pdf.

THE NATURE OF AL QAIDA

The decentralized and ever-evolving nature of the al Qaida network, al Qaida–inspired terrorists, and even completely unrelated terrorist groups complicates ascribing what we might normally consider rational motivation to their behavior. In terms of the Islamic-oriented groups, the desire to fulfill aggressively their perceived religious duties further feeds into their rapidly shifting priorities, increasing the difficulty of predicting their future means of attack. But we do have several prominent declarations that indicate the fundamental tenets of the radical Islamist agenda.

Osama bin Laden himself stated in his 1998 declaration of "Jihad Against the Jews and Crusaders" that his major motivation was to "defend Islam" by removing the United States and its allies from the Middle East. The goal of removing the United States is to enable bin Laden's more specific plan to overthrow "apostate" regimes in the Middle East and replace them with religiously "pure" governments that do not separate religion from politics because, according to him and his followers, there essentially is no politics, only religion.

Indeed, bin Laden believes that striking the United States is but a means of achieving his regional goals, asserting it is the U.S. government's policies that require the use of violence to defend Islam. During an interview in November 2001, bin Laden stated: "The American people should remember that they pay taxes to their government, they elect their president, their government manufactures arms and gives them to Israel and Israel uses them to massacre Palestinians. The American Congress endorses all government measures and this proves that the entire America is responsible for the atrocities perpetrated against Muslims. The entire America, because they elect the Congress."

In the same interview bin Laden described his belief that all injured civilians are essentially collateral damage, saying: "In my view, if an enemy occupies a Muslim territory and uses common people as a human shield, then it is permitted to attack that enemy. For instance, if bandits barge into a home and hold a child hostage, then the child's father can attack the bandits and in that attack even the child may get hurt."

Al Qaida and its adherents have even more ambitions plans, however, than simply removing the U.S. influence in the Middle East and displacing regional regimes. As described by the pro-jihad, anti–U.S. English-language Web site "Jihad Unspun," al Qaida's mandate is "to form a pan-Islamic Caliphate throughout the world to overthrow 'non-Islamic' regimes and to expel Westerners and non-Muslims from Muslim countries."[4] The caliphate refers to the broad expansion of an Islamic state, essentially a single theological empire within which there are no state borders and all Muslims live together, shielded from the outside world. As Harvard's Jessica Stern has noted:

> To achieve these shifting goals, the movement aims to create a clash not only among civilizations but also within civilizations. The ultimate objective is to "purify" the world—replacing the "new world order" with a caliphate of terror based on a fantasized simpler, purer past. For professional terrorists, the mission becomes a marketing strategy aimed at dividing and conquering enemies, maximizing adherents, and forging new alliances.[5]

Taken together these insights create a framework for understanding al Qaida's actions, which are rational within their own construct of the West "oppressing Islam" by "stealing its oil" and corrupting its culture by promoting modernity. It also makes it clear why al Qaida targets the U.S. economy and why they are willing to accept all civilian casualties, including Muslim ones, as "collateral damage." Nonetheless, given the strict antimodernity of most of those seeking to implement such a strategy—and the fact that the Islamic caliphate would control vital natural resources presumably stretching from at least southern Spain across the Middle East and North Africa and into Indonesia and beyond—this is clearly not a development that the rest of the world can allow to take place. That is why this clash of civilizations is likely to last a lot longer than most Americans realize.

---

[4]Jihadunspun, at http://www.jihadunspun.com/theplayers/bio/alqaeda.html.
[5]Jessica Stern, "Caliphate of Terror," *Harvard* magazine (July–August 2004), http://www.harvard-magazine.com/on-line/070480.html.

THE CHANGING FACE OF TERROR

One of the most important issues in dealing with terrorism is the fact that our enemy is an organic, adaptive foe who changes its means and methods of operation as quickly as we develop new tactics that affect their existing practices. For example, within days of press reports about U.S. capabilities to eavesdrop on Osama bin Laden's satellite phone, he stopped using these phones and has regressed to complex systems of couriers and so-called "double-blind" messengers, meaning that each link in the chain knows neither the person from whom they received the message nor the person to whom they have passed it. The enemy, learning that we were using its communications channels against him, adapted his behavior to maintain his advantage of freedom of movement.

This crucial aspect is all too often underplayed in both the popular media and ongoing analysis by the intelligence community. Consider the oft-stated fact that the United States and its allies in the War on Terrorism have captured or killed some two-thirds of al Qaida's senior leadership since 9/11. While true, this statement is also irrelevant; if there were a finite supply of replacement leaders, then we would know that we were, in fact, making progress, and that the enemy's command-and-control structure was being degraded with each new victory. However, with a seemingly endless supply of willing jihadists to replace those who are captured or killed, and with a time horizon for the war that will span several decades or more, having rounded up several of them is not necessarily bringing us closer to a state of victory. Of course, attacking the leadership is a valid and worthy goal that needs to be pursued with absolute vigor; but it is just important to realize that the enemy is reactive and able to adapt, lest we become complacent in our analysis of their tactics, trends, and leaders.

THE NEW BREED

This ability to adapt and alter tactics is also the reason that racial profiling for terrorist suspects is not an effective approach. Al Qaida and others have begun the recruitment of new, nontraditional terrorists to carry out their surveillance, reconnaissance, and even their attacks. While we agree with comedian Dennis Miller that "recognizing that 19 of the 19 hijackers on 9/11 were Muslim males is not profiling, it is minimally observant!" the fact remains that the enemy knows the United States and its allies are on the lookout for Middle Eastern males between the ages of twenty and thirty-five. And knowing this they are turning to the farthest reaches of their recruitment base, aiming specifically to find so-called "blue-eyed" Islamists—meaning individuals with more Caucasian features and preferably U.S. or European citizenship, as well as followers throughout Indonesia, Thailand, and elsewhere with a dramatically more Asian, as opposed to Arab, appearance. This is why the threat of alleged dirty bomber, Jose Padilla, was such a shock to the system—a Hispanic American who became a prison convert to Islam was able to move around our nation with near impunity, and there are many more like him. If that single case becomes a trend, then we will have to take a hard look at how we enforce counterterrorism laws here at home, even those involving U.S. citizens.

In a related twist, there has also been a relatively small but nonetheless potentially very powerful upturn in the use of females for both pre-event activities and for executing actual attacks. Israel has fallen prey to the tactics of female suicide bombers several times in recent years. The same phenomenon includes the so-called Black Widows of Chechnya, who had lost their families and were willing to carry out attacks, as well as a deadly May 2005 shooting spree against a tourism bus in Egypt, which was carried out by the sister and the fiancée of a recently killed male terrorist. This trend has obvious and potentially severe consequences for the West, given our present predilection to avoid detailed scrutiny and physical searches of females.

Sleeper cell: There will usually be a small, inconspicuous advance team, perhaps a family of four or five, that will hold jobs and act as normal members of the community. They will scout the area and determine if it is suitable for an operation.

Logistics cell: Depending on the nature of the event and desirability of leaving agents in place after the attack, the sleepers may or may not also serve as the logistics team. In either case, be it the sleeper cell or another team brought into the area specifically for the mission, the logistics team arranges for items like rental apartments and cars, airline tickets and passports or visas, and handles the funding and other needs of the group.

Surveillance cell: These teams play the critical role of scouting out the various potential attack locations and determining the feasibility of the target. Their research enables the mission's overall leader, who may or may not be in the same country, to more formally design the attack plan.

Munitions cell: For certain attacks the munitions is just acquiring weapons, which can be handled by the logistics team. However, in many other instances this role is played by a bomb maker who, like the assault team, arrives just days before the attack. The bomb maker, whose specialist training makes him too valuable to sacrifice in the attack or risk being caught after the fact trying to leave, generally departs the country a day or two before the attack, as was the case in the North Africa Embassy bombings in 1998.

Operational/Assault cell: This is the actual team or teams that will conduct the operations, having been specially trained in the mountains of Afghanistan or other militant jihadi camps. Generally they are brought in from out of the country just days before the assault, and often the lower members of the cell don't even know the details and plans for the attack until the last minute.

The Cellular Command Structure

When military or government experts speak about the small, substate nature of terrorist groups they are quite correct—relative to the infrastructure present for a traditional, formal state-sponsored military. However, sometimes this characterization of the relative size of terrorist movements leads to a misunderstanding about terrorist groups, prompting the mistaken belief that the attacks they carry out are accomplished by only the very few individuals actually involved in the physical attack. While the actual bombing or other violence is often committed by a small inner core, the cellular structure of the terrorist networks requires both a pervasive recruitment and indoctrination network as well as outwardly law-abiding individuals willing to perform pre-attack reconnaissance, surveillance, and planning. Using these concentric circles of activity minimizes the time that the specially trained strike team (whose members are more likely to be noticed by immigration and law-enforcement officials) has to be in the target area in advance of the attack, thereby minimizing their likelihood of being intercepted.

There are typically several levels of involvement in any terrorist attack, ranging from the tacit supporter who provides basic information or perhaps couriers messages for the team to the reconnaissance team, the specialist bomb makers, and the actual operatives who move in to carry out the attack. Planning for an attack can take anywhere from a few months to many years, depending on the accessibility of the target, the freedom of movement of various operators, and the availability of needed materiel. As with many things, the actual process of completing an attack requires that a significant number of small tasks be accomplished in a particular sequence. The difficult part for the law-enforcement or military team tasked with stopping these attacks is that the enemy has devised levels of involvement where individual actors know only their part in the scheme; with each circle essentially anonymous and insulated from the others, terrorists have minimized the chances that any one actor being captured or turning into an informant will result in the capture of the other members of the cell.

THE TERRORISTS' ARSENAL

Terrorists are, on the whole, generally conventional in their selection of weapons, with guns and improvised bombs being high among the weapons of choice. Nonetheless chemical, biological, and nuclear weapons present by far the deadliest per-incident threat to human life. It is important to remember, however, that 9/11 was carried out using fear, aggression, and box cutters to turn civilian airliners into guided missiles, so even future attacks not involving WMD will not be limited to the traditional forms of weapons described here. As described in the pro-jihad, anti-U.S. Web site "Jihad Unspun," al Qaida and its affiliates possess a variety of capabilities, including:

- T54 tanks, 124-mm heavy artillery, multibarrel rocket launchers, 76-mm antitank guns, Stingers, and SA-7 surface-to-air missiles.
- Large variety of munitions left over from the Soviet campaign, stockpiled in hidden locations in Afghanistan, Pakistan, and Sudan.
- Ocean-going vessels for arms transportation.
- Ground vehicles armed with surface-to-air missiles.
- Biochemical warheads.
- Radioactive warheads.
- Biological weapons, such as anthrax and E. coli.
- Contact poisons in KGB-like pellets used in assassinations.
- Sophisticated explosive capabilities used in bombing operations.
- Cyber capability for targeting critical infrastructure.
- Human warheads, in the form of martyrs, used for spectacular operations.[6]

Worst Case Scenarios: WMD

Every single day, terrorists are seeking to buy, steal, or manufacture the necessary ingredients for chemical, biological, and nuclear weapons. Their activities are going largely unnoticed in Third World arms bazaars, poorly regulated storage facilities in the former Soviet Union, and illicit laboratories in Pakistan and elsewhere. While any scenario by which terrorists acquire such capabilities is a truly horrifying one, the daunting fact is that it has happened in the past and it continues to happen. Clear and convincing evidence of chemical and biological efforts have been found in former al Qaida laboratories throughout Afghanistan, and even when the labs have been captured, the knowledge of how to create the weapons lives on with the al Qaida members. This proliferation will continue to happen until one day, without warning, the terrorists will strike in an unforeseen and deadly way.

The story of A. Q. Khan—the Pakistani nuclear scientist (and hometown hero) who, in large measure, developed Pakistan's nuclear weapons

---

[6] Jihadunspun, "Al-Qaida Special Forces" at http://www.jihadunspun.com/theplayers/bio/alqaeda.html.

program and then sold other countries the knowledge and even parts to aid in the nuclear weapons manufacturing processes—is a terrifying example of the means by which terrorists are most likely to acquire weapons of mass destruction. Khan, who created a for-profit weapons proliferation syndicate operating in the shadows of Pakistan's covert nuclear program, began his efforts during the 1970s. It was only in April of 2000, however, that the Western intelligence community began to really track Khan's activities, including the probable sale of uranium enrichment material to Libya. Apparently, by 2003 the network used to supply these activities was global in scope, stretching from Germany to Dubai and from China to South Asia, and involved numerous middlemen and suppliers. Eventually, following U.S. pressure on Pakistan's president Musharraf, A. Q. Khan was arrested and admitted selling nuclear technology to Iran, Libya, and North Korea. Due to domestic political reasons President Musharraf has resisted anything more severe than "house arrest" of A. Q.[7]

Chemical

An understanding of WMD attacks begins with a realization that, while WMD are different from conventional weapons, they are also different from each other. Chemical weapons are largely effective only in somewhat confined spaces or, at worst, relatively small geographic areas. For this reason chemical weapons, to a degree, can be thought of as "bus-stop bombs," meaning that, as with a conventional explosion, you don't want to be near the bus stop where the weapon is detonated, but if you are far enough away and able to evacuate, you'll be fine.

[7]For more details on A. Q. Khan and WMD proliferation, see Global Security's article on him available at www.globalsecurity.org/wmd/world/pakistan/khan.htm.

Nuclear

Nuclear weapons, on the other hand, are much more significant in terms of both their immediate damage and their lingering effects; you don't want to be in the same city as a nuclear explosion. Significant nuclear effects are difficult to predict, however, because the effect varies due to the amount and type of radioactive material used, the method of detonation, the height of the device when detonated, and the weather. Also, nuclear weapons and materials give off a radiation signature and are perhaps the easiest form of weapon that can be detected by today's technology.

As an associate editor for the *The Washington Post* has observed: "Listening to him on tape after tape, it is difficult to doubt bin Laden's intent. There is evidence that he and his allies have experimented with chemical and biological weapons, typically low-level toxins. But in public, bin Laden talks mainly about nuclear bombs."[8] Worse yet, nuclear devices apparently can be bought or stolen in several places throughout the former Soviet Union and Central Asia. During open testimony in Congress in 1997, Rep. Curt Weldon stated:

> I thought it would be useful if our delegation of six members of Congress also met with General Lebed to get an assessment from his perspective of stability in Russia's military. We asked for the meeting. And we had a private, two-hour, closed meeting in his office. There was no media present. There was no press conference before or after our meeting. It was a very private discussion. There were a number of things that General Lebed raised: One of the things he mentioned was that he was given the responsibility, when he was secretary to the Security Council for Boris Yeltsin, to account for 132 suitcase-sized devices. He wasn't raising this issue to alarm us or to make some big international media story. He was raising the issue as one of a series of concerns that he had, which he felt we should work on together. And he said that in his work, out of the 132 devices, he could only locate

---

[8] Steve Coll, "Nuclear Nightmares," *The Washington Post,* February 6, 2005, p. B1.

48. And we asked him about the others, and he shrugged his shoulders and said, I don't know.[9]

Similarly, a February 2005 *TIME* magazine article notes that nuclear scenarios are the ultimate nightmare for counterterrorism officials, cautioning:

> Osama bin Laden says it is a religious duty to obtain a bomb, and most experts believe that if al-Qaeda were to succeed, the group wouldn't hesitate to use it. Though building even a crude nuclear weapon is time consuming, the wide availability of raw material and scientific expertise means that it is plausible for terrorists someday to get their hands on one. "The simplest nuclear bomb," says Ivan Oelrich, director of the security project at the Federation of American Scientists, "is very simple indeed."[10]

Biological

It is the biological threats that are of the most concern, however. They are the ones with the most potential to drastically alter our lives. If chemical weapons are bus-stop bombs, and you don't want to be in the same city as a detonated nuke, you don't want to be on the same continent as a bio attack. That is because biological agents, and smallpox in particular, spread from person to person, often before identifiable signs of infection even appear. Given today's rampant use of interconnected transportation systems, this means biological weapons can spread beyond any containable area within days, if not hours. If you think of what mad cow and the bird flu did to the global economy, one can hardly imagine what would happen in terms of

[9]Statements during the October 2, 1997, testimony of Dr. Alexie Yablokov, former Science Advisor to Boris Yeltsin, before the Research and Development Subcommittee of the House National Security Committee, chaired by Rep. Curt Weldon, available at http://www.pbs.org/wgbh/pages/frontline/shows/russia/suitcase/yablokov.html.

[10]Massimo Calabresi, "The Other Nuke Nightmare," February 6, 2005, http://www.time.com/time/covers/1101050214/wterror.html.

halted trade and economic devastation if a serious biological event hit the United States.

Means of Delivery

It should be noted for the record that, to date, terrorists have proven fairly inept at actually delivering these weapons for mass effect. The Japanese millennial cult Aum Shinrikyo, for example, botched several attempts to use biological weapons before it released sarin nerve gas on Tokyo's subway system in 1995, an attack that killed 12 and wounded many thousands. Nonetheless, this is cold comfort in an era when the terrorists have declared their intent to do America grievous harm. The delivery means for WMD attacks could include anything from a so-called smallpox martyr entering the country to infect others, a contaminated food shipment, or a nuclear device smuggled into a major port in the hull of a cargo vessel.

CONVENTIONAL ARMS[11]
Guns and Other Small, Medium, and Heavy Weapons

Terrorists' use of semiautomatic pistols, revolvers, rifles, and fully automatic shoulder weapons runs the gamut for involvement in everything from assassinations, sniping, armed attacks, and outright massacres. Terrorists use both professionally manufactured and improvised firearms that can be divided into subcategories of small arms, medium-sized, and heavy weapons. Weapons such as the AK-47 Kalashnikov assault rifle and the M60 heavy machine gun are within the manufacturing capabilities of local arms makers on the northwest frontier of the Indian subcontinent, and primitive mortars and rocket launchers are sometimes manufactured by various unregulated entities. Grenades (either hand grenades or rocket-

---

[11]Portions of this section are adapted from a United Nations report available at www.unodc.org/unodc/terrorism_weapons_conventional.html.

propelled) are also part of the terrorist arsenal, though the use of missiles is rare and only a relative few groups are known to be in possession of surface-to-air, shoulder-fired missiles that can bring down helicopters, fighter aircraft, and civilian airliners.

- **Small arms:** This category includes rifles, shotguns, submachine guns, and light machine guns. Small arms also include true assault rifles, all of which by definition fire rifle cartridges and are capable of fully automatic fire; false "assault rifles," which are merely look-alikes incapable of fully automatic fire and no different, other than in appearance, from semiautomatic hunting rifles; and submachine guns (fully automatic weapons firing handgun rather than rifle cartridges). Handguns (pistols and revolvers) are sometimes known as sidearms. The term "small arms" also includes most firearms under the level of medium machine guns, or as a loose rule, belt-fed, crew-served machine guns. Most small arms are designed originally for military use, but many are designed specifically for personal protection, including law enforcement, hunting, and other shooting sports.
- **Medium-size infantry weapons:** These include medium-sized machine guns (many of which are belt-fed), smaller sized mortars, rocket-propelled grenades, and smaller caliber wire-guided missiles.
- **Heavy infantry weapons:** Heavy-caliber machine guns, mortars, and wire-guided missiles; shoulder-held antitank missile launchers; and some rockets below the category of artillery.

Several of the more commonly used terrorist weapons are discussed below in more detail:

- **AK-47 Soviet assault rifle:** The AK-47, essentially a true assault rifle, was accepted as the standard rifle for the Soviet army in 1949 and retained that status until it was succeeded by the AKM. During the Cold War, the USSR supplied arms to anti-Western insurgent terrorists. The AK-47 became a symbol of left-wing revolution; between thirty to fifty million copies and variations of the AK-47 have been produced globally, making it the most widely used rifle in the world.

■ **RPG-7 rocket-propelled grenade:** The RPG-7 was issued by forces of the former USSR, the Chinese military, and North Korea, and was used in many countries receiving weapons and training from the Warsaw Pact members. The RPG-7 proved to be a very simple and functional weapon developed from the World War II German *panzerfaust,* employing a shaped charge, and is effective against a fixed emplacement and in an antivehicle/antiarmor role. Its effective range is thought to be approximately five hundred meters when used against a fixed target, and about three hundred meters when fired at a moving target. The RPG-7 is being used extensively by terrorist organizations in the Middle East and Latin America and is thought to be in the inventory of many insurgent groups. The RPG-7 is available in illegal international arms markets, particularly in Eastern Europe and the Middle East.

■ **FIM-92A Stinger missile:** The US-made Stinger is a man portable infrared-guided shoulder-launched surface-to-air-missile (SAM). It proved to be highly effective in the hands of Afghan Mujahideen guerrillas during their insurgency against the Soviet intervention. Its maximum effective range is approximately 5,500 meters. Its maximum effective altitude is approximately 5,250 meters. It has been used to target high-speed jets, helicopters, and commercial airliners.

■ **SA-7 "Grail" missile:** Sold by the thousands after the demise of the former Soviet Union, the SA-7 Grail uses an optical sight and tracking device with an infrared seeking mechanism to strike flying targets with great force. Its maximum effective range is approximately 6,125 meters and its maximum effective altitude is approximately 4,300 meters. It is known to be in the stockpiles of several terrorist and guerrilla groups.

TERRORIST TACTICS, TECHNIQUES, AND PROCEDURES: IEDS*

Historically, when terrorist groups have attacked large gatherings and high-profile events, they have done so with conventional improvised explosive devices (IEDs). More specifically, IEDs have been used in preelection attacks in Iraq, Spain, and Chechnya. IEDs are low tech and therefore relatively easy to transport. Terrorists will employ novel methods to conceal IEDs, such as hiding them in jackets, shoes, belts, vests, gym bags, and briefcases. Oftentimes, IED attacks are suicide missions.

Al Qaida has also used vehicle-borne improvised explosive devices (VBIEDs) to conduct attacks. Over the past year and a half, large-scale VBIED attacks have been carried out against U.S. allied countries overseas by al Qaida or al Qaida–affiliated operatives. Moreover, there has been continued reporting from across the United States of the theft of high-profile vehicles, to include tanker trucks, rental trucks, and emergency vehicles—all of which could be used as the basis for a VBIED attack. Establishing a perimeter around the polling sites would reduce the effect of such an attack.

Terrorist groups around the world have used simultaneous attacks to defeat security measures and increase the effect of an attack. For instance, the November 2003 attack against a Saudi Arabian residential compound was a multilayered attack; an initial group of operatives shot their way into the residential compound to weaken security while another group of operatives followed by driving an ambulance filled with explosives into the compound. The terrorist attack in Bali, Indonesia, in October 2002, is an example of a simultaneous attack. Terrorists could adopt these same techniques during future attacks to defeat security measures, divert security personnel, and/or increase the effect of an attack.

*Adapted from an unclassified DHS advisory, January 2005.

IEDs and Other Explosives

Improvised explosive devices (IEDs) were used in the 1993 bombings of the World Trade Center, the 1995 attack on the Alfred P. Murrah Federal Building in Oklahoma, the 1998 attacks on the East African Embassies, the 2000 attack on the USS *Cole,* and the 2003 Earth Liberation Front (ELF) bombings in California. Car and truck bombs, in particular, have become very powerful weapons, in part because the operators need not be as well trained, but also because recent advancements in cell-phone triggers and remote detonation are literally taking the suicide out of suicide bombings by enabling the attacker to survive the attack. Terrorists often use incendiary devices such as Molotov cocktails, which are not much more than flammable liquid with a scrap of cloth as the detonating mechanism. They also make use of letter and parcel bombs, though these are less effective and less controllable than bombs delivered directly.

Most bombs assembled by terrorists are improvised from other devices, the raw material required for explosives being stolen or misappropriated from military or commercial-blasting supplies, or made from fertilizer and other readily available agricultural and household ingredients.

IEDs have a trigger, a fuse, and a main charge, and often these three components are integrated into a single whole. The trigger that activates the fuse may be operated by anything from a push-button mechanism to a cell phone, timer, or even photoelectric or pressure-sensing devices. The fuse then ignites the charge that causes the explosion, which consists of a violent pulse of blast and shock waves. The deadly effects of the IED are sometimes worsened by the addition of fragments of material, such as scrap iron or ball bearings that amplify the bomb's lethality by adding shrapnel to the fragmentation propelled outward by the explosion.

HOW EXPLOSIVES WORK

Explosives destroy by the combination of the blast, the vacuum pressure, the fragmentation, and the shock wave released when their chemical substances undergo a rapid chemical change, producing gases, heat, and light. They are classified as low or high order, primarily according to the detonating velocity at which this change takes place, with 3,300 feet per second as the line of demarcation between low-order explosives, which are said to burn, and high explosives, which burn so quickly they are said to detonate. The burning of low-order explosives gives off a gas that, when confined, in turn produces the explosion. Some low-order explosives, such as black powder, are spark sensitive. Others, such as AMFO (ammonia nitrate fuel oil) require a detonator. High-order explosives, on the other hand, must be triggered by a detonator or blasting cap but do not require confinement of the gases to initiate the explosion. Whether the process is high or low order, when an explosive is detonated the chemical explosive material is instantaneously converted from a solid (or liquid, such as nitroglycerine) into a rapidly expanding mass of gasses.

High-order detonation describes a complete detonation of the explosive at its highest possible velocity, while low-order detonation is either an incomplete detonation or a complete detonation at lower-than-maximum velocity. The difference in the velocities of the gasification also determines whether the explosive will produce a pushing power (low explosives) or a shattering power (high explosives).

Several powerful and potentially damaging effects accompany explosive detonations, the strongest of which is called blast pressure effect. This happens when the explosion occurs very hot and the expanding gases are formed very quickly, creating a blast pressure wave.

Pressure waves have two distinct phases, both of which can cause tremendous damage. The first is the positive phase, which is the relatively short period when the blast wave delivers violent outward force. The second, or negative, phase lasts three times longer but is of less intensity than the positive phase. It is formed by the out-rushing air being compressed and forming a vacuum at the point of detonation. This vacuum causes the displaced air to reverse its movements and return to the point of detonation, which accounts for much of the debris that is found at the seat of the explosion.

Other aspects of explosive detonation include:

- **Fragmentation:** When the bomb casing breaks into little pieces that fly everywhere and cause damage and injury, especially to people.
- **Overpressure:** When the pressure from the wave itself or the reflected wave pressure is too great for a structure or physical form to bear. The effects of overpressure on the human body vary depending on the distance from the explosion, the nature of the surroundings, and the age and physical condition of the individual.
- **Secondary blast effects:** When blast waves are shattered, reflected, or shielded by reflective surfaces. The reflective blast wave from surfaces surrounding it may actually reinforce the original wave by overlapping it in some places (e.g., corners of a room).
- **Ground and water shock:** When an explosive is initiated while buried in the earth or submerged under water. Because both earth

and water are less compressible than air, they propel the shock wave farther and with more force than air, making the structural damage substantially greater. In fact, since water cannot be compressed at all, it will transmit energy much faster and farther than any other substance.

The following article by G. Gordon Liddy foretold of terrorist attacks on America twelve years and two days in advance of 9/11. The article originally appeared on page 44 of the January 1989 issue of *Omni magazine.*

RULES OF THE GAME
by G. GORDON LIDDY

Could terrorists cripple the United States?
A former Washington aide tells the White House how.

THE WHITE HOUSE
TOP SECRET

PENUMBRA IKON ZOAR JENNIFER HELOS
SENSITIVE
NODIS
09 September 1999

MEMORANDUM FOR THE PRESIDENT
FROM: AXEL JOHNSEN [CHIEF OF STAFF]
SUBJECT: HOW AMERICA WAS SHUT DOWN

This memorandum is a summary of, and attached to, the comprehensive damage report, physical and political, on the coordinated terrorist sabotage attack on the night of second August. The political section has, as ordered, been expanded to include a report on the Capitol Hill riot of last Thursday, which cost thirteen lives, including those of the speaker of the House and a congressman, before order was finally restored.

U.S. Commercial Aircraft Industry: 90 Percent Inoperative
The rendering of U.S. jet equipment inventory unusable cannot be attributed to the events of second August. The intelligence community and the Federal Bureau of Investigation are, however, unanimously in agreement that the two are part of the same overall operation. This conclusion is based primarily upon the evidence taken from the body of a female slain by SEAL Team 3 on second August in the San Diego area while she was participating in the attack on the national electrical power distribution system (next heading). But for this fortuitous event, the sudden structural failure of several aircraft belonging to each U.S. carrier would still be blamed on age (à la the 1988 Aloha aircraft incident, when metal fatigue caused the roof of a Boeing 737 to

rupture in flight). As it is, we have had to ground the U.S. civil commercial aviation fleet for an indefinite time, but at least we know what to look for.

Japanese intelligence has confirmed that the body of the woman slain by the SEALs is that of a member of their "Red Army" group. On her person was an item at first thought unrelated to her mission: what appeared to be a U.S. made Magic Marker, which, although not dried out, did not mark. The fluid it contained has been identified by researchers at the Defense Advanced Research Projects Agency (DARPA) as nearly chemically identical to our classified liquid metal embrittlement (LME) agent. Unfortunately, prior to being added to the classified technologies list, the LME agent was discussed in open literature.

With the aid of the LME marking device, a terrorist could gain, and obviously has gained, access to aircraft and by the simple process of drawing a virtually undetectable line across fuselage components subject to stress, could cause the metal under the line to become brittle enough to fail shortly after it is next subjected to the stress of flight.

It will take a long time to check every aircraft, unless under interrogation any of the few prisoners we were able to take will talk. They are being questioned by CIA, over the protests of the FBI, because in this rare instance CIA methods are justified for domestic use and are not in the FBI repertoire.

We have been able to achieve 10 percent capacity of normal civil or commercial air transport only because the smaller turbine, commuter aircraft were not attacked, nor were the aircraft of foreign carriers, a number of which have generously leased us spare aircraft at extortionate rates.

Even assuming the best, the fear of the American public for the safety of our civil fleet will have a lasting, very economically damaging effect.

Nation's Capitol and Seven Largest Metropolitan Areas Blacked Out Indefinitely

Since the devastating New York City blackout of 1977, much has been done by way of redundancy to protect entire nets from chain-reaction failures. Nevertheless the terrorists exploited a vulnerability brought to governmental attention several administrations ago (and ignored since) by Dr. Robert H. Kupperman of the Center for Strategic and International Studies. The terrorists did their homework very thoroughly.

Kupperman's point is as follows: In order to achieve economies of scale, generated electrical power is transmitted over long distances at extremely high voltage (EHV). Think of a power line as a water pipe. In electrical terms, amperage is the flow of water through the pipe. Voltage is the pressure. The higher the pressure, the greater the amount of water a given pipe can transport. To get water under pressure requires a pump. To get electricity under pressure requires a transformer. EHV requires an EHV transformer, both to step the voltage up at the beginning of its journey and down at its destination.

There are only about 500 EHV transformers in the entire nation. Their locations are shown on a map available to the public. Most are protected by no more than a chain-link fence and warning signs that serve to confirm exactly what they are. EHV transformers are sophisticated pieces of equipment not manufactured in the United States. The lead time for delivery of a new one from abroad is 18 months. They can be put out of operation by a high-powered rifle.

Thus a small number of terrorists—a few using .458 Winchester magnum rifles (as was the woman killed by the SEALs), and the rest Israeli-made copies of our Marine Corps' new 40mm lightweight, polymer/ceramic, near-handgun-size grenade launchers—took out the few key EHV transformers around Washington, DC, New York City/Newark, Boston, Chicago, Dallas/Fort Worth, Atlanta, Oakland/San Francisco, and Los Angeles. San Diego was saved when an element of SEAL Team 3, on a security penetration test mission, came upon one of the terrorists who panicked and fired on them. After killing her, the SEALs grasped her mission, alerted their superiors, and in short order we had nearly half the few prisoners captured to date.

The aftermath of the EHV attack has been devastating. There is no power for the water supply pumps. The effects of arson are impossible to control. Martial law is barely able to maintain order now that the stores are looted and burned. Vigilante justice is rampant. Sanitation has broken down, and the rats are out of control in New York City. It will take six months to a year, under emergency conditions, to acquire and replace the transformers and restore the electrical power.

North-South Rail Traffic in Eastern United States Severed; Much of Strategic Rail Corridor Network (STRACNET) Out

Unfortunately all major north-south railroad traffic in the eastern United States funnels through two choke points: a single strategic railroad bridge over the Potomac River between Washington, DC, and Virginia and the rail complex at Cincinnati. On the night of second August, terrorist-planted pressure mines—set so that they would go off only under the weight of a full train—took out the Potomac Bridge, and the Cincinnati choke point was severed by use of an expert combination of low-order (ammonium nitrate combined with heating-grade fuel oil) and high-order (both C, and dynamite) explosives.

Rebuilding is under way, but as you read this, the accordion effect, coupled with the fact that power outages make it impossible to pump automotive fuel, promises substantial interruption of freight delivery, especially of food staples, for some time to come.

Natural Gas Supply for Industrial, Utility, Commercial, and Residential Use in Northeastern and Atlantic Coastal U.S. Cut by 75 Percent, Restoration to Take a Year

Seventy-one percent of domestic natural gas is produced in Texas and Louisiana. Texas consumes a substantial amount of its own production. The remainder is exported interstate via pipelines combining both lengths of pipe and compressor stations. Louisiana, by contrast, consumes little of its production; the bulk of it, combined with excess Texas gas transported from next door, is shipped by pipeline interstate to the northeastern and Atlantic coastal markets. Thus the terrorists, by targeting just the key compressors and a few pipeline river crossings (easily identified by large warning signs saying, WARNING—DO NOT ANCHOR—PIPELINE) entirely within the state of Louisiana, caused a catastrophe. From Louisiana the pipe network fans out into the Northeast and Atlantic coast. The key compressors are in Louisiana at the base of the fan. They have no protection at all.

As with the EHV transformers, many of the gas compressors were manufactured abroad. Replacement lead times are long. Very few are in inventory. The damaged compressors, destroyed easily by Soviet RPG-7's rifle-propelled grenades), cannot be repaired. Even after gas transmission restoration, it will take nearly a year just to relight the industrial pilot lights in large utility and manufacturing installations.

Computer Database Erasure of Wall Street, Six Federal Reserve Banks, Two IRS Service Centers, Several of Largest Commercial Banks, and Numerous Corporations Produces Fiscal Chaos

The same small teams that attacked the EHV transformers serving New York, Washington, Dallas, Atlanta, Boston, Chicago, and San Francisco then used man-transportable electromagnetic pulse generators (EMPGs) to erase computer databases in those cities. The extent of the havoc is now becoming clear as all but the cash monetary system collapses.

A Special Operations Capable Marine Expeditionary Unit (SOCMEU) exercising in Louisiana was alerted by the demolition of a natural gas pipeline at a river crossing. By dawn they killed six and captured four from two separate five-man terrorist teams. Captured with one team was its EMPG.

The EMPG, cruder and more bulky than our own classified device, appears to be of Soviet origin. While both theirs and ours use superconductors, theirs is coupled with an explosion, whereas ours uses an implosion for greater yield.

The best minds we have are trying to find ways to reconstruct what was lost through retrieval of partial data from unaffected network components. They are working first on the governmental losses. It may, for example, be possible through the use of old paper records that may survive in local offices, as well as any correspondence in the hands of individual citizens, to reconstruct some of the Social Security system. We may, however, have to ask Congress to consider some sort of postcatastrophic forgiveness or moratorium, and a fresh start for some of the private sector.

The loss of Social Security records causes the most severe effect on civilians; the government is more devastated by the loss of IRS records. Many experts have for years been worried about computer viruses. Their threat is minor compared to that of the EMPG, which erases everything: records of Treasury bonds, VA checks, pension plans, military pensions. Some military installations are protected from EMPGs, but none of the civilian military ones are, such as those installations where records of military pensions are kept.

Who Did It and How?

Intelligence community and Department of Defense (DoD) estimates of the total number of terrorists involved in the coordinated attack vary from 100 to 250. We shall not know the exact number for a long time, if ever. Although the terrorists are being hunted by both the FBI and civil authorities on the theory of criminal law violation, as by DoD Special Warfare (SPECWAR) assets—such as the SEALs, SOCMEU, and the Army's Delta Force—on the theory of military attack and under martial law, the CIA believes that in the continuing chaos following the assault most participants slipped out of the country, probably via Mexico.

Although worldwide there are more than 3,000 terrorists belonging to about 50 organizations, the intelligence community pinpoints only about five groups with a combined membership of about 200 highly trained men and women as being capable of the second August attack. While there are different estimates of the number of international terrorist groups, here we are including the PLO, IRA (which became totally Marxist, so now there exists the provisional IRA, called the Provos, which is the majority and socialist), Japanese Red Army, the French Action Directe, the Islamic Jihad. Some groups are bogus, like Black September, which was created by the PLO so that it could deny its role in the Olympics massacre. It is, however, unlikely that they could all be recruited for this operation.

Noting that all those captured by the SOCMEU in Louisiana were black aliens, CIA has assigned a high degree of credibility to the information passed on by Mossad that the entire Louisiana attacking force was recruited from black citizens of Communist African nations who were students at the Soviets' Patrice Lumumba University and that the recruits' training took place at the same bases that are used to train the PLO as well as other terrorist groups.

Mossad advances the foregoing based upon three factors: that the attack was Soviet sponsored and directed (CIA is not so sure. They like the Qaddafi revenge theory better—that he arranged the attack to avenge the death of his daughter in 1986 when we bombed his palace);

that the existing pool of 200 sufficiently trained terrorists could not be recruited en masse for one operation; and that groups of blacks could pass unnoticed in Louisiana, given the existing residual racism in the region.

This led to the white commanding officers ignoring the input of competent black police in the South, who detected the presence of black aliens immediately and submitted their field intelligence reports on this matter—the typical police operations procedure. (FBI records tend to lend support to this theory. According to reports from the New Orleans field office, black police officers in Louisiana picked up rumors of strange blacks moving about, but when they reported them to their white superiors, they were either ridiculed or completely ignored.)

It is the consensus, therefore, that the terrorists were recruited from among the two hundred who constitute the transnational threat, further supplemented by a contingent of trained-for-the-event Communist black Africans.

The Soviet initiation theory is lent credence by the possession of the EMPG devices. Other than us, only the Soviets are known to have them, and although Israel could probably build one, it would most likely employ our implosion/superconductor technology rather than that of the cruder, less efficient Soviet model.

DARPA suggests Soviet responsibility based not only on the EMPG technology but also on the captured communications equipment. It nearly mirrors our latest classified gear but with construction techniques peculiarly Soviet. The transceivers operate using a constant sweep of an exceptionally large number of frequencies so that no one frequency is used for more than a microsecond at a time, rendering effective interception virtually impossible. Both Israel and Switzerland have equipment operating on the same principle. We have acquired specimens of both, and the transceivers in question are definitely neither.

The question of responsibility remains in doubt, in view of the foregoing. CIA avers that only the black Africans can be believed to have acted from ideological conviction; international terrorists are really, regardless of their rhetoric, not ideological, despite undistributed extreme left or right dispositions. They do it for personal, psychosocial reasons—because they "like" it.

The how of it is relatively simple. The terrorists were outfitted with appropriate clothing, alias documentation, and pocket litter and infiltrated into the nation with the most porous border on Earth. Armament in total (including AK-47 assault rifles, RPG-7's, handguns, ammunition, and miscellaneous mines and other ordnance) amounted to a small mass compared with the bulk of such regularly smuggled contraband as marijuana. All the odd laws we passed against "plastic" guns did nothing to halt the march of technology, specifically the production of plastic polymer and ceramic guns. While weapons made of these materials are a bit delicate for use in traditional hand-to-hand fashion—i.e., to strike the enemy with—ceramic/plastic construction offers a number of benefits. Ceramic/polymer weapons are impervious to rust, extreme heat, and the elements; and they are self-cleaning.

What we have accomplished with our restrictive laws on this technology was to lose a large new industry and all the jobs that go with it. Even without resorting to such high-tech weapons, it is relatively straightforward to get a standard-construction gun through the airport magnetometers and roentgen machines, which are a joke. In a previous terrorist attack on an aircraft, for example, the protagonists took a common semiautomatic pistol apart and immersed its pieces in molten leaded crystal. This passed as an opaque object through the airport machines. Once airborne, one of the terrorists went into the plane's bathroom, broke the glass, and reassembled the pistol. There is no substitute for human inspection by trained personnel.

Which leaves the question of why. To understand that requires a recapitulation of what has been done to us; what has been accomplished from the point of view of whoever was behind the attack.

Our biggest cities and the huge areas surrounding them (the Boston/New York/Baltimore/Washington metropolitan areas interconnect) are without electrical power, have been so for a month, and will continue to be so for many more. Food has spoiled because there is no refrigeration. (Gas-powered refrigerators have run out.) Fuel cannot be pumped. What traffic there is is gridlocked because there are no operational traffic signals.

Garbage is piled up. Rats are running rampant. Emergency generators at hospitals are out of fuel, and the hospitals are running out of supplies. Freight cannot be moved. Factories are out of operation. Food produced in relatively unaffected areas cannot be marketed or even effectively distributed as relief in the affected areas—because there is no electricity, and combustion engines need fuel. Police, mistakenly now wedded to and dependent upon the automobile, are crippled. The people, weaned on what passes for news on television and radio, are without it.

Virtually every citizen in the vast areas affected by the attack is now jobless because factories have no fuel or power. The homes in the North are without heat and light, with winter coming on. The economy as we know it is at a halt, and the banking system is shut down. Denied such basics of civilization as police, fire, and health care, people are frantic. They have looked to Washington, and Washington has been able to do nothing. We cannot even communicate effectively with these people. Even battery-powered portable radios are failing as their batteries give out.

As you know, according to Kupperman and other observers, the "prayer" of public officials has always been that a disaster will be either so immense as to be perceived as an "act of God" and thus engage the loyalty and team spirit of both the government and a patient populace, or so small that it will go away by itself. The dread of officials is the one in between, affecting more than one choke point, the one with which government cannot cope. It is dreaded because it damages the faith of the people in their government and way of life.

The current situation is a nightmare. The people know this was not an act of God. What has happened is so immense as to be almost incomprehensible to them. The people expect their government to do something about it—to fix the problem and punish those responsible. And the American people are not patient. Their faith in what the Founding Fathers wrought is ebbing fast. It is this last factor that occasioned the following.

The Capitol Hill Riot

DoD, working with the Secret Service, has taken elaborate precautions to protect the White House from the angry mobs that looted and burned the K Street corridor. The service has taken additional steps to protect the White House. This is beyond the work that has been done in past years, including the concrete barriers and extensive sensor deployment. As you are aware, if a would-be intruder stood in Lafayette

Park and looked at the executive mansion, he would be observed via high-powered TV monitors secreted in the little vent housings on the roof of the White House. Beyond this, should an individual set foot anywhere on the lawn area, sensors would display exactly where he or she was. Should evacuation become necessary for you or members of your staff, there is the escape tunnel from the White House into the Treasury—which has been recently checked and is fully operational. It was anticipated that the focus of resentment would be upon your office and the White House, the symbol of authority of the national government throughout our history. We know now that that has changed.

Gradually, over the past few administrations, as Congress passed law after law for the people and the executive branch to follow but excepted Congress itself (the civil rights acts, the Fair Labor Standards Act, the minimum wage laws, etc.) and as Congress continued to act as if the rest of the laws of the land did not apply to its members (and indeed, the Constitution itself, as Congress usurped more and more of the powers of the executive branch), the perception of the people shifted like the needle of a compass toward a more powerful magnet. The Capitol Building came to supplant the White House as the foremost symbol of power as well as the actual locus of power.

Thus the rage and frustration of the people was not directed at you but at Congress. Speaker of the House Galloway, bravely defying the urgent advice of the Capitol police, sought to confront and calm the mob sacking the Capitol Building and beating individual members. The mob, shouting obscenities and references to the speaker's recent press conference—at which he denied new charges of illegality in his solicitation of campaign contributions—used electrical cable from a nearby construction repair site to hang him from a lamppost.

Action

We have got to reunite the country without delay. Already for millions, their faith in government and our way of life has been destroyed. We can keep that from happening to the majority of the population. The present situation serves as an opportunity to do that and to achieve the return of power to the presidency. As a bonus, we can be rid of Communist Nicaragua. The armed forces are intact and functioning. A quick strike by all three divisions of the Marine Corps (the Army will scream, but we need them here to deal with the emergency) will get rid of the *comandantes* within 90 days. It will focus the public's attention outside and let us get a handle on things domestic. This recommendation is concurred to by all of your Cabinet save the Department of State.

The aim of this action is to divert the country from its domestic woes. This is a perfect job for the Marines—it is the sort of mission that they are intended to perform. The general plan of battle is for one division to land via amphibious assault of Nicaragua's Atlantic coast, and another on the Pacific side, with a third division in reserve. The division landing on the Pacific coast would capture Managua. The Sandinistas are expected to take to the countryside. The two divisions would then employ a classic pincer movement to trap the Nicaraguan forces between them.

The legal scenario that such action would prompt is as follows. Congress passed the War Powers Act, to which no President has yet yielded. Nor has any President tested it, either legally or politically. The legal test for those opposed to this act centers on the theory that if you read it together with the decision of the Supreme Court that struck down the congressional veto, then the War Powers Act is unconstitutional and thus can be ignored by the President. In short, we could just do it and then tell those against our action to take us to court. Strategically, from a legal point of view it is important to note also that because Nicaragua is small, if you use overwhelming power and get the job done and the U.S. troops out within 90 days, the War Powers Act never goes into effect, and the point is moot.

"Delay in the use of force, and hesitation to accept responsibility for its employment when the situation clearly demands it, will always be interpreted as a weakness. Such indecision will encourage further disorder, and will eventually necessitate measures more severe than those which would have sufficed in the first instance." *The United States Marine Corps Small Wars Manual* (1940), page 27, paragraph (d).

Your father and any other veteran of WWII would remember.

THREE

▼

Overview of Significant Terrorist Groups

The foot soldiers will not necessarily be Arab, nor will there always be a disciplined mastermind like Mohammed Atta leading them. The next attacker could be a man with a midwestern accent, or a man who makes up for his lack of aplomb with sheer rage. He could be someone like Padilla, whose metamorphosis— from a pudgy Catholic boy to a radical Muslim accused of conspiring to kill his fellow citizens—started out all too commonly.

AMANDA RIPLEY, *TIME* MAGAZINE

Based on intent, capabilities, and actual historical attacks, it is most appropriate to begin an overview of the groups threatening the United States and its interests with al Qaida and its affiliates. Yet despite America's understandable preoccupation with al Qaida, there are several al Qaida affiliates and half a dozen non-AQ-affiliated international terrorist groups that could conceivably strike the United States. This is in addition to dozens or more Islamic splinter groups and smaller cells that are believed to be operating well under the international police community's radar screen, not to mention the ecoterrorists and domestic U.S. hate groups. (The latter died down following Oklahoma City but are apparently on the rise again following the expansion of the government's search-and-seizure powers post–9/11).

The following is an overview of the major international and domestic terror groups that threaten the United States today.[1]

AL QAIDA

Established by Osama bin Ladin in the late 1980s to bring together Arabs who fought in Afghanistan against the Soviet Union, it helped finance, recruit, transport, and train Sunni Islamic extremists for the Afghan resistance. Its current goal is to establish a pan-Islamic caliphate throughout the world by working with allied Islamic extremist groups to overthrow regimes it deems "non-Islamic" and expelling Westerners and non-Muslims from Muslim countries—particularly Saudi Arabia. It issued a statement under the banner THE WORLD ISLAMIC FRONT FOR JIHAD AGAINST THE JEWS AND CRUSADERS in February 1998, saying it was the duty of all Muslims to kill U.S. citizens—civilian or military—and their allies everywhere. It merged with Egyptian Islamic Jihad (Al-Jihad) in June 2001. It was first designated as a terrorist organization by the U.S. Department of State in October 1999.

Activities: Al Qaida conducted the bombings in August 1998 of the U.S. Embassies in Nairobi, Kenya, and Dar es Salaam, Tanzania, that killed at least 301 individuals and injured more than five thousand others. It claims to have shot down U.S. helicopters and killed U.S. servicemen in Somalia in 1993 and to have conducted three bombings that targeted U.S. troops in Aden, Yemen, in December 1992.

Al Qaida is linked to the following plans that were disrupted or not carried out: to assassinate Pope John Paul II during his visit to Manila in late 1994, to kill President Clinton during a visit to the Philippines in early 1995, to bomb in midair a dozen U.S. transpacific flights in 1995,

---

[1]Much of this information is adapted from the official U.S. State Department Report "Patterns of Global Terrorism 2003" (at www.state.gov/s/ct/rls/pgtrpt/2003).

and to set off a bomb at Los Angeles International Airport in 1999. It also plotted to carry out terrorist operations against U.S. and Israeli tourists visiting Jordan for millennial celebrations in late 1999. (Jordanian authorities thwarted the planned attacks and put twenty-eight suspects on trial.) It directed the attack on the USS *Cole* in the port of Aden, Yemen, on October 12, 2000, killing 17 U.S. Navy members and injuring another 39.

In December 2001, suspected al Qaida associate Richard Colvin Reid attempted to ignite a shoe bomb on a transatlantic flight from Paris to Miami. On September 11, 2001, nineteen al Qaida suicide attackers hijacked and crashed four U.S. commercial jets—two into the World Trade Center in New York City, one into the Pentagon near Washington, D.C., and a fourth into a field in Shanksville, Pennsylvania, leaving nearly 3,000 individuals dead or missing.

In 2002 it carried out the bombing on November 28 of a hotel in Mombasa, Kenya, killing 13 and injuring 80. It probably supported a nightclub bombing in Bali, Indonesia, on October 12 that killed 202 and injured 80. It was responsible for an attack on U.S. military personnel in Kuwait on October 8 that killed one U.S. soldier and injured another. It directed a suicide attack on the *MV Limburg* off the coast of Yemen on October 6 that killed one and injured twelve. It carried out a firebombing of a synagogue in Tunisia on April 11 that killed 15 and injured 20.

In 2003 it carried out the assault and bombing on May 12 of three expatriate housing complexes in Riyadh, Saudi Arabia, that killed 34 and injured at least 40. It assisted in carrying out the bombings on May 16 in Casablanca, Morocco, of a Jewish center, restaurant, nightclub, and hotel that killed 43 and injured over 100. It probably supported the bombing of the J. W. Marriott Hotel in Jakarta, Indonesia, on August 5 that killed 14 and injured 149, and was responsible for the assault and bombing on November 8 of a housing complex in Riyadh, Saudi Arabia, that killed 17 and injured 122. It conducted the bombings of two synagogues in Istanbul, Turkey, on November 15 that killed 25 and injured 300, and the bombings in Istanbul of the British Consulate and HSBC Bank on November 20 that resulted in 28 dead and 450 injured.

In 2004, the Saudi-based al Qaida network and associated extremists launched at least eleven attacks, killing over sixty people, including six Americans, and wounding over 225 in Saudi Arabia. It remains focused on targets associated with United States and Western presence and Saudi Security forces in Riyadh, Yanbu, Jeddah, and Dharan. Attacks consisted of vehicle bombs, infantry assaults, kidnappings, targeted shootings, bombings, and beheadings. Other al Qaida networks have been involved in attacks in Afghanistan and Iraq.

Strength: Al Qaida probably has several thousand members and associates. The arrests of senior-level al Qaida operatives have interrupted some terrorist plots. It also serves as a focal point, or umbrella organization, for a worldwide network that includes many Sunni Islamic extremist groups, some members of al-Gama'a al-Islamiyya, the Islamic movement of Uzbekistan, and the Harakat ul-Mujahidin (HUM).

Location/Area of Operation: Al Qaida has cells worldwide and is reinforced by its ties to Sunni extremist networks. It was based in Afghanistan until coalition forces removed the Taliban from power in late 2001. Al Qaida has dispersed in small groups across South Asia, Southeast Asia, and the Middle East and probably will attempt to carry out future attacks against U.S. interests.

External Aid: Al Qaida maintains moneymaking front businesses, solicits donations from like-minded supporters, and illicitly siphons funds from donations to Muslim charitable organizations. United States and international efforts to block al Qaida funding has hampered the group's ability to obtain money.

AL QAIDA-AFFILIATED TERRORIST GROUPS[2]
Abu Sayyaf Group (ASG)

The ASG is a small, brutally violent Muslim separatist group operating in the southern Philippines. Some ASG leaders allegedly fought in Afghanistan during the Soviet war and are students and proponents of radical Islamic teachings. The group split from the much larger Moro National Liberation Front in the early 1990s under the leadership of Abdurajak Abubakar Janjalani, who was killed in a clash with Philippine police on December 18, 1998. His younger brother, Khadaffy Janjalani, has replaced him as the nominal leader of the group, which is composed of several semiautonomous factions. It was first designated in October 1997.

Activities: The ASG engages in kidnappings for ransom, bombings, beheadings, assassinations, and extortion. Although from time to time it claims that its motivation is to promote an independent Islamic state in western Mindanao and the Sulu Archipelago—areas in the southern Philippines heavily populated by Muslims—the ASG has primarily used terror for financial profit. Recent bombings may herald a return to a more radical, politicized agenda, at least among the factions.

The group's first large-scale action was a raid on the town of Ipil in Mindanao in April 1995. In April 2000, an ASG faction kidnapped twenty-one persons—including ten Western tourists—from a resort in Malaysia. Separately in 2000, the group briefly abducted several foreign journalists, three Malaysians, and a U.S. citizen.

On May 27, 2001, the ASG kidnapped three U.S. citizens and seventeen Filipinos from a tourist resort in Palawan, Philippines. Several of the hostages, including one U.S. citizen, were murdered. During a Philippine military hostage rescue operation on June 7, 2002, U.S. hostage Gracia

---

[2]U.S. Department of State, "Patterns of Global Terrorism 2003" (at www.state.gov/s/ct/rls/pgtrpt/2003).

Burnham was wounded but rescued, and her husband, Martin Burnham, and Filipina Deborah Yap were killed during the operation. Philippine authorities say that the ASG had a role in the bombing near a Philippine military base in Zamboanga on October 2, 2002 that killed three Filipinos and one U.S. serviceman and wounded twenty others. It is unclear what role ASG has played in subsequent bombing attacks in Mindanao.

Strength: Estimated to have two hundred to five hundred members.

Location/Area of Operation: The ASG was founded in the Basilan Province and operates there and in the neighboring provinces of Sulu and Tawi-Tawi in the Sulu Archipelago. It also operates in the Zamboanga peninsula, and members occasionally travel to Manila. In mid-2003, the group started operating in the major city of Cotobato and on the coast of Sultan Kudarat on Mindanao. The group expanded its operational reach to Malaysia in 2000 when it abducted foreigners from a tourist resort.

External Aid: Largely self-financing through ransom and extortion, the ASG may receive support from Islamic extremists in the Middle East and South Asia. Libya publicly paid millions of dollars for the release of the foreign hostages seized from Malaysia in 2000.

Jemaah Islamiya (JI)

Jemaah Islamiya is a Southeast Asian–based terrorist network with links to al Qaida. The network recruited and trained extremists in the late 1990s, following the stated goal of creating an Islamic state comprising Brunei, Indonesia, Malaysia, Singapore, the southern Philippines, and southern Thailand. It was first designated as a terror group in October 2002.

Activities: Investigations linked the JI to bombings in December 2000, when dozens of bombs were detonated in Indonesia and the Philippines, killing 22 in the Philippines and 15 in Indonesia, as well as an attack against the Phillipine ambassador to Indonesia in August.

In December 2001 Singapore authorities uncovered a JI plot to attack the U.S. and Israeli Embassies and British and Australian diplomatic buildings in Singapore.

The Bali bombings on October 12, 2002, left more than 200 dead; it was reportedly the final outcome of meetings in early 2002 in Thailand, where attacks against Singapore and soft targets, such as tourist spots in the region, were considered.

In June 2003 Thai authorities disrupted a JI plan to attack several Western embassies and tourist sites there. It was also responsible for the bombing of the J. W. Marriott Hotel in Jakarta on August 5, 2003.

The capture in August 2003 of Indonesian Riduan bin Isomoddin (aka Hambali), JI leader and al Qaida Southeast Asia operations chief, damaged the JI, but the group maintains its ability to target Western interests in the region and to recruit new members through a network of radical Islamic schools based primarily in Indonesia.

Strength: Exact numbers are currently unknown, and Southeast Asian authorities continue to uncover and arrest additional JI elements. Estimates of total JI members vary widely from the hundreds to the thousands.

Location/Area of Operation: JI is believed to have cells spanning Indonesia, Malaysia, the Philippines, southern Thailand, and Pakistan and may have some presence in neighboring countries.

External Aid: Investigations indicate that, in addition to raising its own funds, JI receives money and logistic assistance from Middle Eastern and South Asian contacts, nongovernmental organizations, and other groups—including al Qaida.

Lashkar-e-Tayyiba (LT) (Army of the Righteous)

The LT is the armed wing of the Pakistan-based religious organization, Jamat ud-Dawa (JUD)—a Sunni anti-U.S. missionary organization formed in 1989. The LT is led by Hafiz Muhammad Saeed and is one of the three largest and best-trained groups fighting in Kashmir against India; it is not connected to a political party. The United States, in October 2001, announced the addition of the LT to the U.S. Treasury Department's Office of Foreign Asset Control (OFAC) list—which includes organizations that are believed to support terrorist groups and have assets in U.S. jurisdiction that can be frozen or controlled. The group was banned, and the Pakistani government froze its assets in January 2002. The LT is also known by the name of its associated organization, Jamaat ud-Dawa (JUD). Musharraf placed JUD on a watchlist in November 2003. It was first designated in December 2001.

Activities: The LT has conducted a number of operations against Indian troops and civilian targets in Jammu and Kashmir since 1993. The LT claimed responsibility for numerous attacks in 2001, including an attack in January on Srinagar airport that killed five Indians along with six militants; an attack on a police station in Srinagar that killed at least eight officers and wounded several others; and an attack in April against Indian border security forces that left at least four dead. The Indian government publicly implicated the LT—along with JEM—for the attack on December 13, 2001 on the Indian Parliament Building, although concrete evidence is lacking. The LT is also suspected of involvement in the attack on May 14, 2002 on an Indian army base in Kaluchak that left 36 dead.

Al Qaida lieutenant Abu Zubaydah was captured at an LT safehouse in Faisalabad in March 2002, suggesting some members are facilitating the movement of al Qaida members in Pakistan.

Strength: Has several thousand members in Azad Kashmir, Pakistan; in southern Jammu and Kashmir and Doda regions; and in the Kashmir valley. Almost all LT cadres are Pakistanis from madrassas across Pakistan, or Afghan veterans of the Afghan wars. They use assault rifles, light and heavy machine guns, mortars, explosives, and rocket-propelled grenades.

Location/Area of Operation: Based in Muridke (near Lahore) and Muzaffarabad.

External Aid: Collects donations from the Pakistani community in the Persian Gulf and United Kingdom, Islamic NGOs, and Pakistani and other Kashmiri business people. The LT also maintains a Web site (under the name of its associated organization Jamaat ud-Dawa) through which it solicits funds and provides information on the group's activities. The amount of LT funding is unknown. The LT maintains ties to religious/military groups around the world, ranging from the Philippines to the Middle East and Chechnya through the fraternal network of its parent organization Jamaat ud-Dawa, formerly Jamat ud-Dawa (JUD). In anticipation of asset seizures by the Pakistani government, the LT withdrew funds from bank accounts and invested in legal businesses, such as commodity trading, real estate, and production of consumer goods.

NON-AL QAIDA-AFFILIATED ISLAMIC TERROR GROUPS
Armed Islamic Group (GIA)

An Islamic extremist group, the GIA aims to overthrow the secular Algerian regime and replace it with an Islamic state. The GIA began its violent activity in 1992 after the military government suspended legislative elections in anticipation of an overwhelming victory by the Islamic Salvation Front (FIS), the largest Islamic opposition party. First designated as a terror group in October 1997.

Activities: Frequent attacks against civilians and government workers. Since 1992 the GIA has conducted a terrorist campaign of civilian massacres, sometimes wiping out entire villages in its area of operation, although the group's dwindling numbers have caused a decrease in the number of attacks. Since announcing its campaign against foreigners living in Algeria in 1993, the GIA has killed more than hundred expatriate men and women—mostly Europeans—in the country. The group uses assassinations and bombings, including car bombs; and it is known to favor kidnapping victims. The GIA hijacked an Air France flight to Algiers in

December 1994. In 2002 a French court sentenced two GIA members to life in prison for conducting a series of bombings in France in 1995.

Strength: Precise numbers unknown; probably fewer than one hundred.

Location/Area of Operation: Algeria and Europe.

External Aid: None known.

Al-Gama'a al-Islamiyya (Islamic Group, IG)

Egypt's largest militant group, active since the late 1970s, appears to be loosely organized. It has an external wing with a worldwide presence. The group issued a cease-fire in March 1999, but its spiritual leader, Shaykh Umar Abd al-Rahman, incarcerated in the United States for the 1993 bombing of the WTC, rescinded his support for the cease-fire in June 2000. Al-Gama'a has not conducted an attack inside Egypt since August 1997. Rifa'i Taha Musa—a hard-line former senior member of the group—signed Osama bin Ladin's February 1998 fatwa calling for attacks against U.S. civilians.

The IG since has publicly denied that it supports bin Ladin and frequently differs with public statements made by Taha Musa. Taha Musa has, in the last year, sought to push the group toward a return to armed operations; but the group, which is still led by Mustafa Hamza, has yet to break the unilaterally declared cease-fire. In late 2000 Taha Musa appeared in an undated video with bin Ladin and Ayman al-Zawahiri, threatening retaliation against the United States for Abd al-Rahman's continued incarceration. The IG's primary goal is to overthrow the Egyptian government and replace it with an Islamic state, but Taha Musa also may be interested in attacking U.S. and Israeli interests.

Activities: Group specialized in armed attacks against Egyptian security and other government officials, Coptic Christians, and Egyptian opponents of Islamic extremism before the cease-fire. From 1997 until the cease-fire, al-Gama'a launched attacks on tourists in Egypt, most notably the attack in

November 1997 at Luxor that killed fifty-eight foreign tourists. It also claimed responsibility for the attempt in June 1995 to assassinate Egyptian president Hosni Mubarak in Addis Ababa, Ethiopia. Al-Gama'a has never specifically attacked a U.S. citizen or facility but has threatened U.S. interests.

Strength: Unknown. At its peak the IG probably commanded several thousand hard-core members and a like number of sympathizers. The 1999 cease-fire and security crackdowns following the attack in Luxor in 1997 probably resulted in a substantial decrease in the group's numbers.

Location/Area of Operation: Operates mainly in the Al-Minya, Asyut, Qina, and Soha governorates of southern Egypt. They also appear to have support in Cairo, Alexandria, and other urban locations, particularly among unemployed graduates and students. They have a worldwide presence, including the Sudan, the United Kingdom, Afghanistan, Austria, and Yemen.

External Aid: Unknown. The Egyptian government believes that Iran, bin Ladin, and Afghan militant groups support the organization. They also may obtain some funding through various Islamic nongovernmental organizations (NGOs).

HAMAS (Islamic Resistance Movement)

Formed in late 1987 as an outgrowth of the Palestinian branch of the Muslim Brotherhood. Various HAMAS elements have used both violent and political means—including terrorism—to pursue the goal of establishing an Islamic Palestinian state in Israel. Loosely structured, with some elements working clandestinely and others openly through mosques and social service institutions to recruit members, raise money, organize activities, and distribute propaganda. HAMAS's strength is concentrated in the Gaza Strip and the West Bank.

Activities: HAMAS terrorists, especially those in the Izz al-Din al-Qassam Brigades, have conducted many attacks—including large-scale suicide bombings—against Israeli civilian and military targets. HAMAS maintained the pace of its operational activity during 2002–4, claiming numerous attacks against Israeli interests. HAMAS has not yet directly targeted U.S. interests, although the group makes little or no effort to avoid targets frequented by foreigners. HAMAS continues to confine its attacks to Israel and the occupied territories.

Strength: It has an unknown number of official members but tens of thousands of supporters and sympathizers.

Location/Area of Operation: HAMAS currently limits its terrorist operations against Israeli military and civilian targets in the West Bank, Gaza Strip, and Israel. The group's leadership is dispersed throughout the Gaza Strip and West Bank, with a few senior leaders residing in Syria, Lebanon, Iran, and the Gulf states.

External Aid: They receive some funding from Iran but rely primarily on donations from Palestinian expatriates around the world and private benefactors, particularly in Western Europe, North America, and the Persian Gulf region.

Hizbollah (Party of God) aka Islamic Jihad

Also known as Lebanese Hizbollah, this group was formed in 1982 in response to the Israeli invasion of Lebanon. This Lebanon-based radical Shi'i group takes its ideological inspiration from the Iranian revolution and the teachings of the late Ayatollah Khomeini. The Majlis al-Shura, or Consultative Council, is the group's highest governing body and is led by Sect. Gen. Hassan Nasrallah. Hizbollah is dedicated to liberating Jerusalem and eliminating Israel and has formally advocated the ultimate establishment of Islamic rule in Lebanon. Nonetheless, Hizbollah has actively participated in Lebanon's political system since 1992. Hizbollah is closely allied with and often directed by Iran, but it has the capability and willingness to act alone. Although Hizbollah does not share the Syrian regime's secular orientation, the group has been a strong ally in helping Syria advance its political objectives in the region. First designated in October 1997.

Activities: Known or suspected to have been involved in numerous anti-U.S. and anti-Israeli terrorist attacks, including the suicide truck bombings of the U.S. Embassy and U.S. Marine barracks in Beirut in 1983 and the U.S. Embassy annex in Beirut in September 1984. Three members of Hizbollah—'Imad Mughniyah, Hasan Izz-al-Din, and Ali Atwa—are on the FBI's list of the twenty-two Most-Wanted Terrorists for the hijacking in 1985 of TWA Flight 847, during which a U.S. Navy diver was murdered.

Elements of the group were responsible for the kidnapping and detention of U.S. and other Westerners in Lebanon in the 1980s. Hizbollah also attacked the Israeli Embassy in Argentina in 1992 and the Israeli cultural center in Buenos Aires in 1994. In fall 2000 Hizbollah operatives captured three Israeli soldiers in the Shab'a Farms and kidnapped an Israeli noncombatant, who may have been lured to Lebanon under false pretenses.

In 2003 Hizbollah appeared to have established a presence in Iraq, but for the moment its activities there are limited. Hizbollah secretary general Hassan Nasrallah stated in speeches that "we are heading . . . toward the end and elimination of Israel from the region" and that the group's slogan is and will continue to be "death to America." Hizbollah's television station, al-Manar, continued to use inflammatory images and reporting in an effort to encourage the intifada and promote Palestinian suicide operations.

Strength: It has several thousand supporters and a few hundred terrorist operatives.

Location/Area of Operation: It operates in the southern suburbs of Beirut, the Bekaa Valley, and southern Lebanon and has established cells in Europe, Africa, South America, North America, and Asia.

External Aid: Receives financial, training, weapons, explosives, political, diplomatic, and organizational aid from Iran and diplomatic, political, and logistic support from Syria. Receives financial support from sympathetic business interests and individuals worldwide, largely through the Lebanese diaspora.

The Palestine Islamic Jihad (PIJ)

Originated among militant Palestinians in the Gaza Strip during the 1970s. Committed to the creation of an Islamic Palestinian state and the destruction of Israel through holy war. Also opposes moderate Arab governments that it believes have been tainted by Western secularism. First designated in October 1997.

Activities: PIJ activists have conducted many attacks, including large-scale suicide bombings, against Israeli civilian and military targets. The group has not yet targeted U.S. interests and continues to confine its attacks to Israelis inside Israel and the territories although U.S. citizens have died in attacks mounted by the PIJ.

Strength: Unknown.

Location/Area of Operation: Primarily Israel, the West Bank, and the Gaza Strip. The group's leadership resides in Syria and Lebanon, as well as other parts of the Middle East.

External Aid: It receives financial assistance from Iran and limited logistic assistance from Syria.

NON-ISLAMIC TERRORIST GROUPS
Aum Supreme Truth (Aum), aka Aum Shinrikyo

A cult established in 1987 by Shoko Asahara, the Aum aimed to take over Japan and then the world. Approved as a religious entity in 1989 under Japanese law, the group ran candidates in a Japanese parliamentary election in 1990. Over time, the cult began to emphasize the imminence of the end of the world and stated that the United States would initiate Armageddon by starting WWIII with Japan. The Japanese government revoked its recognition of the Aum as a religious organization in October 1995, but in 1997 a government panel decided not to invoke the Antisubversive Law against the group, which would have outlawed the cult. A 1999 law gave the Japanese government authorization to continue police surveillance of the group due to concerns that the Aum might launch future terrorist attacks. Under the leadership of Fumihiro Joyu, the Aum changed its name to Aleph in January 2000 and claimed to have rejected the violent and apocalyptic teachings of its founder. First designated in October 1997.

Activities: On March 20, 1995, Aum members simultaneously released the chemical nerve agent sarin on several Tokyo subway trains, killing 12 persons and injuring up to six thousand. The group was responsible for other mysterious chemical accidents in Japan in 1994. Its efforts to conduct more attacks using biological agents have been unsuccessful. Japanese police arrested Asahara in May 1995. Asahara was sentenced in February 2004 and received the death sentence for his role in the attacks of 1995. Since 1997, the cult continued to recruit new members, engage in commercial enterprise, and acquire property, although it scaled back these activities significantly in 2001 in response to public outcry. The cult maintains an Internet home page. In July 2001, Russian authorities arrested a group of Russian Aum followers who had planned to set off bombs near the Imperial Palace in Tokyo as part of an operation to free Asahara from jail and then smuggle him to Russia.

Strength: The Aum's current membership is estimated to be less than one thousand persons. At the time of the Tokyo subway attack, the group claimed to have nine thousand members in Japan and as many as forty thousand worldwide.

Location/Area of Operation: The Aum's principal membership is located only in Japan, but a residual branch comprising perhaps a few hundred followers has surfaced in Russia.

External Aid: None.

Revolutionary Armed Forces of Colombia (FARC)

Growing out of the turmoil and fighting in the 1950s between liberal and conservative militias, the FARC was established in 1964 by the Colombian Communist Party to defend what were then autonomous Communist-controlled rural areas. The FARC is Latin America's oldest, largest, most capable, and best-equipped insurgency of Marxist origin. Although only nominally fighting in support of Marxist goals today, the FARC is governed by a general secretariat led by longtime leader Manuel Marulanda (aka "Tirofijo") and six others, including senior military commander Jorge Briceno (aka "Mono Jojoy"). It is organized along military lines and includes several units that operate mostly in key urban areas such as Bogota. In 2003 the FARC conducted several high-profile terrorist attacks, including a February car-bombing of a Bogota nightclub that killed more than 30 persons and wounded more than 160, as well as a November grenade attack in Bogota's restaurant district that wounded 3 Americans. First designated in October 1997.

Activities: Bombings, murder, mortar attacks, narcotrafficking, kidnapping, extortion, hijacking, as well as guerrilla and conventional military action against Colombian political, military, and economic targets. In March 1999 the FARC executed three U.S. indigenous rights activists on Venezuelan territory after it kidnapped them in Colombia. In February 2003 the FARC captured and continues to hold three U.S. contractors and killed one other American and a Colombian when their plane crashed in Florencia. Foreign citizens often are targets of FARC kidnapping for ransom. The FARC has well-documented ties to the full range of narcotics trafficking activities, including taxation, cultivation, and distribution.

Strength: Approximately nine thousand to twelve thousand armed combatants and several thousand more supporters, mostly in rural areas.

Location/Area of Operation: Primarily in Colombia, with some activities—extortion, kidnapping, weapons sourcing, logistics, and R & R—in neighboring Brazil, Venezuela, Panama, and Ecuador.

External Aid: Cuba provides some medical care and political consultation. A trial is currently under way in Bogota to determine whether three members of the Irish Republican Army—arrested in Colombia in 2001 upon exiting the FARC-controlled demilitarized zone *(despeje)*—were guilty of providing advanced explosives training to the FARC. The FARC and the Colombian National Liberation Army (ELN) often use the border area for cross-border incursions and use Venezuelan territory near the border as a safe haven.

DOMESTIC U.S. TERRORIST GROUPS[3]

It must be remembered, sadly, that in the history of the United States our own countrymen have carried out most of the terrorist acts against our citizenry. This includes such dastardly deeds as Timothy McVeigh's role in the Oklahoma City bombing, the Unabomber's bizarre two-decade mail-bomb campaign, and Eric Rudolph's role in bombings of abortion clinics and a park adjacent to the 1996 Atlanta Olympic Park. Additionally, the late 1990s saw an increased period of activity by left-wing "eco-terrorist" movements, which are dominated by two groups, the Earth Liberation Front (ELF) and the Animal Liberation Front (ALF). They have targeted a wide range of groups, including automobile dealerships, construction sites, and animal research laboratories, and have caused significant structural and financial damage throughout the United States. But domestic threats also include more recent events such as the D.C. sniper attacks of 2002, and the October 2001 mailing of the anthrax letters that killed several innocent

[3]The following descriptions of domestic U.S. terror groups come from the Memorial Institute for the Prevention of Terrorism's excellent "terrorism knowledge base," available to the public at www.tkb.org. TKB offers a wealth of knowledge on all manner of terrorism and related concerns, domestic and international, including links to court filings and additional documentation.

Americans and frightened thousands more. While these examples show the power of the one- or two-man operation, there is a much more insidious risk, that of the organized groupings of various domestic terror groups. As with all modern terrorists their lethality has increased through harnessing modern technology, and their potential to wreak havoc and cause significant damage must not be underestimated. What follows is a brief overview of the most significant of the known groups, though many of today's groups are secretive and as yet relatively obscure.

American Front (AF)

BASE OF OPERATION: United States

FOUNDING PHILOSOPHY: American Front (AF) is a skinhead group that was founded by Bob Heick around 1990. According to some sources, the group was founded in Portland, Oregon, while other sources locate AF's roots in San Francisco, California. Within a few years, AF had spread across the Northwest and beyond. AF members have been arrested in Napa, San Francisco, Sacramento, Pennsylvania, Florida, Maryland, and Washington. Heick, a high school dropout, first encountered racist-skinhead culture in Britain in 1984. At the time, the racist organization National Front was winning a war with antiracist skinheads for control of the British skinhead movement. When Heick returned to the United States, he launched his own skinhead organization, American Front. Membership in American Front is by application only, and the application implies that if a member betrays the organization, the punishment is "death by crucifixion [sic]" (www.cgiaonline.org). This is a common attitude among skinheads, who are most brutal toward those who try to leave the movement.

AF members have committed heinous crimes. In 1991 police officers searching a Beaverton, Oregon, residence from which AF members had been evicted found a "hit list" of Portland police officers who were to be targeted. In California and Washington, during July of 1993, there was a series of bombings targeting public meeting places for blacks, gays, and Jews in California and Washington. American Front members Wayne Paul

Wooten, Jeremiah Gordon Knesal, and Mark Kowaalski were convicted of committing two of those attacks: the bombing of the Elite Tavern (a gay club) on July 22 and the bombing of an NAACP meeting hall on July 20. According to U.S. attorney Mike Yamaguchi, Wooten, Knesal, and Kowaalski were part of a larger conspiracy to incite race war. The bombings seem to have been timed to coincide with the sentencing of the police officers convicted in the Rodney King case, presumably to take advantage of heightened racial tension.

CURRENT GOALS: American Front's new leader is James Porazzo. Porazzo moved AF to Harrison, Arkansas, and made it the most explicitly Third Positionist group in America. The idea behind "Third Position" philosophy is to unify the extreme right and extreme left in their fight against the global capitalist system. Third Positionists are both socialist and racist. Porazzo advocates "socialist revolution in a racialist context," explaining, "We propose a workable, realistic alternative, and that is Separatism! White autonomy, Black autonomy, Brown autonomy and death to the current twisted system. . . . The only other obvious route would be an eventual winner take all race war: I don't think anyone with any sense would want that . . . [L]et me make it clear that American Front would rather fight the REAL ENEMY—the system. [The system we must fight is] the dictatorship of the dollar. [The forces of global capitalism are controlled by] the Zionists and the Race that spawned them . . . a filthy, evil people the world would be better without. [Charging interest] is a filthy Jewish practice."

Animal Liberation Front (ALF)

BASE OF OPERATION: Canada, United Kingdom, United States

FOUNDING PHILOSOPHY: The original Animal Liberation Front (ALF) formed in England in 1976, splintering off from the Hunt Saboteurs Association (HSA) to form a more militant organization. The FBI claims that the American branch of the ALF began its operations in the late 1970s, but the group became more high profile in 1982, and then made the FBI's domestic terrorism list in 1987 with a multimillion-dollar arson attack at a veterinary lab in California. ALF carries out direct action against animal abuse in the form of rescuing animals and causing financial loss to animal exploiters, usually through the damage and destruction of property. Because ALF actions are against the law, activists work anonymously, either in small groups or individually, and they do not have any centralized organization or coordination. The Animal Liberation Front consists of small, autonomous groups of people all over the world who carry out direct action according to the ALF guidelines. Any group of people who are vegetarians or vegans and who carry out actions according to ALF guidelines have the right to regard themselves as part of the ALF, according to their Web site and other materials.

Similar to activities in the United Kingdom and Canada, the American ALF has attacked medical and scientific research laboratories, butcher shops, and retail furriers. The organization has claimed credit for the theft of research animals and the destruction of research equipment and records, as well as acts of vandalism and arson. In August of 2003, ALF activists claimed responsibility for the release of ten thousand mink from a mink farm in Washington State. In North America and the United Kingdom, the most militant members of the ALF are young and from middle-class backgrounds.

CURRENT GOALS: The ALF's short-term aim is to save as many animals as possible and directly disrupt the practice of animal abuse. Their long-term aim is to end all animal suffering by forcing animal-abuse companies out of business. The organization claims to be nonviolent, and activists are encouraged to take precautions not to harm any animal (human or otherwise).

ALF goals, according to their Web site, are as follows: (1) To liberate animals from places of abuse, i.e., laboratories, factory farms, fur farms, etc., and place them in good homes where they may live out their natural lives free from suffering, (2) to inflict economic damage on those who profit from the misery and exploitation of animals, and (3) to reveal the horror and atrocities committed against animals behind locked doors by performing nonviolent direct actions and liberations, (4) to take all necessary precautions against harming any animal, human and nonhuman.

Aryan Nations (AN)

BASE OF OPERATION: United States

FOUNDING PHILOSOPHY: Aryan Nations (AN) is an umbrella group for factions of the Klan and other right-wing extremists. Aryan Nations founder Richard Butler dubbed Aryan Nation's headquarters in Hayden Lake, Idaho, the "international headquarters of the White race," and the white supremacist community seems to agree. The RAND Institute describes Aryan Nations as the "first truly nationwide terrorist network."

Aryan Nations advocates Christian Identity, white supremacy, and neo-Nazism. Its goal is to form "a national racial state. We shall have it at whatever price is necessary. Just as our forefathers purchased their freedom in blood so must we. We will have to kill the bastards."

Until Aryan Nations lost its Hayden Lake property in 2000, the compound was the site of regular white supremacist festivals known as the World Congress of Aryan Nations. The festivals trained attendees in urban terrorism and guerrilla warfare and gave prominent white supremacists a chance to network. The group ran an "Aryan Nations Academy" in the early 1980s to teach young people the principles of white nationalism. The group has been reaching out to prisoners with a message of white supremacy since 1979.

CURRENT GOALS: During the 1990s, Aryan Nations suffered from internal struggles, and several key leaders departed. In September of 2000, a jury awarded Victoria and Jason Keenan $6.3 million in damages because the two had been chased and shot at by Aryan Nations guards outside the Idaho compound. Butler and Aryan Nations were bankrupted, and the Idaho compound was seized. The group has currently splintered into three factions: one headed by Butler, one located in Pennsylvania and led by August Kreis and Charles Juba, and a group calling itself The Church of the Sons of YHVH/Legion of Saints (Church of the Sons of Yahweh), led by Ray Redfeairn and Morris Gulett.

Aryan Resistance Army (ARA)

BASE OF OPERATION: United States

FOUNDING PHILOSOPHY: The Aryan Resistance Army (ARA) was a militant group of Aryan Nations members and Christian Identity followers who committed twenty-two bank robberies in the Midwest during 1994 and '95. They were one of many cells of violent racists that adopted the "leaderless resistance" structure advocated by KKK leader Louis Beam. They were, by some accounts, the most paramilitary and radical neo-Nazi group in the United States during their two-year robbing spree.

The ARA was named after the Irish Republican Army and claims to have adopted its tactics and goals from the IRA. It is clear, however, that the ARA was a far more extreme group than its Irish role model. The ARA's goals were nothing less than the overthrow of the U.S. government, the extermination of Jews, and the establishment of an Aryan state in North America. Members were required to read *The Turner Diaries,* a white supremacist fantasy novel that served as the inspiration for both Timothy McVeigh and The Order, a white supremacy group. Their main base of operations was Elohim City, an Oklahoma haven for militant racists. Timothy McVeigh called Elohim City two weeks before the bombing, and the possibility of a connection between McVeigh and the ARA is the subject of volumes of speculation by militia watchers and conspiracy theorists.

The ARA's primary activities were robbing banks and stockpiling weapons and ammunition. During a typical bank robbery, an ARA member would enter with a pipe bomb and a pistol and threaten to kill both employees and customers of the bank. ARA members seem to have had a sick sense of whimsy. They often committed robberies in costume, dressed as Santa Claus, the Easter Bunny, ATF or FBI agents, and Middle Eastern men. Part of the proceeds from the robberies were used to fund "White Terror Productions," a racist record label that recorded a CD dedicated to Sam and Vicki Weaver (who were killed at Ruby Ridge) and Richard

Wayne Snell (a racist militant who was executed on the day of the Oklahoma City bombing for his role in an earlier plot to bomb the Alfred P. Murrah Federal Building.

CURRENT GOALS: The FBI was not actually aware of the existence of the ARA until one of its members was apprehended, since the group had not claimed responsibility for any of its robberies. When Richard Lee Guthrie was arrested in January of 1996 as a suspect in one of the twenty-two robberies that the ARA had committed, he told police about the ARA and gave them the location of four of his accomplices. Police then arrested Pete Langaan, Mark Thomas, Scott Stedeford, and Kevin McCarthy. Mike Brescia was arrested a year later. Guthrie hanged himself in his cell soon after fingering his associates. The other five members of ARA were all sent to prison for their crimes.

No further crimes have been connected with members of the Aryan Resistance Army, and, as far as authorities know, the group ceased to exist when its six known members were arrested. According to Mike Reynolds of the Southern Poverty Law Center, however, it is likely that associates of the group remain at large. "These people had a support system. They had safehouses and very good false documents. They were clearly preparing for something beyond bank robberies."

Black Panthers

ALIASES: Black Panther Party for Self-Defense

BASE OF OPERATION: United States

FOUNDING PHILOSOPHY: The Black Panther Party was formed in October 1966 in Oakland, California. The organization, formed by Huey Percy Newton and Bobby Seale, supported black nationalism in the United States and criticized the United States as a racist, capitalist state. The Black Panthers believed that the U.S. government and economic structure systematically oppressed black people. Thus, the Black Panthers' "Ten Points," which detailed the group's beliefs and objectives, demanded freedom for all imprisoned blacks, exemption of black people from military service, and full employment of the black population. The Ten Points also reflect the group's leanings toward communism.

While the Black Panthers always advocated self-defense (in fact, the group's original name was the Black Panther Party for Self-Defense), the group stepped up its aggressive tactics following the April 1968 assassination of Martin Luther King Jr. The Black Panthers did not subscribe to King's belief in nonviolent protest and began to arm their group members and provide military training. The Black Panthers gained support from some Americans due to their confrontational approach, as well as their programs for lower-class people such as the Free Breakfast for Children program. Beyond the Black Panthers' militaristic speech, certain group members had criminal records and had even jumped bail. This situation led to a series of confrontations with police, wherein both police officers and Black Panthers were killed. The police confrontations and internal fractionalization severely limited the Black Panthers' operational capabilities. In the late 1960s and early 1970s, the Black Panthers leadership fled the country or went into hiding within the United States. There were a series of high-profile airline hijackings; Black Panthers forced planes to Cuba, Algeria, and North Korea, where they requested political asylum.

CURRENT GOALS: The Black Panthers had approximately two thousand members in 1970, spread out throughout the United States. However, due to efforts by law enforcement and internal Black Panther rivalries, the group's leadership had either been captured or killed, was in hiding, or had fled the United States entirely by the early 1970s. By 1972 the Black Panthers was no longer operational. Some former Black Panthers members then joined the terrorist organization, Black Liberation Army. The New Black Panthers, formed in the 1990s, is not associated with the Black Panther Party of the 1960s–70s.

The Covenant, Sword and Arm of the Lord (CSA)

BASE OF OPERATION: United States

FOUNDING PHILOSOPHY: The Covenant, Sword and Arm of the Lord (CSA) was a Christian Identity survivalist group founded by James Ellison. Ellison, a former minister, ran a Christian retreat on his property, located near the Missouri-Arkansas border. In 1978 Ellison had a vision of the race war that he believed would soon engulf America, and he transformed his retreat into a white supremacist paramilitary training camp dedicated to the principles of Christian Identity. According to Ellison, the CSA would be an "Ark for God's people" during the coming race war. By God's people, Ellison meant white Christians. Jews, he told his followers, were not really God's chosen people but rather a demonic and inferior race.

CSA recruited at gun shows, where they invited people to sign up for CSA's "Endtime Overcomer Survival Training School." Students who attended CSA training were taught weapons usage, urban warfare, wilderness survival, and "Christian martial arts." CSA also made money at gun shows by selling homemade machine guns, silencers, and explosives. The organization's other source of cash was theft. Ellison encouraged his disciples to steal, citing the Israelites plundering of the Philistine's tents, after David killed Goliath, as biblical justification.

CURRENT GOALS: Beginning in 1983 the CSA embarked on a crime spree that included the firebombing of an Indiana synagogue, an arson attack on a Missouri church, and the attempted bombing of a Chicago gas pipeline. On April 19, 1985, three hundred federal officers surrounded the CSA compound and demanded that the one hundred or so heavily armed residents surrender. After a tense four days of negotiations, the CSA peacefully surrendered. Inside the compound authorities found homemade land mines, U.S. Army antitank rockets, and a large supply of cyanide that the CSA was apparently planning to use to poison the water supply of an unspecified city.

Eight of the captured leaders and members, including Ellison, were convicted and imprisoned, effectively destroying the group.

Earth Liberation Front (ELF)

MOTHER-TONGUE NAME: Earth Liberation Front (ELF)

BASE OF OPERATION: Canada, United Kingdom, United States

FOUNDING PHILOSOPHY: The Earth Liberation Front (ELF) is an international underground organization consisting of autonomous groups of people who carry out direct action according to the ELF guidelines. It was founded in 1992 in Brighton, England, by Earth First! members who refused to abandon criminal acts as a tactic when others wished to move Earth First! into the mainstream. The group jumped to North America in the mid-1990s. Historically, the group has concentrated efforts on the timber industry and animal rights issues. More recent actions indicate that some ELF factions are also targeting suburban sprawl, with New York a hotspot for this type of activity. Within the past year, a number of underconstruction condominiums and luxury homes have been set on fire by ELF operatives. Subsequent press releases describe "an unbounded war on urban sprawl," adding that "we will not tolerate the destruction of our island" and "if you build it, we will burn it." There is not a centralized organization or membership to speak of in the ELF, so individuals or cells are driven only by their personal decisions to carry out actions.

CURRENT GOALS: According to the ELF Web site, which guides individual member's actions: "Any direct action to halt the destruction of the environment and adhering to the strict nonviolence guidelines, listed below, can be considered an ELF action. Economic sabotage and property destruction fall within these guidelines":

1. To inflict economic damage on those profiting from the destruction and exploitation of the natural environment.

2. To reveal and educate the public on the atrocities committed against the earth and all species that populate it.
3. To take all necessary precautions against harming any animal, human and nonhuman.

The ELF advocates "monkey wrenching," a euphemism for acts of sabotage and property destruction against industries and other entities perceived to be damaging to the natural environment. "Monkey wrenching" includes tree spiking, arson, sabotage of logging or construction equipment, and other types of property destruction. Economic damage is often accomplished via acts of vandalism, ranging from breaking windows and gumming locks to setting fires and damaging equipment. Public education is typically achieved by means of anonymous press releases following acts of sabotage. Spray paint is also used to communicate messages and to claim responsibility at the site of sabotage.

Fourth Reich Skinheads

BASE OF OPERATION: United States

FOUNDING PHILOSOPHY: In July of 1993, the FBI arrested eight members of the Fourth Reich Skinheads. The group's members had been plotting to attack several racially symbolic targets in Los Angeles, including the First African Methodist Episcopal Church. They were also planning to assassinate Rodney King, Louis Farrakhan, and Al Sharpton. They had already bombed several houses in Lakewood and Paramount and attacked the Temple Beth Synagogue in Westminster.

The group's purpose was to provoke a reaction from the African-American and Jewish communities that they hoped would be violent enough to begin a race war. The Fourth Reich Skinheads were members of the World Church of the Creator, a racist group in Florida that encouraged its members to fight a "racial holy war" (or RAHOWA) against "mud" races.

Fourth Reich Skinheads, like most skinhead groups, were a loosely organized network of young white people, most of whom were male.

According to some estimates, the group may have had as many as fifty members, while others believe it may have been as few as eighteen. Police investigated the possibility that Fourth Reich Skinheads were tied with some of the other skinhead terrorists that were active on the West Coast in the summer of 1993, such as Jeremiah Gordon Knesal of the American Front. No evidence of any organizational structure connecting the various skinhead groups was found.

CURRENT GOALS: Fourth Reich Skinheads has ceased to exist as an organization for two reasons. First, five of its members, including group leader Christopher Daniel Fisher, were sent to prison for their involvement in the plot; second, thirteen members were required to participate in "Operation Grow Hair," a program designed by the U.S. district attorney to challenge the group's racist views. Participants in the program met with their intended targets, members of the First AME Church and Holocaust survivors. The speakers discussed and debated the skinheads' bigoted beliefs, and organizers believe the program was a success. "Operation Grow Hair" has become a model for dealing with skinhead groups.

Montana Freemen

BASE OF OPERATION: United States

FOUNDING PHILOSOPHY: The Montana Freemen were a group of farmers and shysters who practiced Posse Comitatus theories of common law and sovereign citizenship. The Montana Freemen refused to recognize the authority of the federal government and asserted their own right as "sovereign citizens" to print money and issue arrest warrants.

CURRENT GOALS: In September of 1995 two Freemen cells merged near Justus, Montana. Local tax protest leaders Leroy Schweitzer, Rodney Skurdal, and Daniel Peterson moved in with the Clark family. Schweitzer and Skurdal were infamous for teaching classes on how to pass fraudulent checks and file bogus liens. Earlier that year the Clark family, who owed

$1.8 million in mortgage payments and taxes, had convened a "common law court" and issued warrants threatening the life of the local sheriff and the county judge. When the two groups joined forces, they renamed the Clarks' farm, their base of operations, "Justus Township," and continued to threaten local authorities and teach seminars on how to execute classic Posse Comitatus scams.

Local law enforcement realized they would have to confront the Freemen, but Justus's sheriff didn't have the manpower to ensure that the confrontation went smoothly. The FBI, suffering from what the press dubbed "Weaver Fever" (the fear that a confrontation with militants would go as badly as the Ruby Ridge standoff had) was also reluctant to get involved. Local residents began to resent the apparent impunity with which the Freemen were flouting federal authority. "Call the IRS and ask them why they haven't seized their property," a local car dealer insisted. "Why do they get special treatment? I think the federal government has a responsibility to the people who are paying taxes."

Finally, on March 25, 1996, the FBI arrested Leroy Schweitzer and Daniel Peterson, and demanded the dozen or so Freemen for whom they had arrest warrants leave Justus Township. The Freemen refused, and a standoff, which was to last eighty-one days, began.

The FBI was determined not to make the same mistakes that were made at Ruby Ridge. The standoff was managed by the FBI's Critical Incident Response Group, which implemented lessons learned during the Ruby Ridge confrontation. Agents wore civilian clothes instead of camouflage and drove civilian vehicles instead of armored cars. Federal officials made repeated, televised pleas to the Freemen to surrender peacefully. Instead of surrounding the Clark ranch, FBI agents merely stopped and questioned anyone who tried to enter or leave. Finally, the FBI notified paramilitary groups across the country before arresting a single Freeman, which preempted conspiracy theories and actually won the support of some militias. Several prominent figures in the militia community, such as the attorneys of Randy Weaver and families who died at Waco, actually served as negotiators in attempts to end the standoff.

At first, the Freemen showed no signs of willingness to compromise and deliberately made unreasonable demands to stall negotiations. For example, they insisted at one point that they would only negotiate if Supreme Court nominee, Robert Bork, acted as a mediator. The also issued a press release declaring independence from the "de facto corporate prostitute also known as the United States." The standoff dragged on for weeks, then months, without any sign of a breakthrough. On day seventy-one, the FBI cut power to the Freemen Ranch. Finally, on June 13, 1996, the remaining members of the Freemen surrendered peacefully, and the FBI arrested those for whom it had warrants, effectively ending the existence of the Montana Freemen.

Oklahoma Constitutional Militia

ALIASES: Universal Church of God

BASE OF OPERATION: United States

FOUNDING PHILOSOPHY: The Oklahoma Constitutional Militia (OCM) was a small, antigovernment, anti-Semitic group whose only planned attack was foiled by an FBI informer. They believed that the New World Order existed and posed a direct and immediate threat to them. Militia leader Willie Ray Lampley expected Russia to invade the United States through Mexico during his lifetime, and he encouraged his followers to stockpile supplies and arms in preparation for the invasion. The Militia's members were all followers of the racist teachings of Christian Identity, and the group was also known as the Universal Church of God. Lampley visited Elohim City, a compound at which the leaders of American white supremacy networked and discussed their shared beliefs.

The militia formed in 1994, when Lampley and Larry Wayne Crow met and forged a friendship based on their shared religious views. The two soon began to attend militia meetings and published religious pamphlets. Lampley believed he was a prophet, and Crow, who testified for the prosecution at Lampley's trial, claims that Lampley thought it was his duty to act on God's alleged condemnation of supposedly sinful people such as homosexuals, abortion doctors, and civil rights activists.

CURRENT GOALS: Lampley, Crow, Lampley's wife, Cecilia, and John Dare Baird were arrested in November of 1995 for conspiring to bomb several targets, including gay bars, abortion clinics, and civil rights groups, such as the Southern Poverty Law Center (SPL) and the Anti-Defamation League. Authorities found the supplies for an ammonium nitrate bomb in the Lampleys' home in Vernon, Oklahoma. Crow, who claims he had left the group, negotiated a plea bargain with the prosecution and testified against the other three group members. Lampley and his codefendants claimed that they'd been entrapped by FBI agent Richard Schrum. Lampley insisted that it had been Schrum's idea to build the bomb. Cecilia Lampley, John Baird, and Willie Ray Lampley were all convicted of conspiring to construct a homemade bomb. Willie Ray Lampley was also convicted on two additional counts. The Oklahoma Constitutional Militia ceased to exist after the arrest and trial of its only known members.

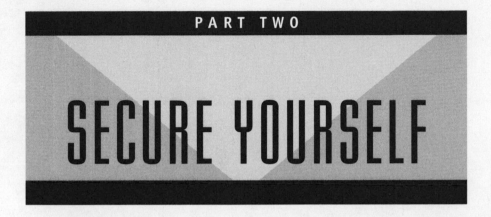

PART TWO

SECURE YOURSELF

FOUR

▼

Risk Assessment and Total Security Management (TSM)

The extent to which the nation as a whole can depend on critical infrastructure is in question. A lot of people assume it is all going to be OK. Everything is not always going to be OK.

ROY MAXION, CARNEGIE MELLON UNIVERSITY PROFESSOR AND NOTED

CRITICAL INFRASTRUCTURE PROTECTION EXPERT

RISK MANAGEMENT

The goal of the risk-management process is to determine a rational basis for deciding which mitigation measures to enact (and at what concrete costs) versus how much risk to accept (and at what potential costs). A company, for example, can hire a personal security detail to protect its CEO from physical assault, but if that CEO works in an inadequately protected facility, he or she can still be injured or killed in an attack against the headquarters building, thereby negating the investment in the security detail. Alternatively, the CEO could survive an attack that nonetheless destroys expensive research and development logs or a one-of-a-kind piece of manufacturing equipment that takes so long to replace that the company's competitors gain a market advantage or, worse, drive it out of business.

RISK MANAGEMENT ALTERNATIVES

Do Nothing
■ No cost
■ Greatest risk

Reasonable Mitigation Measures
■ Some cost
■ Reduced risk

Harden the Facility
■ Greatest cost
■ Least risk

Such threats have to be weighed against the reality that limited resources and normative business practices preclude hardening all targets at all times. In this example, as in real life, the optimal answer will vary for each company. Company A may not have the funds to address the problem at all and therefore will have to accept greater operational risk, understanding that a single anomalous event could destroy the company; Company B may decide to harden existing facilities or accelerate construction on additional off-site production capacity, while Company C may decide to move its productive capacity offshore or relocate its headquarters to a less severe threat environment. The optimal solution, and the costs and risks it entails, will vary for each company, but the risk-assessment process for analyzing alternatives remains the same across companies and, for the most part, across industries. The essential element is that a deliberate decision process analyzes the risks and the costs and determines which path to take, as opposed to merely avoiding the issue and allowing inertia, or other factors, to determine the company's de facto level of risk.

The efficient and effective management of terrorism and related risks therefore requires a comprehensive understanding of the various risks and rewards for altering each element, then making calculated decisions to mitigate certain risks while accepting the potential losses from other risks. This is true as well with natural disasters such as hurricanes and tornadoes, and human error such as is often the case in power blackouts. Ensuring that a complete and validated process is used to protect the company's credit rating and investment potential is necessary because the conclusions of the analysis can be communicated to shareholders, employees, and industry analysts.

Security: Net Loss or Essential Function?

The era of terrorism combined with the increasing interconnectedness of the systems that we rely upon to run, monitor, and respond to nearly every activity of our daily lives has given rise to tremendous inherent risk and uncertainty. This risk extends to many businesses as well, where even industry leaders remain surprisingly unprepared for preventing or responding to disruptive events. How much risk should be accepted in order to reasonably mitigate most risks while continuing to carry out normal business operations? In other words, how much security is enough?

Ten years ago technology and security analysts began discussing the inherent dangers created by our ever-more-interrelated control systems. President Clinton responded to this emerging threat through Executive Order 13010, which created the President Commission on Critical Infrastructure Protection (PCCIP) to explore the concept of critical infrastructures and national security. Over the intervening decade, and especially with the events of 9/11, a new reality has emerged requiring businesses to become better able to secure their facilities, value chains, and overall business processes. Despite a decade of effort and the additional impetus of the terrorist threat to our nation, not only are security measures still broadly insufficient, but our understanding of the interdependencies among, for example, the railway, port, and energy industries, remains elementary. As a result the next significant event (be it nature, negligence, or terrorism) could potentially and needlessly affect many more thousands of Americans than would otherwise be the case.

Take the transportation industry. Air, rail, and sea transportation have collectively been designated as critical national infrastructures, meaning the government recognizes that their impairment could do grievous harm to the nation and their ability to function is essential to the physical and economic well-being of the nation. This concern is understandable, especially given that according to press reports U.S. intelligence officials believe al Qaida owns and operates some fifteen cargo freighters worldwide, many of which generate profits for the group through legitimate trade but which could potentially be used for attacks anywhere in the world. (One such ves-

sel is believed to have carried and delivered the explosives used by al Qaida
in the 1998 U.S. Embassy bombings in Africa.) Similarly, there is com-
pelling evidence of a link between an al Qaida–affiliated ring of scuba divers
in the Netherlands and possible attacks on U.S. interests. But while billions
and billions of dollars have been poured into securing the nation's airports,
less progress has been made on other equally perilous fronts.

This is especially true in securing maritime cargo. Some four years after
9/11, less than 10 percent of ocean cargo is inspected, and even the several
key ports that process the bulk of the nation's cargo remain woefully unprepared for terrorist strikes or other disruptive events. For example, the names
on shipping manifests not only are screened against disconnected and
incomplete suspect terrorist watch lists, but with no reliable means of
verifying that the names match the workers. And the much heralded
Customs-Trade Partnership Against Terrorism (C-TPAT) remains voluntary
and without sufficient funds for anyone to audit and verify self-reported
vulnerability assessments.

What would happen if a cargo container in the midst of a busy port is
determined to be a risk for containing a chemical, biological, or nuclear device? Where would the potentially contaminated cargo be moved for further inspection, and who would protect it en route from being detonated?
How much of the nearby cargo would also need to be quarantined and
should the facility be closed? Remember that a few envelopes filled with anthrax shut down Congress for weeks and a postal-processing plant for over
two years; is there a means for rapid decontamination and isolation of the
area or will the entire facility be closed?

In 2002 a ten-day Long Beach dockworkers strike upset the cargo-
handling system and, in turn, prevented the movement of parts and supplies nationwide. It cost the U.S. economy an estimated $2 billion per day
because the twenty-nine affected ports handle approximately 21 percent
of goods imported into the United States and about nine percent of all
goods exported. The strike also forced some manufacturers who rely on
foreign parts, including Boeing, GM, and Toyota, to shut down or realign
their assembly processes because they couldn't get necessary parts. Produce was lost at sea as it spoiled, and even after the strike it took weeks
before the domestic rail, truck, and air-transportation networks worked

through the backlog. And there was no damage involved, no crime scene to investigate, no area to be quarantined; just some workers who didn't go to work for ten days. How much would it cost if Long Beach were shut down for several months? How many such incidents can the economy withstand?

Risk Management and the Global War on Terrorism[1]

The business sector's risk-management process seeks to analyze existing and potential vulnerabilities, weigh them against the costs of mitigation alternatives, and determine which risks to minimize and which to accept. The process inherently accepts that some risks are so severe that mitigation is worth relatively high costs (i.e., using armed guards to protect banks and nuclear power plants), while others are less severe and receive comparatively little mitigation (unarmed guards for shopping malls, schools, and office buildings). With years of use as the business world's formula for managing and mitigating risks, this approach is increasingly applicable to public-sector efforts to manage the needs of Homeland Security.

It is not surprising, therefore, that discussions of risk management have become increasingly popular since the advent of the Global War on Terrorism, and all the more so since Michael Chertoff, the second Secretary of the Department of Homeland Security, announced his intention to enforce a national policy of risk-based threat mitigation.

The difference between this approach and the "blanket security" approach necessarily taken by Secretary Chertoff's predecessor is clear: the federal government will look to preempt, disrupt, and prepare for significant future attacks, but the lower-level threats to security are the responsibility of not just state and local actors but the private sector as well. This fact will be all the more important as the terrorists' tactics continue to evolve in response to changing conditions and newly perceived weaknesses. For example, if

[1]Portions of this section are drawn from the article "Securing Communities Through Total Security Management™," authored by J. Michael Barrett and published as an Issue Analysis by the American Legislative Exchange Council in the summer of 2005.

federal and military facilities are too difficult to strike, then the threat shifts to less-protected critical components of the economy, including state-based facilities, infrastructure, iconic businesses, and food and water supplies. What is called for, therefore, is a renewed effort to create public-private partnership for the protection of assets critical to the common good.

Fortunately, like private-sector firms, if individual communities or states can differentiate themselves through measures that deter the enemy from striking them, the benefits of this deterrent effect become significant in evaluating their overall strategies for managing risk. Just as the business world's use of risk management enables analysts and investors to determine relative risk and reward associated with investing in or doing business with firms more secure than their peers, in the public-safety arena such security measures could be used to help citizens determine their relative risk, desired level of safety, and which preparedness steps the citizens themselves should take.

Consider that when Osama bin Laden declared war on the modern world in 1998, he issued a statement calling for the United States and its allies to depart the Middle East. Shortly thereafter his al Qaida terrorists struck two overseas American Embassies, killing a total of 224 innocent people and wounding more than 5,000. But significantly, and because our embassies in the Middle East were at "high alert" status, the terrorists chose not to target our facilities in Israel, Saudi Arabia, Bahrain, or elsewhere in the region; they attacked those in Kenya and Tanzania instead. This happened because terrorists, like all those acting outside the law, select their targets at least partially based on the probability for success. It therefore follows that it is possible to deter terrorists from attacking your community or the facilities within it by implementing appropriate deterrent security measures, which will enable individual communities and/or firms to shift risk away from themselves. Consequently, proper security practices, far from being a drag on public expenditures or economic productivity, have become significant "better business" prerogatives.

At the same time the paramilitary experience, skills, and technologies that enable terrorists throughout Lebanon, Palestine, and now Iraq to use improvised explosive devices and car and truck bombs to such effect are very likely migrating to our shores. Experts inside and outside of the government are increasingly concerned that the future may well be marked by a duality of terrorist threat streams: a continuation of large-scale "spectaculars" like the attacks of 9/11 coupled with massive economic disruptions based on multiple, smaller-scale events, like the disruption of transportation networks with radiological bombs, shooting sprees at shopping malls, bombings of sporting events, and tampering with our agriculture. The result would be an enemy strategy of economic death by a thousands cuts, as terrorist events, both large and small, combine to adversely effect the free flow of goods and services and disrupt each industry's value chain in unforeseen ways.

How Secure Is Your Community?

You won't know until a comprehensive risk assessment and vulnerability analysis has been completed. This is the essential first step in achieving an adequate security posture and sustainable business continuity plans, and, as such, is the key to dealing with today's inherent uncertainties. Here again, the public sector can take a lesson from the private sector, expanding on the narrow focus a single business or industry uses by examining the total security of the "systems within systems" that serve and sustain the community. This includes the power plants, water facilities, telecommunications hubs, and public health and transportation assets that promote the community's safety, security, and survivability.

TOTAL SECURITY MANAGEMENT

The Liddy approach to risk management for security is called "Total Security Management" (TSM), defined as "the business practice of developing and implementing comprehensive risk management and security practices for a firm's entire value chain. TSM calls for an evaluation of suppliers, distribution channels, and internal policies and procedures in terms of preparedness for disruptive events such as terrorism, natural disasters, and accidents."

TSM emphasizes a holistic approach to security by extending the traditional definition beyond securing only one's own facilities, personnel, and supply chains, and is reliant upon an evolving set of standards and ratings to assess the relative preparedness of business-critical infrastructure and processes. Communities must take the same big-picture approach, evaluating their entire chain of critical infrastructure and how interrelated functions affect each other, plus the cascading effects of potential failures. The approach should be one broadly based on an assessment of relevant risks, potential loss of life, economic effect, and realistic threat. Critically, communities must do this in concert with their key private-sector constituents, for communities cannot be secure if they rely on insecure privately held critical infrastructure.

Another key component of TSM is finding solutions that are complementary of, as opposed to in conflict with, the prerogatives of the private sector's business model and the public sector's operational imperatives. For example, banks, casinos, and hospitals have long understood the need for certain levels of security but have invested strategically in ways to maintain an open flow of people combined with a sense of security through appropriate combinations of surveillance equipment, security guards, and insurance policies.

By the same token, security is a field where employee practices play a significant role in proper implementation, in both the public and private spheres. For example, at security's most basic level, radiation detectors only work if the agents are properly trained; high-quality locks for external doors are useless against thieves if employees don't close the doors properly; and proper landscaping and use of set-back distances to protect against car and truck bombs won't be useful unless security teams properly control traffic flow and screen delivery trucks.

Communities and key industry partners must be free to hold open and honest discussions about security, an area where neither communities nor businesses are comfortable exposing their known vulnerabilities. If they don't share knowledge of their known vulnerabilities then there will be no way to combine the information provided to reveal the unknown vulnerabilities, the hidden critical assets, and the "single points of failure" that must be addressed in advance of any disruptive event. But there must not be penalties incurred for being open and honest with those responsible for public safety and security; the right protections will require concerted, aggressive political will, including provisions that protect proprietary corporate information from being used against a firm in either the press or in courtrooms. For example, legislators could consider protecting security-specific deliberations from the Freedom of Information Act (FOIA), thereby encouraging firms to share known issues more widely.

Achieving the full benefits of better security practices will rely upon the degree of buy-in by various key elements both within and external to the government agencies and the businesses involved. From a public policy perspective, it is important that leaders push for appropriate security measures, and, in turn, receive the appropriate credit for making decisions that may require expenditures today, especially when those expenditures will be minimal indeed compared to the losses should an event strike an unprepared community. From the business side, senior leadership also plays a major role in understanding that certain direct, immediate costs will be more than compensated for by gains over time in less tangible areas such as investor confidence and improved credit ratings.

The first step in managing risk is to understand existing vulnerabilities and various mitigation alternatives, but one cannot ignore the business imperatives to find ways where security complements public policy imperatives as well as existing business practices. Given the inherent uncertainty in today's threat-and-security environment, it is imperative that all marketplace players—public, private, and other—rethink the way they approach security. When disaster strikes—be it from avian flu, an accidental but sustained power disruption, or a terrorist event involving weapons of mass destruction—communities that didn't prepare themselves will find themselves much worse off than those that did. And in the long run, just as the marketplace learns to differentiate among firms based on deterrence-and-disaster preparedness, communities and citizens will as well.

RISK ASSESSMENT, LIDDY STYLE

The approach to risk management separates terrorism risks into three key elements: the assets you value and therefore need to protect, the likelihood of you or your industry being attacked, and your vulnerability to attack.[2] This approach promotes effective, predictive risk management by identifying known threats to a company or industry. It also facilitates deeper analysis and focus on previously unrecognized threats emanating from the evolution of new forms of risk and a broader understanding of the systemic effects of the degradation or destruction of key critical infrastructures (power, water, transportation, etc.).

These key components of risk do not act in isolation from each other; quite the contrary, they are closely dependent on and reinforce each other. For instance, colocating your key assets will make a single attack potentially all the more devastating (as with the New York City government's decision to collocate most disaster-recovery offices and many supplies in and around the World Trade Center complex). However, reducing your vulnerability to attack by hardening your facility with increased physical protection should, in turn, make the targeting of your facility less likely.

Perhaps the most important part of the analysis is examining the potential for cascading effects of a single event, such as how the loss of power may preclude the pumping of water to fire-control systems, which by law means plant activities must cease, or the ways in which a seaport's closure will disrupt the flow of parts, preventing the assembly and distribution of final products. This analysis of the physical and logical interrelationships of all the components, both within and outside the organization, is the basis for understanding and avoiding potentially catastrophic events that, on the

---

[2]While this approach offers a viable means of assigning values and apportioning risk, there can be a degree of subjectivity in this analysis because it is difficult to know the full value of an item, fully understand the enemy's mind-set and intentions, or to ensure your vulnerability-mitigation efforts will be effective. The key to success lies in having experienced and knowledgeable industry analysts perform the assessment and assign the values.

Risk = Value of Assets + Likelihood of Attack + Vulnerability to Attack

surface, may not seem as high risk as other events. These key processes must be protected from harm in order to return most efficiently to normal operations. Identifying and mitigating these cascading effects is one of the primary functions of the analysis team.

Building the Team

The most critical aspect of the risk-management process is putting together the right assessment team. It should include paramilitary expertise, structural and other engineers, and industry specialists to properly identify where and how the facility interacts with and relies upon various external functions, such as power, water, and transportation infrastructures. Fortunately, the Department of Defense (DoD) has spent years developing assessment methodologies for assessing at-risk nuclear facilities and other critical national assets. And post–9/11, these approaches have migrated to the private sector.[3]

The key is to understand the real level of threat and to "war game" against the most likely and most severe threats. Tailoring the appropriate team to the task at hand will ensure that the proper threat levels are countered but that security expenditures are not unnecessarily and prohibitively expensive. The team that assesses high-value assets, like nuclear power plants, for example, should be composed of paramilitary specialists trained in special operations weapons and tactics, covert and clandestine intelligence gathering,

[3]Commander James Liddy, a retired career Navy SEAL officer was the head of the U.S. Navy's post–Khobar Towers integrated-vulnerability-assessment team, where he played a primary role in developing the navy's antiterrorism and force-protection standards. His follow-up assignment was to turn his team's methodolody into what became the Joint Staff Integrated Vulnerability Assessment, which has since become the de facto standard for all the services' antiterrorism/force-protection assessments.

and exploitation of IT and physical vulnerabilities. This is because nuclear power plants are known terrorist targets, where an attack has the potential to do significant and lasting harm well beyond the facility itself.

By contrast, an average chemical production facility or less-significant seaport needs to take prudent security measures against the danger of terrorist tactics seen in Saudi Arabia and Iraq, which include small-unit tactics such as truck bombs and armed assaults by five to ten gunmen, but not attacks by world-class paramilitary units that are well-trained and conduct weeks or months of preoperational intelligence collection and exploitation and use specialized weapons and communications equipment.

For many assessments the majority of the assessment team members are not specially trained military commandos, though you often have a Special Forces, Navy SEAL, or Marine Force Recon veteran as the team leader. The remainder of the team is often a combination of industry experts; electrical, mechanical, or physical engineers; veteran law-enforcement agents; and information technology specialists. Using this blend of experts provides the ability to analyze risks from a variety of vectors; understand the interlocking relationships among the physical, transportation, logistical, and IT nodes of the company or community's key components; and propose complementary, practical, and effective risk-mitigation solutions.

Analyzing Asset Value

Analyzing values for assets such as people, production facilities, or distribution channels requires an overall assessment determining relative values for all company assets as well as the systems within which they operate and upon which they rely. The assessment team begins by identifying the critical processes and key "nodes" of production that are of the highest value to the company. These will include certain tangible aspects, such as production and storage facilities, information systems, customer-care centers, and shipping routes and methods. It will also identify less tangible factors, such as the survival of key decision makers, maintaining public image, and sustaining corporate morale.

This process also includes conducting a quantitative risk assessment, collecting readily identifiable data, such as floor plans, computerized assets lists, documentation on policies and procedures, and information on known risks such as natural hazards or terrorist, environmental extremist, or other threats. If appropriate, based on the size and complexity of the organization, a number of specific respondent questionnaires are prepared and distributed to certain employees to identify known problem areas and vulnerabilities. The collected data are also analyzed to define the mission of the organization and the function of each of its components, classifying key assets according to their criticality, sensitivity, and use within the organization. These assets can then be targeted for additional protection through developing redundant power systems, alternate supply and distribution channels, training of back-up personnel, and securing off-site emergency work space for continuity of operations.

Determining Specific Threats

Now that you have determined which assets you must protect, the second step is to assess the threat of attack. This is often the least precise of the evaluations in the risk-assessment process, as it is a function of understanding the enemy's intent and capabilities as well as their probable assessment of a target's relative value in terms of propaganda, economic effect, or some similar value. Even the U.S. intelligence community, which spends billions of dollars a year to gain insight into such issues, is unable to definitively assign degrees of threat beyond rudimentary "rule of thumb" estimates.

For example, is American Airlines a more lucrative target than Jet-Blue because of the name "American," or does the fact that JetBlue uses smaller airports to cut costs lead terrorists to conclude that its airports will be less well protected? Are Washington, D.C., and New York at greater risk for future attacks than Phoenix, Saint Louis, or Denver because Washington and New York are such prominent cities, or are Washington and New York at reduced risk because they are perceived to be better prepared?

THE PROTECTION CHALLENGE*

Agriculture & Food	1,912,000 farms; 87,000 food-processing plants
Water	1,800 federal reservoirs; 1,600 municipal waste water facilities
Public Health	5,800 registered hospitals
Emergency Services	87,000 U.S. localities
Defense Industrial Base	250,000 firms in 215 distinct industries
Telecommunications	2 billion miles of cable
Energy	
Electricity	2,800 power plants
Oil & Natural Gas	300,000 producing sites
Transportation	
Aviation	5,000 public airports
Passenger Rail & Railroads	120,000 miles of major railroads
Highways, Trucking & Busing	590,000 highway bridges
Pipelines	2 million miles of pipeline
Maritime	300 inland/coastal ports
Mass Transit	500 major urban public transit operators
Banking & Finance	26,600 FDIC-insured institutions
Chemical Industry & Hazardous Materials	66,000 chemical plants
Postal & Shipping	137 million delivery sites
Key Assets	
National Monuments & Icons	5,800 historic buildings
Nuclear Power Plants	104 commercial nuclear power plants
Dams	80,000 dams
Government Facilities	3,000 government-owned/operated facilities
Commercial Assets	460 skyscrapers

*These are approximate figures adapted from "The National Strategy for the Physical Protection of Critical Infrastructure and Key Assets," www.whitehouse.gov/pcipb/physical_strategy.pdf.

It is also difficult to assess the relative value of your neighbors and co-tenants. For example, after determining that the local FBI building was too well secured, Timothy McVeigh chose to strike the more accessible Alfred P. Murrah Federal Building, which housed the Bureau of Alcohol, Tobacco, Firearms, and Explosives (BATFE). McVeigh considered the BATFE a legit-imate target because of its role in the fiery massacre of a fundamentalist

Christian sect at Waco, Texas. However, the building also housed numerous completely unrelated facilities, including a child day-care center. Finally, if someone else in your industry is attacked, will it prompt regulatory actions that affect you, and can you better prepare yourself for such actions by performing adequate risk assessments today? Will not preparing yourself or your business potentially increase your liability?[4]

EXAMPLES OF CORPORATE RISK

- Injuries to the public or workforce.
- Direct and indirect financial losses.
- Loss of reputation or business viability.
- Environmental damage.

Despite the difficulty of answering these questions, intelligence and other security experts agree that the tactics we are likely to see in the future will blend the mass-casualty spectacular-attack approach with the less-complex but more frequent truck-and-suicide bombing tactics we see in Israel and Iraq. Furthermore, based on the al Qaida network's stated goals, even if precise calculations are difficult the overall threat is clear: all Americans, and therefore all American businesses, face a high degree of risk.

Vulnerability Assessments

Vulnerability is defined as a weakness that can be exploited to gain unauthorized access or to provide an opportunity to cause harm. If the threat assessment is the most subjective aspect of risk management, then the vulnerability assessment is the part that requires the greatest depth of specialized expertise to turn the "science" of the methodology into an "art." An effective vulnerability assessment will be both broad and narrow in scope, with one track looking at the overall systemic picture of potential loss from key interrelated infrastructures and interdependencies, while a parallel track examines the narrow security features surrounding specific assets, such as the effectiveness of certain surveillance measures or physical barriers.

---

[4] Portions of this section adapted from the Federal Emergency Management Agency's Reference Manual to Mitigate Potential Terrorist Attacks Against Buildings, available at www.fema.gov/pdf/fima/426/fema42.pdf.

Examples of typical vulnerabilities include weaknesses in IT management, physical security, or operational security.

Enumerating Vulnerability

Based on an examination of the organization's related functions and assigned resources, the assessment team then designs a list of likely threats that could cause a significant loss of organizational assets and affect the ability to carry out their mission. For each key asset the severity of major threats and vulnerabilities are considered and a numerical value is assigned to represent the actual percentage of the value of the asset that is subject to loss if the event were to occur. A computation is made of the loss that could be expected for each occurrence of the threat based on presumed degree of harm to the asset's value.

Categorizing Risk

Having determined your threat, key assets, and vulnerabilities, the next phase of risk assessment is to categorize your risks into certain data tables to better identify which ones you need to address. This will enable better expenditures of resources in mitigating certain risks while accepting others. Properly performing such evaluations involves somewhat extensive calculations based on weighted variables for each possible type of attack and for various assets. The extremely simplistic model for risk categorization shown in the following tables is based on a model provided by the Federal Emergency Management Agency (FEMA) as a notional method for categorizing risk. It is based on assigning scores of relative vulnerability and then comparing relative total risk values.

1. **Effect:** Assign a score of 1 to 10 for the values of each asset, with 10 being the highest effect if the asset is lost or destroyed.
2. **Threat:** Assign a score of 1 to 10 for the threat rating, which represents a subjective judgment based on experience, capability,

history, intentions, and targeting, with 10 being the highest probability of attack.

3. **Vulnerability:** Assign a score of 1 to 10 for the level of vulnerability for each of the assets you are evaluating, with 10 being extremely vulnerable.

4. **Total risk:** Multiply the three values together to determine the total perceived risk for each asset based on the various types of attacks. The total value determines a total risk category for each factor and, in turn, helps in prioritizing which mitigation measures to implement to address which types of threats.

RISK FACTORS DEFINED	
Very High	10
High	8–9
Medium High	7
Medium	5–6
Medium Low	4
Low	2–3
Very Low	1

Risk Mitigation

The final step in the risk-assessment process is to evaluate appropriate risk-mitigation alternatives. The factors to be considered for various proposed solutions include the likely reduction in threat of a successful attack, implementation and maintenance costs, the effect on daily operations, and any identifiable negative externalities such as decreased efficiency or increased risk to other assets.

Potential solutions may range from altering the existing security rotation to allow for larger evening staff to the installation of better exterior lighting or construction of physical barriers. Often, however, the solution can be as simple as improved awareness of employee and visitor locations inside the facility and better communication with local authorities to ensure mutual understanding of emergency response protocols. A more thorough risk assessment will identify specific mitigation solutions and then detail the costs and savings associated with each proposed additional safeguard in terms of return on investment to help management rationally determine which risks to mitigate and which to accept.

RISK FACTORS TOTAL		
Low Risk	Medium Risk	High Risk
1–60	61–175	>175

A Word About the Risk-Consulting Industry[5]

Many companies find that the most effective way for them to address risk mitigation is to hire a specialty firm that offers expertise in the processes outlined above. While one must be careful to determine in advance their purposes and intents in order to take full advantage of the specialty firms' offerings, the risk-assessment industry generally is divided into three fairly distinct models: traditional, large auditing and consulting firms; other, usually smaller, firms that use automated tools to perform systems processes surveys and make rough estimates of risk values; and firms composed of former military or law-enforcement analysts who offer rapid assessments based primarily on intuition and experience in understanding how adversaries exploit existing vulnerabilities. Any of these three firms may provide the solution you are looking for, although they each provide a somewhat different service.

The first group, marked by marquee industry players known for all types of auditing services, is strongest in terms of business practice realignment and in-depth analysis of processes that affect overall security. They typically provide well-educated business analysts or very bright generalists who have learned security as a matter of course as an "additional category," as opposed to from deep personal experience, and can often spend anywhere from thirty-six to fifty-two weeks on-site conducting large assessments. The typical methodology for any business concern is to engage the clients and conduct interviews and assessments in-person to reveal inefficiencies and failings in current practices, and this model is extended to security. This approach yields significant opportunities for improvement

[5]Portions of this section are drawn from the article "Risk Consultants Aren't All Alike," authored by J. Michael Barrett and published in the *The Journal of Commerce* (May 23, 2005).

and internal reconfiguring, and is most applicable to those firms looking to aggressively restructure and realign their business processes as they relate to security.

The second group is characterized generally by individuals and smaller firms aided by the use of software tools, with each firm usually selecting a specific single-industry focus. These analysts typically automate the survey process, which can cut the total product cost of their consulting services dramatically by limiting the on-site portion of the assessment timeline by as much as two-thirds. This in turn results in a less comprehensive but more affordable means of assessing one's basic needs. Here again you may not be getting a highly trained security specialist conducting the work, but that is not the focus: the focus is on creating surveys so that internal parties can report back on how well existing policies and procedures are adhered to, how secure they feel, and assessing any widely known vulnerabilities. This is the best approach for a firm that is certain it faces relatively low risk, does not wish to invest in the full audit model described above, and is primarily focused on surveying *current* practices rather than a full evaluation of what those practices *should be*.

The third type of firm provides the most comprehensive and specialized risk assessment specifically in terms of security, especially with regard to terrorism or other nontraditional threats. These firms are almost all staffed by former law-enforcement agents or members of the military who have deep and specialized experience and expertise in assessing security, both as the aggressor looking for holes to exploit and as the team assigned to protect a certain area. Their pricing is usually comparable to the second group above, and therefore less expensive than the full auditor approach. Typically their interviews to determine current practices will be less in-depth than those of the first group, opting instead to conduct exercises and simulations to test response times and procedures. They also will focus intently on the client's threats, vulnerabilities, and security posture, drawing on experience to determine what additional safeguards could increase the security posture relative to the most likely, relevant, and significant threats. These audits are the right choice for clients who are focused specifically on defeating significant threats and want to improve their security posture by taking a hard, critical look at existing gaps in physical and procedural mitigation measures.

FIVE

▼

Personal Security

The ultimate measure of a man is not where he stands in moments
of comfort and convenience, but where he stands at times of
challenge and controversy.

DR. MARTIN LUTHER KING JR.

Despite the attacks of September 11, 2001, and the ongoing threat of
WMD terrorism, statistics tell us that on an individual level traditional
violent crime, such as kidnapping and murder, remain the more likely personal security threat. In fact, from 1992 to 1996, federal statistics report
more than 2 million workplace assaults each year, including 395,000 aggra-
vated assaults, 51,000 rapes and sexual assaults, 84,000 robberies, and one
thousand homicides. Additionally, among the American population at
large, while approximately half of all murderers each year are related to
their assailants, the other half were strangers, proving that danger lurks on
many fronts.[1] While it cannot be determined in advance if the threat you
specifically face will come from a large-scale mass casualty attack, from

[1]From Centers for Disease Control, "Violence in the Workplace," July 1996, at www.cdc.gov/niosh/
violcont.html.

smaller suicide and truck bomb attacks, or from a lesser form of street crime, the single most important action for an individual is refining awareness of your surroundings and learning to trust your intuition. If something doesn't seem right, better to act decisively and remove yourself from the threat area than to stick around and be proven correct that yes, you were indeed in danger.

Developing a reliable sense of when things don't seem right and acting on your instincts are invaluable tools in the personal security game, and it is often the simple measures that will do the most to protect you. The best path is always to avoid the potential danger, especially if you are accompanying your family; so if the neighborhood in which you are parking makes you feel uncomfortable, the best course of action is to pay for safe parking or use a valet service rather than take your chances with an undesirable street element. Personal security isn't just about being tough; it's about being smart, too. Tough works when necessary, but there's no reason to put yourself in a situation where the odds are stacked against you.

RESPONSE PREPAREDNESS

- Be aware of your surroundings.
- Take precautions when commuting or traveling.
- Move or leave if you feel uncomfortable or if something does not seem right.
- Develop an emergency response plan.
- Assemble an emergency supplies kit.
- Report unusual behavior, suspicious packages, or strange devices to security personnel.
- Develop a communications plan for the office, home, and while traveling.
- Pay attention to emergency exits in buildings and public transportation.
- Ensure that employees and family members understand the Homeland Security Advisory System and current threat level.
- Identify at least two meeting points for family members.
- Remember to make special accommodations for people with special needs or medical conditions.

RESPONDING TO TERRORISM

Even terrorists respond to the principle that success is a key to every mission—that is why they attacked U.S. embassies in Kenya and Tanzania in 1998 instead of the more secure facilities in Saudi Arabia or Israel. Your primary objective in deterring any attacker, including terrorists, therefore is to reduce the assailant's perceived likelihood of success by making yourself

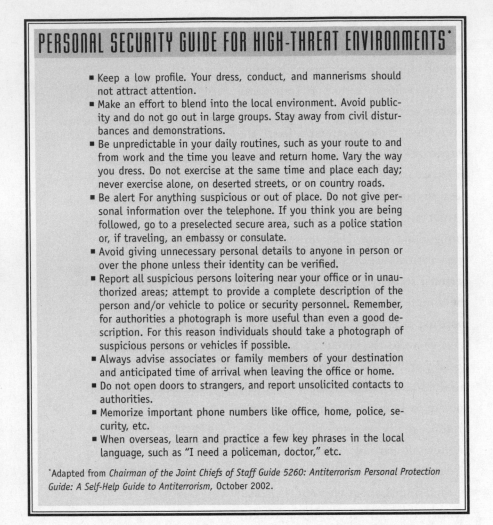

PERSONAL SECURITY GUIDE FOR HIGH-THREAT ENVIRONMENTS*

- Keep a low profile. Your dress, conduct, and mannerisms should not attract attention.
- Make an effort to blend into the local environment. Avoid publicity and do not go out in large groups. Stay away from civil disturbances and demonstrations.
- Be unpredictable in your daily routines, such as your route to and from work and the time you leave and return home. Vary the way you dress. Do not exercise at the same time and place each day; never exercise alone, on deserted streets, or on country roads.
- Be alert For anything suspicious or out of place. Do not give personal information over the telephone. If you think you are being followed, go to a preselected secure area, such as a police station or, if traveling, an embassy or consulate.
- Avoid giving unnecessary personal details to anyone in person or over the phone unless their identity can be verified.
- Report all suspicious persons loitering near your office or in unauthorized areas; attempt to provide a complete description of the person and/or vehicle to police or security personnel. Remember, for authorities a photograph is more useful than even a good description. For this reason individuals should take a photograph of suspicious persons or vehicles if possible.
- Always advise associates or family members of your destination and anticipated time of arrival when leaving the office or home.
- Do not open doors to strangers, and report unsolicited contacts to authorities.
- Memorize important phone numbers like office, home, police, security, etc.
- When overseas, learn and practice a few key phrases in the local language, such as "I need a policeman, doctor," etc.

*Adapted from *Chairman of the Joint Chiefs of Staff Guide 5260: Antiterrorism Personal Protection Guide: A Self-Help Guide to Antiterrorism*, October 2002.

into a "hard" target. The goal is to let them know that you are a more difficult target than someone else that also fits your profile, thereby decreasing your individual risk.

Aggressive Posture

For example, if you are walking out of a restaurant on your way to a car parked on the street and you see a suspicious person watching you, don't avoid his eyes; it is better to look right at him as if you expect him to challenge you. A confident demeanor will cause the typical street vagrant to wonder if you are such an easy mark after all, and your aggressive demeanor will likely cause him to hesitate. If he does not sense fear from you, he is likely to look for easier prey.

If you do become involved in a "street crime," the most likely target is your property, not your person, though since most street criminals work in teams it is likely you will be outnumbered. Simple techniques, such as showing your wallet plainly and then tossing it in one direction while escaping in another direction are important options to keep in mind. If the criminal is not content with your wallet and continues to pursue you, then you are faced with a "flight or fight" situation. Your best move is to act first, catching them off guard. By the time that you perceive it is a threatening situation, odds are they've already moved into place to cut off your avenues of escape and have prepared themselves for a fight. There are no points for gentleman's rules in a street fight; he who takes the initiative has the advantage, so strike first, hit hard, and play dirty. If there are several attackers and you strike decisively at the first, the others may rethink their desire to come after you. In this case, and especially if you are protecting someone who is with you, you must summon your aggressive strength and make do with the objects you have at hand.

Self-Defense Tactics

You can, for example, reach into your pocket and take out a pen (a steel ballpoint is preferred) and, at the moment your would-be assailant attempts physical contact with you, drive the point of the pen into the soft tissue above the collar line—at the base of his neck—in a deliberate and hard hammer fashion. Done right, this will inflict a critical, debilitating wound that causes your attacker to go into shock. At this point you have taken the advantage, and you may elect to flee or to strike again to incapacitate the attacker further. For example, a sharp pencil up into the armpit or, lethally, can be driven straight up through the underchin, through the tongue, into

When Jim Liddy was fourteen he had his life threatened for the first time. It was late in the evening, sometime after ten P.M., and he was walking home from the junior high school near where he lived when a young man passed by him riding a bike. The young man was standing up as he rode and turned back to look at Jim. He appeared to be in his late teens and was wearing torn blue jeans and an untucked button-down flannel shirt. He rode past Jim two more times; each time he would ride off, he would travel a block or so then turn around and come back. On his third pass, he came up behind Jim again, and again he looked back at him as he passed.

Jim sensed the danger, but was unsure what the man wanted. On his third pass he jumped off his bike and ran over toward Jim, pulling out a knife from his back pocket and demanding Jim give him all the money he had. Jim looked at him and immediately began sizing him up; he was older, but that didn't seem unusual—nearly all the people Jim had fought with in his life were older than he. The assailant was also thinner and less muscular than Jim, making the age issue less of a factor. The scenario followed one of the three rules his father had set down early in his upbringing: never start a fight but always finish it; second, never fight anyone younger than you; and third, never fight anyone smaller than you. At just fourteen Jim was not about to break any of those rules. But there was a new factor. The guy had a knife.

So there Jim was, confronted by an individual obviously older, a little bigger, and armed with a knife. As Jim stood there, his adrenaline pumping, the assailant again demanded all Jim's money. Given that his father was in prison and his mother was raising five children on a schoolteacher's salary of around eleven thousand dollars a year, Jim didn't have much in the way of cash. But what he had he was going to keep. So Jim told the man he didn't have any money.

The man didn't believe him. That's when Jim noticed he had positioned himself closer and gotten into a fighting position (generally, when an adversary confronts you his feet are parallel so you haven't lost the advantage yet; once he has moved one foot in front of the other, he is ready to fight). Unfortunately, Jim was still wondering why this predator chose to attempt to rob him of all people. The man again demanded, "Give me your money!" Jim repeated that he didn't have any money, at which point the assailant lunged forward with his knife. Jim was quick enough to step backward, leaning out of the way so that the knife entered his upper right thigh but missed the intended target, Jim's abdomen. Jim felt the burning sting of the knife penetrating his leg, but he also felt the powerful natural reaction of the fight or flight stimulus. He chose to fight.

With his body leaning forward Jim saw that the assailant was now opening himself up as a target. Not yet having received hand-to-hand combat training from the Navy SEALs, Jim didn't know how to best take advantage of this situation. However, the natural instinct to *fight back* kicked in. Jim kicked upward hard and fast with the leg that had been stabbed because the man's hand was still holding the knife. The knife stayed in Jim's thigh as the man jumped back and Jim pulled the knife out of his own thigh and glared at his attacker. That is when the attacker realized he was no longer armed, but now Jim was. At this point you'd naturally assume Jim took the advantage. Instead, he threw the knife as far as he could. This undoubtedly surprised the attacker, and upon reflection it surprised Jim as well! It was probably ultimately for the best, however, as Jim was not yet trained in the skills of knife fighting and this move actually evened the playing field into a normal fistfight. The attacker looked at

Jim, who immediately attacked him. Keeping a little low and moving to one side, Jim hit him hard in the chest with his right fist. Without pause Jim reached down and pulled the man's right leg out from under him. The man fell to the ground, hitting his head on the sidewalk. So as not to lose the advantage Jim jumped on him, putting his knee in the center of his back and pummeling him in the head and the ribs with his fists. When the assailant turned over to protect his face and attempted to get up on his knees Jim grabbed the man's ankle and pulled it up into his buttocks, grabbing him by the hair and slamming his face into the sidewalk four or five times until he no longer resisted. Jim left him bleeding on the sidewalk: wounded, unarmed, and no doubt regretting that he had picked on that particular fourteen-year-old boy.

Later, during SEAL training, Jim came to learn where he had gone wrong. Never give the SOB the advantage of choosing when the fight begins; incapacitate your attacker before he moves against you. Always strike first when confronted with hostile intent. Of all the lessons Jim learned as a Navy SEAL, none was as important as this one. What Jim had done correctly was to deny the attacker the opportunity to regain the offensive. We learn more from our mistakes than we do from our victories. When you learn from a mistake, you have not really failed; as long as you learn, you have advanced yourself in some measure. It is only when you repeat the same mistake over again that you have failed.

the soft palate, and ending in the brain. Your assailant will be dead before he hits the ground. Eight pounds of a pressure-chopping blow to the clavicle (collar bone) will break it and cause your opponent to lose the use of the arm on the same side. Alternatively, you can grab a brick or other nearby object to throw at your assailant. Be careful, however, to stay on main streets that are well-lit and avoid getting trapped in alleys or alcoves, for attracting the attention of others is an inherent part of your survival strategy.

SECURING YOUR HOME

It is an understandable and important concern to want to secure your home and protect your family. While terrorism is a significant threat, other crimes like theft, kidnap, rape, and murder remain all too common. Following a few simple guidelines will help deter criminals from selecting your home as their target. However, for those who feel that they are in need of more aggressive techniques, chapter 6, "Securing Your Workplace," and chapter 7, "Defensive Landscaping and Antiterrorism Architecture,"

REPORTING EMERGENCIES*

Any threat or real risk that puts lives in immediate danger is an emergency and should be reported by calling 9-1-1. Note the exact location of the threat or danger you observed and remember as much detail as you can provide about the emergency. Stay calm and take note of physical descriptions of the perpetrators, license plate numbers, and directions of travel.

You can help save lives by calling 9-1-1 when:

- You see or hear about someone carrying a weapon in an unlawful manner, using verbal threats, or suspiciously exiting a secured, nonpublic area near a train or bus depot, airport, tunnel, bridge, government building, or tourist attraction.
- You see or hear someone use or threaten to use a gun or other weapon, place a bomb, or release a poisonous substance into the air, water, or food supply.
- You see fire, smell smoke or gas, or hear an explosion.
- You see someone forcibly taken or being held by someone holding a weapon or threatening violence.
- You see a suspicious package abandoned in a crowded public place like an office building, airport, school, or shopping center.
- You see a suspicious letter or package in your mailbox.
- You believe a life or property is in immediate danger.

*Adapted from the National Crime Prevention Council's *United for a Stronger America Citizens' Preparedness Guide*.

---

contain access-and-surveillance recommendations for businesses and larger facilities that are relevant for certain homeowners as well.

The first step is to ensure your streets and the areas around your home are well lit and make sure every external door has a sturdy, properly installed dead-bolt look and a peephole to verify who is outside. Also, instead of hiding keys around the outside of your home, give an extra key to a neighbor whom you know and trust. Identify and secure external fixtures such as fuse boxes, circuit breakers, and telephone switches. Install inside metal screens and locking bars for all glass doors and ground-floor windows as well as bars and locks on skylights. You can also prune shrubbery so that it does not hide doors or windows, reducing the area where an attacker can hide and making it more difficult for him to enter illegally without being seen. Remember to cut tree limbs that could grant access to upper-level windows. You should also consider installing or upgrading intruder alarms and fire-protection systems such as sprinklers and emergency

PREPARING AN EMERGENCY RESPONSE PLAN*

1. Make a plan to stay in touch with your family.
   - Choose an out-of-state contact, such as a relative or friend. In an emergency, local phone lines may be busy. It may be easier to make a long-distance call than to make a local call. Your out-of-state contact can help you get in touch with any family members you cannot reach.
   - Make sure every member of your family knows the phone number of your out-of-state contact and has a way to make a long-distance phone call at all times (e.g., a prepaid phone card or a cell phone).

2. Decide on a place to meet if you are separated from your family.
   - If your family is not together when an emergency happens, watch TV or listen to the radio to find out whether you should go home, evacuate to another location, or stay where you are ("shelter-in-place").
   - Pick a meeting place in advance that is away from your home and neighborhood in case it is not safe to meet at home. Pick a backup meeting location in case travel to the first choice is not possible.
   - If an emergency occurs when your children are in school or childcare, it may be safer for them to stay there temporarily.
   - As you develop your plan, consider any family members with special needs (e.g., impaired physical or mental abilities).
   - Include your pets in your plan. Ask friends or relatives outside your area whether they could shelter your pets in an emergency, or contact hotels and motels to inquire about their pet policies.

3. Know emergency plans. Ask about the emergency plans of your:
   - Workplaces.
   - Children's schools and childcare providers.
   - City or town.
   - Places of worship.

*Adapted from "Public Health Emergencies: What You Can Do to Prepare," by the Rhode Island Department of Health.

lighting, and keep first-aid supplies and manual fire extinguishers on hand. The best and cheapest alarm system, by the way, is a big dog.

MAKING AN EMERGENCY RESPONSE PLAN

Pre-event preparedness is the single most important determinant in your survival. Many factors in a terrorist attack will be beyond your control, but the one thing you can control is how well you prepare. Have a plan for where to meet your loved ones, a plan with several "rally points" so you can find each other in case the event requires evacuation. Identify reliable safe points with access to telephones, radios, and basic medical care, such as a police or fire station or a large hotel that is open around the clock. Determine a communications strategy, such as a relative's phone number, and ensure that your entire family has the number with them at all times. Work with your employers, your children's schools, and other establishments to ensure you understand their plans and that you will be confident in what will happen in response to an event.

Emergency Preparedness Training

There are certain basic functions to sustain life that are the indicators to whether or not you should initiate CPR. If the victim is conscious, ask them if you may help them. If the victim appears to be unconscious, lean very close to them and tap then and then ask very clearly, "Do you need help?" If there is no response begin by checking the "ABCs" of first aid when you approach a victim:

- Airway. Is the victim's airway clear?
- Breathing. Is the victim breathing?
- Circulation. Does the victim have a pulse?

Be aware, as well, that certain jobs require an individual in those positions to administer first aid when they come across a victim of an accident or a nefarious act, including schoolteachers, athletic coaches, life guards, and even babysitters. This job-related requirement is called the "Duty to Act." If someone in one of these positions comes upon a victim of an accident they are required to render assistance or else they could be found legally liable. In cases where a person has assumed responsibility for other people's lives, they must act and render assistance in an emergency.

Another important rule is the "Good Samaritan Law," which protects a normal citizen who is trying to help from becoming involved in a lawsuit. The Good Samaritan laws are based on the following key points: Have you obtained permission or, in the case of an unconscious victim, made a reasonable attempt to obtain permission to administer help? Did you act in the manner of a reasonable and prudent person in similar circumstances and conditions? Be aware, however, that not every state has such provisions, so you should check to find out about local laws.

Finally, there are a few good rules of thumb to remember in emergency situations:

- Never move a victim unless his life was endangered if you did not move him.
- Call for emergency medical services (EMS) as soon as possible. If you can't or are in the process of saving lives, have someone else call for EMS as soon as possible.
- If you start first aid on a victim, do not stop until a more qualified person has arrived on the scene and takes over for you, or your life is endangered by continuing to give aid.

Stocking an Emergency Kit

A closely related issue is the need to have an emergency supply kit with food, water, a change of clothes, a medical kit, and flashlights. These are the most basic of supplies, but given the reality of the threat and the criticality of being prepared you should also consider a much more substantial emergency kit—one in your home, another in your car, and a third at your place of work. (See the "Terrorism

AMERICAN RED CROSS EMERGENCY KIT RECOMMENDATIONS

- Flashlight with extra batteries.
- Battery-powered or hand-cranked radio.
- Food (enough for three meals).
- Water (at least one gallon).
- Medications (six-day supply of all prescriptions).
- Family-size first-aid kit.
- Emergency "space" blanket (Mylar).
- Personal hygiene items.
- Garbage bags, ties (for personal sanitation).
- Complete change of clothes.
- Extra pair of eyeglasses.

Response Handbook" section of this book for a more detailed list of emergency supplies you should have on hand.)

Safe Rooms

In establishing a safe room for your house you need to find an internal room that can accommodate your family comfortably for a sustained period of time, where you can install a telephone, and where you have enough room to store a sizable emergency kit and food and water for five days. You should also have latex gloves, medical supplies, clothes, flashlights with extra batteries, a radio, and a toilet and plastic bags for sanitation.

Fire Safety at Home

It is appropriate at this point to make mention of fire-safety precautions because many incidents involving terrorist and other threats involve explosions or other disruptive events (like shoot-outs or diversionary fires) that increase the likelihood of a building or home catching fire. Even without terrorists or other assaults, every year some 30,000 Americans are injured and another 4,800 die from fires. The key to not becoming one of them is to ensure you have working smoke detectors and fire extinguishers, have your home checked for faulty electrical wiring or overloaded circuits, and avoid storing flammable items in or near your house.

HOME SECURITY CHECKLIST*

- If you have a fence or tight hedge, is it effective against intrusion?
- Is your fence or wall in good repair?
- Are the gates solid and in good repair?
- Are the gates properly locked during the day and at night?
- Do you check regularly to see that your gates are locked?
- Have you eliminated trees, poles, ladders, boxes, etc., that might help an intruder to scale the fence, wall, or hedge?
- Have you removed shrubbery near your gate, garage, or front door that could conceal an intruder?
- Do you have lights to illuminate all sides of your residence, garage area, patio, etc.?
- Do you leave your lights on during hours of darkness?
- Do you check regularly to see that the lights are working?
- If your community has a guard, does his post properly position him to have the best possible view of your grounds and residence?
- Does your guard patrol your grounds during the hours of darkness?
- Do you have dogs or other pets that will sound an alarm if they spot an intruder?
- Have you considered installation of a camera system with record capabilities or dummy camera system as a deterrent?
- Are your perimeter doors made of metal or solid wood?
- Are the doorframes of good solid construction?
- Do you have a peephole in your main entrance door?
- Are your perimeter doors properly secured with good heavy-duty dead-bolt locks?
- Are the locks in good working order?
- Can any of your door locks be bypassed by breaking the glass or a panel of light wood?
- Have you permanently secured all unused doors?
- Are your windows protected by solid steel bars, ornamental or some other type of shutters?
- Do you close all shutters at night and when leaving your residence for extended periods of time?
- Are unused windows permanently closed and secured?
- Are your windows locked when they are shut?
- Are you as careful of second-floor or basement windows as you are of those on the ground floor?
- Have you secured sliding glass doors with a broom handle "charlie bar" or good patio door lock?
- If your residence has a skylight, roof latch or roof doors, are they properly secured?
- Does your residence have an alarm system?
- Have you briefed your family on good security procedures?
- Do you know the phone number of the police or security force that services your neighborhood?

*Adapted from the *U.S. Department of State Guide to Overseas Housing Security.*

Daily Routines and Predictability[2]

According to the U.S. State Department, your most at-risk activities are your daily routines, such as the time you leave for work in the morning, because that is when your timing and route selection are most predictable for those who may wish to do you harm. If you develop regular habits and preferred routes of travel, your enemy will be better enabled to use surveillance to learn and predict your patterns, placing you at greater risk. Understanding and countering threats to your personal safety requires much individual effort. Surveillance may last for days or weeks; naturally, those with rigidly set routines and who take few security precautions will take the least amount of time. The likelihood of a surprise attack also is greatest when entering or exiting vehicles because these are situations where you are most likely to be distracted by the items you are carrying, thinking about your route, or worrying about getting somewhere on time.

There are a great many inherent security problems with passenger vehicle travel, especially for the vast majority of us who travel without regular security protection. Because vehicles are often left in driveways, parked on public streets, or in other relatively isolated areas with no positive control or protection, terrorists or criminals can easily gain entry to the vehicle and sabotage it with the intent to maim, kill, or ensure it will break down to enable a future attack. These factors make vehicles the ideal place for your enemy to apply scare tactics, deliver warnings, or carry out their attack. Vehicles also can be easily recognized by year, make, and model, and a trained terrorist can accurately assess any protection modifications and security devices. Using adequate resources, common vehicles can be discreetly followed, which also makes it possible for potential attackers to make repeated "dry runs" with a low risk of detection. Under such conditions, different methods of attack can be formulated and tested until success is ensured. While traveling in a passenger vehicle you also have limited pro-

---

[2]Portions of this section adapted from the Bureau of Diplomatic Security, Overseas Security Advisory Council (OSAC), "Personal Security for the American Business Traveler Overseas," November 1995.

tective resources, making it easier for terrorist groups to ensure numerical superiority.

Be Aware of Possible Surveillance[3]

Your personal habits make you predictable in terms of planning an operation to do you harm, be it for kidnap, ransom, or murder. If you believe that you are at high personal risk, but will not be protected by specialty guard services, then you need to learn to take an active role in your security and safety. Most criminals and terrorists prefer not to enter your home because it is a less-controlled environment for them, especially if you follow the deterrent strategies for strategically using exterior lighting, landscaping, and similar security precautions detailed later in this book. As a result, after conducting surveillance against you, your adversary's most likely window of opportunity to harm you is during your daily commute or as you enter or exit your car at your home.

Detecting surveillance generally requires a fairly constant state of alertness and must therefore become a routine habit. A good sense of what is normal versus what is unusual and learning to trust your instincts could be your most important security precaution. Above all, do not hesitate to report any unusual event. There are three forms of surveillance: foot, vehicular, and stationary, of which foot surveillance is often the easiest to detect. Well-established routines enable your enemy to use the methods that are much more difficult to detect, however, such as stand-off distances when trailing your vehicle in another vehicle and allowing for the easy determination of when and how to emplace stationary teams, which are often inside of vans with commercial logos on them or in nearby rental units with a clear line-of-sight to your residence or work. Additionally, because it can be hard

[3]The U.S. military has spent years refining terrorism preparedness and personal security training based on numerous specific events that have occurred overseas. With the threat of terrorism having come to our homeland it is imperative that we bring those lessons learned to our defense here at home. Accordingly, parts of this chapter are based on several versions of the Department of Defense's "CJCS Guide 5260, Antiterrorism Personal Protection Guide: A Self-Help Guide to Antiterrorism," available at www.dtic.mil/cjcs_directives/cdata/unlimit/gude5260.pdf.

to take notes while driving, you should carry a minicassette recorder with you in your car to dictate details of a suspect surveillance car such as color, make, model, license plate, description of occupants, etc.

Recognizing and Reporting an Attack

The actions taken in the first few critical minutes and hours following an attack often mean the difference between life and death. First responders call this period the "golden hour" because appropriate actions can make such a significant improvement in the eventual effect of the overall event. Individuals need to know whether they should evacuate or shelter-in-place and where to turn for advice from the state, local, and federal response teams, but also they need to help others by appropriately and immediately reporting any incidents that occur. Aside from personal security the most good you can do for your fellow Americans is to learn how to recognize and immediately report an event. That will best enable the government to begin mobilizing its resources to deal with the incident, which could include everything from sending ambulances and hazardous materials (HazMat) teams to activation of the Strategic National Stockpile and the deployment of elite counterterrorism units.

VEHICLE SECURITY

AUTO TIPS

- Keep vehicles in good repair.
- Always keep gas tank at least half full.
- Ensure tires have sufficient tread and enough air.
- Do not display personalized name license plates in car window.
- Avoid decals or stickers that readily distinguish your car.
- Keep a self-defense weapon within reach of the driver's seat.

Always lock your car when parking it, even if you will only be away from it for a moment. Adversaries may want to implant a listening or tracking device in your vehicle and you must take the simple precautions that will impede their efforts. If possible, avoid leaving your car on the street overnight and park it in well-lit areas. As mentioned previously, never get out without checking for suspicious persons and, if in doubt, drive away and find a better situation for yourself. You should also be sure to get a key chain with a quick-release feature so you can leave only your vehicle's valet key, and not your residential keys, with parking attendants or valets. If you have a garage with a direct entrance to the house it is always better to close the garage door and then enter/exit the house immediately, especially if you often have packages or other items that occupy your hands and make you less prepared to defend yourself.

Make a habit of checking your vehicle and the surrounding area before entering and starting the vehicle by conducting a precautionary inspection. You should check to see if there are any external signs of tampering, such as fingerprints, smudges, scratches, or other signs. Check beneath your vehicle for any tampering or bombs by looking for wires, tape, or anything else out of the ordinary. If you believe you are in direct, immediate risk and suspect someone may have tampered with your vehicle's brakes or tires then you should check the tightness of your lug nuts and examine tires for stress marks or other evidence.

Before approaching your vehicle be sure to check the surrounding area to determine if anything of a suspicious nature exists, and before entering it always glance inside to see if anything is out of place and look for suspicious or unfamiliar items. If you have an alarm system you should check to see if it was triggered in your absence. You can also install two bolts (perpendicular to each other) through the exhaust pipe to prevent the insertion of an explosive in the tail pipe. Remember, if you do find something out of the ordinary, DO NOT TOUCH IT! Contact the local authorities for assistance. However, if you have more than one vehicle and find someone has tampered with one, you should immediately inspect the other and caution your wife, husband, coworkers, and children accordingly.

Everyday Driving Tips

Vary routes to work and home and vary the timing of your travels, being careful to try and travel with companions and also to avoid late-night travel.

Plan your route and alternate routes in case of emergency or detour, avoiding isolated roads or dark alleys whenever possible. Know the location of emergency service providers along your route and make a habit of riding with seatbelts buckled, doors locked, and windows closed. Also be sure you have a battery charger for your cell phone and an earpiece so you can keep your hands free while calling for assistance.

Never allow your vehicle to be boxed in when driving and maintain a minimum eight-foot interval between yourself and the vehicle in front of you, as well as half a car length to preserve freedom of movement when stopping at traffic lights. Be alert while driving or riding, and stay in outer lanes where you have maximum freedom of movement, rather than curbside lanes where you are more restricted. Even if you have a vehicle emergency, unless it becomes unsafe to proceed, you should avoid stopping on the side of the road. Drive slowly, even on a flat tire, until you reach a well-lit public place where you can get help or perform repairs. You should also know how to react if you are being followed by checking during turns to see if you can spot surveillance, being sure to get the best possible description of the car and its occupants so you can report the incident to the authorities. You also need to learn to recognize events that can signal the start of an attack or aggressive maneuver against you. When one of these events occurs, start mentally preparing a course of action and an evasion route in case an attack develops. These events may include, but are not limited to:

- Cyclist falling in front of your car.
- Flagman or workman stopping your car.
- Unusual or false police or government checkpoint.
- Disabled vehicle and/or accident victims on the road.
- Unusual detours.
- An accident in which your car is struck.
- Cars or pedestrian traffic that box you in.
- Sudden activity or gunfire.

Planning Your Route

If you believe the risk warrants it, you should develop and utilize counter-ambush procedures for vehicle travel. As described above, your greatest window of vulnerability is when you are on the move, typically during predictable movements such as going from home to work or to a regularly scheduled activity. While it is often impractical or impossible to alter your start and end points for such activities, you can vary the route you take and thereby lessen your periods of exposure to maximum risk. In so doing, you make it less likely that the middle portion of your journey will be subject to risk, and therefore can concentrate on maximizing your preparedness efforts around your journey's common beginning and end points.

The key elements of a counter-ambush plan include identifying primary and alternate routes, dangerous choke points and safe areas. Efforts in this regard are greatly aided in developed countries by the presence of MapQuest® and other electronic map and travel planning aids,[4] and one important objective is to identify tall buildings or other distinctive landmarks that will aid you in terrain recognition and provide you a point of reference should you be in an emergency and need to rapidly determine where you are relative to your home, office, or other predesignated safe area. Your next step is to identify the known areas where your choices are limited, such as when leaving your driveway or entering a cul-de-sac, being careful to note that this may be when you are at your greatest risk because of limited maneuverability. You should then identify and try to minimize choke points, which are areas where your flow is impeded by traffic, sharp curves in the road, or other exogenous variables like a railroad crossing. For an organized and determined enemy, each choke point becomes an excellent opportunity for an ambush.

---

[4]See chapter 8, "Executive Security and Hostage Survival/Recovery," for more detailed advice on developing safe routes as well as other executive security techniques that can be adapted for personal use.

Emergency Driving Techniques

If you do find yourself under attack while driving, look for any nearby authorities and sound the horn to draw attention to yourself, which may cause some assailants to hesitate or select another victim. You should also develop a simple procedure to tell any regular travel companions or family members that something is wrong so they can immediately begin to assist you in your response. If you are moving and it appears that aggressors are threatening you, immediately put another vehicle between you and your pursuer to provide room to maneuver. At the first opportunity, execute an immediate turn and escape, jumping the curb at thirty- to forty-five-degree angles, being careful to travel a maximum of thirty-five miles per hour at curb effect so as not to pop your tires. If the adversary pursues and moves to block your path, then consider ramming the blocking vehicle, but only if you cannot get by on either side. Some cars will not fare well and may leave you stranded, which is no better than you were before the ramming.

Ramming another vehicle, however, is an inherently dangerous move and should only be used as a last resort. This is especially true considering that many newer vehicles have airbags that may deploy during a collision, a chain of events that often includes an onboard computer immobilizing the vehicle. Nevertheless, the deployment of airbags is based on the force created by a certain type of crash, and ramming a vehicle at the proper speed may dissipate the force of the crash enough to prevent the airbag from deploying. So while the airbag may deploy, and that may stop the vehicle, if the consequences of not ramming are grave enough, then it remains a viable last option.

If you decide to ram the vehicle and do so properly, it can be an extremely effective tool. The first move is to stop your car twelve to fifteen feet in front of the blocking vehicles and put your car into its lowest gear to maximize engine torque, being sure to hold the gear shift in place manually to avoid the car slipping out of gear during effect. From this distance you are also able to gain enough momentum to break free from the cars in your path but not likely to be moving so fast as to do grievous harm to yourself or passengers. Step hard on the accelerator and, continuing to apply full pressure to the gas pedal, strike the fender area in front of the front tire or behind the rear tire in order to maximize the force of your car against the edges of the other vehicle. This should cause the car to spin out of the way and free your path with less likelihood of entangling the two cars. Keep your foot pressed to the floor to ensure your vehicle clears the scene as quickly as possible and does not get hung up on the blocking vehicle as you depart the scene.

Post-Incident Safe Areas

Immediately after clearing the accident scene, go to the closest safe haven, such as a police or fire station or even a luxury hotel that has a strong security presence and is well lit and will have appropriate means of communications available. Do not try to travel too far as you may have punctured your fuel tank or oil pan and don't want to break down and become stranded. Also, while you'll want to immediately alert your family and coworkers of potential dangers to them, don't return home without the authorities or other armed security in case the adversary had a fallback plan of getting to you there. Report the incident to the nearest police, security force, or another emergency responder who will have communications with the authorities, for the chances are you now need to seek professional security.

Special Vehicle Equipment

All drivers should ensure each of their vehicles contains routine items such as a fire extinguisher, medical kit, flashlights, and spare blankets and clothes for warmth. Most everyone may also want to consider having a steel baton, small baseball bat, or other personal defense weapon hidden under the driver's seat in case of emergency. For individuals at significantly heightened personal risk, however, thought should be given to acquiring vehicles that meet certain specifications. For instance, hardtop cars are inherently safer than convertibles, and you should select a vehicle that offers an inside hood latch, locking gas caps, and an escape latch in the trunk. You can also add extra plating to protect the radiator and the undercarriage and steel-belted radial tires with inner tire devices that permit vehicle movement even with a flat tire. You can also purchase an after-market alarm system with a separate battery for back-up power, point-to-point radios, and communications gear, etc. Finally, determine whether or not you wish to carry a firearm in your vehicle and be aware that the "right-to-carry" rules differ greatly from state to state.

SECURITY WHILE TRAVELING

The world is getting smaller every day as the ongoing transportation and communications revolutions make travel between practically all spots on the globe easier, faster, and all the more common. However, as we travel more and more for business and pleasure to locations farther and farther from established destinations, it is important to remember that many nations simply do not have the same kinds of protections offered by professional police forces that we enjoy in America. Indeed, in many countries it is the police themselves that you have to be concerned with, at least in terms of petty crimes, for they all too often supplement their pay by extorting relatively wealthy foreigners, especially those who would likely be more inclined to pay rather than remain in the country and sue for justice. Examples of the basic steps travelers should take include counter-surveillance awareness of your surroundings, varying your travel routes, and making wise decisions with respect to when and where you travel alone.

For several decades overseas travelers have faced some minimal risk of getting caught up in terrorist attacks resulting from local political tensions. While this threat remains, the much more significant risk is the worrying increase in attacks specifically against "Western" targets. Since the mid-1990s Osama bin Laden's al Qaida network and associated groups have carried out multiple attacks against such targets as trains in Spain, hotels in Africa, banks and consulates in Turkey, and expatriate communities in Saudi Arabia. Other Islamic extremists have directly targeted tourists, such as in November of 1997 when 68 foreign tourists were gunned down at the pyramids in Luxor, Egypt, by al-Gama'a al-Islamiyya, or in 2002 when Jemaah Islamiya targeted Australian backpackers at a nightclub in Bali, Indonesia, killing 202 tourists.

Despite ongoing military and law-enforcement successes against terrorist networks, the threat from terrorism persists. As America and other Western targets become increasingly difficult to enter and significant buildings and events are better defended, it is likely that we will see a continued attacking of weak spots.

Understand the Likely Risks

So what else can you do to minimize your risk while traveling? Most precautions are common sense. Make sure you are aware of the political and social situation in the country you are going to and consider obtaining a guidebook from the Lonely Planet or Frommers series to read up on warnings about common local scams and criminal tricks. If on a prolonged trip, or if you have reason for concern after being in-country, then contact the local American Embassy or consulate in your host country. One of the most important tips for traveling is to

CULTURAL AWARENESS

- Get a good guidebook that will tell you about the history, customs, and culture of the country you are visiting.
- Find out about local laws, customs, and culture.
- Take a phrase book and try speaking the local language.
- Always ask permission before taking photographs; in some cultures it is forbidden to photograph women.
- Do not behave so as to draw undue attention to the fact you are a foreigner.

travel light so that you can keep a close eye on all your possessions—and on events taking place around you. You can also heed some of the more specific advice in the pages that follow, including security tips for airports, commercial transportation, and evenings out on the town.

Individuals should also need warnings and travel advisories from the U.S. government. The Department of State assesses the threat to U.S. residents and visitors in each country where the United States maintains diplomatic representation with one of three designators: High, Medium, or Low. An analysis of the political, terrorist, and criminal environment of a country determines the level assigned to it, and is updated quarterly.

- High-threat country: The threat is serious and forced entries and assaults on residents are common, or an active terrorist threat exists.
- Medium-threat country: The threat is moderate, with some forced entries and assaults on residents occurring, or the area has the potential for terrorist activity.
- Low-threat country: The threat is minimal, forced entry of residences and assault of occupants is not common, and there is no known terrorist threat.

Airport Safety

Safety precautions begin at the airport, where you must be especially aware of suspicious activity, particularly in the less developed countries, where the police presence tends to be much less reliable than in the United States. Indeed, even after all the post–9/11 security measures, in July 2002 a forty-one-year-old Egyptian man opened fire inside Los Angeles International Airport, killing two people and injuring several others, demonstrating that even in the United States, airports are not invulnerable to violence.

Be conscious of visibly nervous passengers who are behaving unusually or whose attire is inappropriate for the weather (i.e., long, heavy jackets in the summer, etc.). Also pay attention to any unattended luggage or other object, including unattended janitor's carts or kiosks that could contain a bomb. To the extent possible, avoid lingering near open public areas. In general, you are safer once you have passed through the metal detectors and security screening, so after checking in proceed immediately through security to your gate area. Look for airport security personnel or telephones and other means of communicating your concerns to them, if warranted, and always be aware of emergency exits and objects that could provide cover for you and your family or travel companions in the event of an attack, such as couches or sheltered alcoves.

If you do find yourself in an airport during an attack of any sort, your best immediate action is to dive to the floor and seek cover behind any nearby object that can protect you from fragmentation or bullets. Running during the immediate onset of an event only increases the likelihood that you'll be injured by flying glass or targeted by gunmen; better to first get on the floor or behind a thick couch or wide column and assess the situation. This will also help minimize your chances of being caught up in secondary explosions that were intended for simultaneous detonation with the beginning of the attack. If you think you see or hear multiple small explosions, it could be from grenades, pipe bombs, Molotov cocktails, or the like, so be sure to stay behind a protective barrier and minimize exposure by crouching and staying as compact as possible. Once a couple of minutes have passed without additional gunfire or explosions, and especially if there is obvious structural damage or fire, it may be safer to get out than to remain where you are. If that is the case, stay low to the ground and move rapidly from cover to cover to protect yourself. However, remember that with terrorist attacks it will likely be impossible for emergency response personnel to distinguish you from the attackers, so do not attempt to assist or interfere with their efforts. Instead, raise your hands to show them you do not pose a threat, and carefully and deliberately follow their instructions.

Staying in Hotels

When selecting a hotel keep safety and security in mind, especially when staying in certain less secure environments. Though local hotels often have more charm, the better-known international hotels have a reputation to maintain and accordingly they are quite vigilant about stopping petty crime and nuisances from affecting their guests' stay. These international chain hotels also conform to international insurance regulations for items such as fire and smoke alarms, and around-the-clock, English-speaking staff. Choose to stay in rooms on the second through fifth or sixth floors, as this will generally keep you out of reach of criminal activity from the street but still within reach of most fire truck ladders. Never loudly discuss your business or travel plans in public areas where they may be overheard, including when talking to the desk clerks or concierge. Do not discuss your room number while standing in the lobby or leave your room key on restaurant or bar tables. Keep your room neat so you will notice disturbed or missing items quickly. You should also use the door chain or bolt lock whenever you are in your room and place a small wedge under the door as an extra security measure. Also be sure to look through the door's peephole before opening the door to visitors or room service.

Before leaving a hotel room, place a small piece of transparent tape on window frames and connecting doors to indicate if they've been opened in your absence. Place the "Do Not Disturb" sign on the outside of your room whenever you are going out in the evening (or during the day, if your room has already been cleaned), and leave a light and the television on whenever you leave the room. If you are staying at a hotel that still openly exhibits room keys on the wall behind the front desk, keep your key with you to avoid letting potential thieves or others know that you are not in your room. Rather than taking jewelry or other valuables with you or leaving them in the room, use the hotel safe and get a written receipt with specific descriptions of your items. For lesser valuable items you can also use in-room safes, but only if they operate with a personal code you set yourself. When returning to your room, make sure that your side of all connecting doors are securely locked, and also use a small wedge to block these doors.

MONEY, CREDIT CARDS, AND TRAVEL DOCUMENTS

Recognizing that theft is a major cause of most of the random violence against travelers, you should use a money belt or secure inside pocket to keep your cash and wallet from being taken. You can also separate your money, placing a small amount of cash in one front pocket for paying taxis, fast-food, and the like, and keeping your credit cards and larger bills in a wallet in your other front pocket. If you have more than one credit card, it is also a good idea to leave one of them hidden securely in your hotel room or in the hotel safe so that you will have emergency access to money in the event that you do lose your wallet or purse. Similarly, keep your passport and travel tickets in the hotel safe and carry copies with you, if necessary. Be careful to change money in banks or other established, legal foreign-exchange locations, as it is often illegal to exchange currency with unauthorized persons, and you run a high risk of receiving counterfeit bills.

Out on the Town

When traveling overseas you want to avoid being alone because isolation makes you an easy target. On the other hand, being among a huge mass of fellow tourists makes you part of a lucrative target, such as the victims of the attacks at Luxor, Egypt, noted earlier. You should also learn to be conscientious of local dress patterns, such as how in many parts of the world adult males never wear shorts or women wear skirts below their knees. This is not to deny your culture, but rather to minimize the likelihood you are the one targeted if violence erupts. You should also avoid the spectacle of spontaneous gatherings or demonstrations; security forces in most of the world show none of the usual restraint of American police, and being in the wrong place at the wrong time can sometimes be enough for a conviction in certain parts of the world. Think back to the 1989 Tiananmen Square atrocity and choose instead to head

SAFETY ON FOOT

- Plan your route and alternates so you won't appear lost or confused.
- Avoid distractions; criminals often work in pairs or teams.
- Be alert if approached by a stranger and project an air of somber confidence.
- Never go near or lean into a car when asking or giving directions.
- Identify police and fire stations and late-night or twenty-four-hour restaurants and hotels as possible "safe havens."
- If you are being followed, do not go home; go instead to a busy well-lit area.
- If you think someone is following you, switch directions or cross the street.

across town or back to your hotel. It is also a good idea to understand the local telephone systems (many international payphones require you to insert a local calling card, even for toll-free calls) and how and who to call for assistance in an emergency.

One of the most exciting aspects of traveling is running into friendly locals who offer to "show you the town." In certain countries, this is often as innocent and welcoming as it sounds, though in much of the world you have to be wary of criminal intent. In particular, beware of overly friendly locals offering to take you to a "special" restaurant. In the past, such ruses have been used in order to offer victims drugged refreshments, allowing criminals to easily take your possessions or commit even worse acts.

COMMERCIAL GROUND TRANSPORTATION

As with most personal security strategies, your goal while traveling is to present yourself as the most difficult possible target to your potential enemies. This includes maintaining alert, aware body language, varying your routines, and carefully analyzing your alternatives. In particular, when traveling by commercial bus, taxi, or subway you should try to avoid being alone, and yet not put yourself amid such a dense mass of people that you lose your freedom of action. In other words, you desire to have the safety of fellow citizens without the risks inherent in being trapped or restricted by too large a crowd.

When available, to reduce the risk of fraud and danger use hotel shuttles instead of taxis. When you do choose to travel by taxi be sure to learn the markings for official, registered taxis, as many countries have both legitimate taxi services and other "freelance," unregistered drivers. While many of these are simply honest individuals working extra hours to supplement their income, it is still not as safe as using a regulated cab service and therefore not worth the risk. Consult current guidebooks or on-line traveler advice sites for estimates on average taxi fares from the airport to major destinations, and ask the hotel desk staff for an estimate before taking taxis to local destinations. If the taxis do not have meters, always negotiate the fare to your destination up front before getting into the cab, being careful

TAKING ACTION

In the early 1980s, Jim Liddy was attending Fordham University, a Jesuit school in a somewhat rough neighborhood of New York City. One night in his junior year, as he and his brother, Tom, were plowing through homework in their dorm room, they heard a woman's scream pierce the otherwise quiet night. Jim and Tom knew instinctively from the pitch and intensity of the scream that this was no college prank—it was a violent attack and someone needed help.

Jim and Tom raced out their room and up a flight of stairs, where they found a female classmate crying and bleeding profusely from a stab wound to her chest. While Tom attended to the young woman and evaluated the severity of her injury, Jim raced off in pursuit of the assailant. One of the girls on the floor recognized Jim and yelled, "He went down there!" pointing to the stairwell. Jim raced downstairs to the ground floor, ran past the still-seated security guard, and out of the building. He looked down the street and began running in the direction that was the fastest way to get off the university property, looking out for anyone moving away from the campus in a hurry. Two blocks later Jim and a friend who had joined the chase saw a vagrant who was looking for a place to hide yet very much in a hurry.

The man threw away his knife between two buildings and was running down the street when Jim caught up to him, tackling him against the curb. While his friend recovered the knife, Jim quickly frisked the man, checking for any additional weapons. Finding none, Jim pulled the man's arm behind his back, pushing his wrist up to the back of his head until he grimaced with pain; Jim later admitted he'd wanted to hear the guy's arm snap. After all, this pervert had stabbed and attempted to rape an innocent young woman and he deserved to pay. Jim's good judgment soon took over, and he proceeded to keep pressure on the man as he escorted him back to campus.

Knowing that pain can be an effective means of controlling an unwilling detainee, Jim kept up the pressure to maintain the advantage over the assailant. Sadly, when he tried to turn the suspect over to the security guard, the guard wanted nothing to do with the matter. Apparently the guard wasn't interested in public safety or doing the right thing and instead just wanted to collect his paycheck. "Give me the handcuffs, then!" Jim directed the security guard, taking charge of the situation and ensuring justice was done until someone better trained and of higher authority could relieve him. Jim forced the would-be rapist's head down on the ground and pulled his other hand behind his back, controlling him with a knee in the back while he handcuffed him. Meanwhile Tom, satisfied that the victim was now in stable condition, proceeded to lecture the suspected rapist on how lucky he was that he was still able to breathe. Just how fortunate was an open question because he was soon to be turned over to the NYPD, and New York's finest doesn't like rapists any more than the rest of the civilized world. Jim and Tom like to think the rapist's day did not get any better.

It was later learned that the perpetrator had committed at least five other campus rapes in the past several years and was sentenced to twenty-five years to life for his crimes. Jim, Tom, and their friend who'd helped pursue the assailant were later honored for "endangering their lives to pursue and capture an armed and dangerous felon." Jim maintains that he was just doing the right thing, saying he'd have been ashamed of himself if he hadn't gotten the SOB. Luckily, the right guy was in the right place when action was needed, and he was ready and willing to respond forcefully when the need arose.

not to allow taxi drivers to put your luggage into the trunk until you have agreed upon the fare.

You should also avoid being predictable by consistently using the same taxi company *except* in certain countries where the professionalism and safety standards of preferred taxis outweigh the desire to minimize predictable selections. Seek to travel with a companion whenever possible and, to the degree possible, specify to the driver the specific route you want the taxi to take, thus identifying yourself as an aware, in control passenger who is unlikely to be an especially easy target for petty crime.

Throughout much of the world, trains and subways are more common means of travel than in the United States. For short trips by rail or subway sit near aisles or doors and stay awake and alert. When traveling long distances or overnight by train and with companions, try to take turns sleeping so at least one person can keep an eye on your valuables. Also be sure to arrange for a separate compartment for you and your companions, and consider additional security measures such as tying a piece of rope or cord around the door handle and securing the other end to the bottom of the seat or another fixed object so the door cannot be opened without your notice.

AFTER A ROBBERY

If your money, passport, or anything else is stolen, report it at once to the local police in order to obtain a police statement about the loss, which you will need to claim against your insurance. If it is cash that is stolen you are out of luck, so consider also carrying at least a minimal amount of funds in traveler's checks, which are promptly replaced by the issuing agent.

What Uncle Sam Will (and Will Not) Do

According to the U.S. State Department Web site, when a crisis occurs the State Department headquarters in Washington, D.C., creates a "task force" to bring together all the people necessary to work on that event. Usually this task force will be in touch by telephone twenty-four hours a day with our ambassador and Foreign Service officers at the embassy in the country affected. The immediate job of the State Department's Bureau of Consular Affairs is to respond to the thousands of concerned relatives and friends who begin to telephone the State Department immediately after the news of a disaster is broadcast, and the State Department relies on its embassies and consulates abroad for hard information. The Bureau of Consular Affairs collects the names of the Americans possibly involved in the disaster and passes them to the embassy and consulates. Officers at the post attempt to locate these Americans in order to report on their welfare. The officers work with local authorities and, depending on the circumstances, may personally search hotels, airports, hospitals, or even prisons. As they try to get the information, their first priority is Americans dead or injured. As the State Department notes, however, this information is often slower in coming than that from the media, which therefore becomes the preferred method for families back home.

In the case of an American injured abroad, the embassy or consulate notifies the task force, which, in turn, notifies family members in the United States. The Bureau of Consular Affairs then assists in sending private funds to the injured American and frequently collects information on the individual's prior medical history to forward to the embassy or consulate. When necessary, the State Department assists in arranging the return of the injured American to the United States commercially, with appropriate medical escort, via commercial air ambulance or, occasionally, by U.S. Air Force medical evacuation aircraft. The use of Air Force facilities for a medical evacuation is authorized only under certain stringent conditions, and when commercial evacuation is not possible. The full expense must be borne by the injured American or his family; the State Department does not provide money or loans, so you have to find a way to have funds transferred to you.

When an American dies abroad, the Bureau of Consular Affairs must locate and inform the next of kin. The Bureau of Consular Affairs also provides guidance to grieving family members on making arrangements for local burial or return of the remains to the United States. The disposition of remains is affected by local laws, customs, and facilities, which vary widely and are often different from those in the United States.

The State Department will also help Americans abroad to evacuate from a dangerous situation, especially if normal commercial transportation is disrupted. As necessary the embassy and consulates will work with the task force in Washington to charter special air flights and ground transportation to help Americans depart, although the U.S. government cannot order Americans to leave a foreign country. Should you choose to stay against the advice of the government, or to enter areas such as Iran where American citizens are not currently permitted, you risk the State Department being unable to assist you should you get into trouble.

SIX

▼

Securing Your Workplace

Regardless of your size, location, or technology, terrorists could
involve you, your employees, and your business in their evil plot.
They could hijack one of your trucks loaded with flammable
materials and crash it into a public school, steal hazardous
chemicals from your worksite to bring harm to a neighboring city,
or drive a delivery truck with a bomb onto your property.

SOUTH CAROLINA'S *WORKPLACE SECURITY GUIDE*, FEBRUARY 2003

The attacks of September 11, 2001, accounted for 2,886 workplace fatalities, which was just one-third of the total 8,786 workplace fatalities
of 2001.[1] Even more startling, when you remove accidental workplace
deaths, *each week* an average of 20 workers was actually *murdered* in the
United States in 1997. Another approximately 1 million workers are victims of nonfatal workplace assaults each year, meaning that with nearly
18,000 assaults per week we Americans face enormous security problems
at the places where we work, recreate, and do our shopping. Furthermore,

---

[1]U.S. Department of Labor, Bureau of Labor Statistics, Census of Fatal Occupational Injuries (CFOI)—
Current and Revised Data, at http://stats.bls.gov/iif/oshcfoi1.htm#19922002.

from a business perspective, the nonfatal workplace assaults alone result in more than 876,000 lost workdays and $16 million in lost wages annually.

At the same time, in early 2005 Osama bin Laden again reiterated his challenge to the civilized world, calling on Iraqi militant Abu Musab al-Zarqawi and his followers to take their attacks to the U.S. homeland. Both at home and abroad U.S. businesses are at the forefront of exposure to terrorist threats, especially as government and public facilities increase their security postures, in turn making often less-secure businesses into more attractive targets. According to the U.S. State Department's annual report "Patterns of Global Terrorism," U.S. businesses are being targeted significantly more often than any other category of entities, with a full 30 percent of international terrorist incidents against U.S. interests targeting American businesses.

The foregoing are just statistics, and statistics are all too easy to ignore. How would you fight back if your workplace erupted in violence, your company's trucks and warehouses were targeted for theft, or you and your fellow workers were at risk of being caught up in terrorist acts? The solution begins with taking practical steps to both deter terrorists through sound, recognizable security practices and reducing the likelihood of workplace violence and its effect through adequate planning and training.

The first and most important step in reducing workplace violence is to establish a clear, enforceable and zero-tolerance policy that is in place at all times. However, setting a policy is just not enough. With threats of the magnitude outlined above, a more active policy is required, one that incorporates an all-hazards emergency-response plan and provides the appropriate, flexible response framework that you need. This will include an enhanced combination of security measures, administrative protocols, and employee and management training in response to a variety of threats.

WORKPLACE DISASTER-PREVENTION STRATEGIES

As we have seen all too often, a major threat to individuals comes in the form of disgruntled current or former coworkers. While the majority of workplace homicides are robbery-related crimes (71 percent), coworkers or former coworkers commit approximately one-in-ten of these murders. Corporate America learned this tragic lesson during several spectacular episodes of workplace violence in the early 1990s. It is no wonder that when many major companies now dismiss an employee they have them escorted by security guards while they gather their belongings and leave the building. Unfortunately, many small and medium-sized firms cannot afford such measures, and even large companies are often inadequately protected

BUILDING ACCESS

- Properly screen visitors and employees.
- Control after-hour access.
- Utilize an Intrusion Detection System (IDS).
- Report suspicious persons and activities to your security people and the authorities.
- Remain vigilant around the building and at home.

against determined attackers who return at a later time. Basic precautions taken in advance, however, can vastly improve your response options. In addition to increased perimeter security and changing the codes on keypad door locks, management can also work with local law enforcement or private security firms to coordinate response activities well in advance of any incident. The best of the workplace security tactics, techniques, and procedures are listed, so review the set of standard guidelines below that can be customized for any situation.

Workplace security requires a comprehensive approach. Tactics and procedures are not always enough. Taking the next steps, such as designing safety features into your floor plans, ensuring your guard force is adequately trained, and implementing building-access restrictions, are very effective means of enhancing your workplace security. Security plans and training should also be conducted at least annually, and it is important to regularly update contact rosters for outside agencies you may need to call. These include emergency and nonemergency numbers for police, FBI, fire, and nearby hospitals. Where appropriate, you may even consider inviting officials from these organizations to your worksite and offering them a tour of your facility, so they are more familiar with your physical layout and security situation if they ever need to respond in an emergency.

Administrative Procedures

Using security guards or receptionists to screen persons entering the workplace and controlling access to actual work areas can be a good administrative means of protecting the work environment. Similarly, increasing the number of staff on duty at various times and for certain off-hour shifts is an appropriate solution for securing retail or other service environments, although limiting worker access on weekends or late at night when their presence precludes the use of more aggressive security measures, such as dogs or fully-armed alarm systems, may also reduce the risk of violence against your employees. Finally, you should consider means to more aggressively implement and monitor practices, such as escorting visitors and tracking their activities against their appropriate level of access.

You may also want to consider establishing policies and procedures for assessing and reporting threats that will allow you to track and assess threats and violent incidents in the workplace. These policies will clearly indicate a zero-tolerance of workplace violence and provide a mechanism by which incidents can be formally reported and handled. In addition, these procedures will allow employers to assess the effectiveness of various prevention strategies. These policies should also include guidance on recognizing the potential for violence, methods for defusing or de-escalating potentially violent situations, and instruction about the use of security devices and protective equipment. Access to and from the building, elevators, stairs, and even elevated or covered walkways to and from parking facilities should always lead into well-monitored areas.

Deadly Deliveries

In October of 2001, letters laced with anthrax were distributed through the U.S. postal system, ultimately killing five innocent Americans, infecting more than a dozen, and prompting the preventive treatment of almost thirty thousand. The events also closed down parts of the U.S. Capitol complex for over a month. Well before the anthrax attacks of 2001, and even before the days of "Unabomber" Ted Kaczynski, however, the threat of explosives delivered by innocuous letters and packages has been a significant concern for a variety of industries. Some major American companies receive literally hundreds of suspect packages a year, in addition to those packages that target abortion clinics or are mailed by "environmental" terrorists. As a result it has become incumbent upon every office manager, business owner, and responsible citizen to learn how to handle suspect packages. The threat of mass-casualty terrorism and developments in chemical and biological warfare only heighten this risk.

According to the U.S. State Department's Diplomatic Security Service, letter and mail bombs do not often contain timers or other delayed-trigger devices; rather, they are almost always "victim activated," meaning that a victim or intended target must activate the device through the way they handle or open the package. Furthermore, such bombs can range from the size of a cigarette package to an oversized parcel, with previous bombs having been disguised as letters, books, dolls, and small statues.

A set of general procedures can be applied to address the vast majority of such incidents, however. First, use the suspicious-package detection tips in the accompanying box to recognize any suspicious packages, and train all mailroom employees in proper response techniques, including immediately reporting all suspicious events to security or the authorities. Additionally, never cut tape, strings, or other wrappings on a suspect package or immerse a suspected letter or package in water as either could cause an explosive device to detonate. If possible, isolate the space where the package is located;

CHARACTERISTICS OF SUSPICIOUS PACKAGES*

- Unusual or unknown place of origin.
- Handwritten labels, foreign handwriting, or misspelled words.
- Incorrect titles or title with no name.
- Abnormal or unusual size or shape.
- Differing return address and postmark.
- Protruding strings, aluminum foil, or wires.
- Unusual odor.
- Evidence of powder or other contaminants.
- Crease marks, discoloration, or oily stains.
- Ticking, beeping, or other sounds.
- Marked with special instruction such as "Personal," "Confidential."

*Adapted from *Chairman of the Joint Chiefs of Staff Guide 5260: Antiterrorism Personal Protection Guide: A Self-Help Guide to Antiterrorism*, October 2002.

and if there is even a remote chance you have been contaminated, wash your hands thoroughly with soap and water. Next, if the letter or package has already been moved, put on disposable gloves and place it in a plastic bag or some other container to prevent leakage of contents. If you are not certain whether the package has been moved, avoid touching or moving the suspicious package or letter. Finally, and very importantly, make a list of all personnel who were in the room or area when the suspicious envelope or package was recognized. This is done in case they may have been exposed. If the package is contaminated, time will be critical to saving lives and preventing further contamination. Finally, wait for the authorities to come and determine if further tests or sanitization of the area are required.

Access, Surveillance, and Perimeter Control[2]

Good access control is designed to decrease the facility exposure to criminal activity. Proper attention to security considerations during the design phase will reduce the accessibility to an installation, keeping unauthorized persons out of areas where they don't belong. Access routes to and from the workplace are important areas to assess in terms of inherent vulnerabilities. An inventory of all exits and entrances should be made, with special attention to unlocked and unguarded access to areas where potential attackers can hide. This issue has implications for the design of buildings and parking areas, landscaping, and the placement of garbage areas, outdoor refrigeration areas, and other storage facilities that workers must use during a work shift.

Numerous commercially available security devices can also reduce the risk of assaults and other threats to workers and facilitate the identification and apprehension of would-be perpetrators. These include closed-circuit television cameras, automated alarms, two-way mirrors, card-key access systems, panic-bar doors locked from the outside only, and geolocation devices

---

[2]See chapter 7, "Defensive Landscaping and Antiterrorism Architecture," for more detailed information on how to utilize environmental security procedures to combine physical features with technological solutions.

for mobile workplaces. Access-control equipment, such as keypads and cipher locks, can be used on all employee entrances to minimize unauthorized access. In many settings it is appropriate to require all employees and contractors to wear picture identification badges, which should be updated annually so the pictures are recent. You also should make all badges unique in design and tamperproof, and require employees who leave the company to turn in badges during their exit interview. Remember to periodically review, reissue, and reassign badges and access passes, however, as badges tend to get lost over time and people are often slow to report them missing. Additionally, body armor and other personal protective equipment have saved thousands of military and police lives and may be appropriate for certain members of your security and perimeter control team at medium- to high-threat facilities.

Guards/Patrols

In order to control access at approved points of entry, use gates, turnstiles, fencing, and a security guard or a monitoring system to control access, and provide your guards with a quick, reliable means of contacting local law-enforcement agencies. Post a security guard at the main building entrance or at entrances to specific offices, and ensure that guards have a clear view of employee entrances at all times. Develop clear guidance for each manned security post to give the security guard a clear understanding of his/her responsibilities. You should contract with a reputable security firm and perform regular auditing of all security procedures at least bimonthly, with annual audits by a certified security professional. Identify and use bars or special covers to protect all drainpipes large enough for an intruder to gain entry to your facility and use cameras or security officers to routinely monitor such areas. Finally, for more aggressive deterrence, you may want to weigh the dramatically increased benefits of having armed guards and/or trained guard dogs.

Guard Dogs

Guard dogs often provide many outstanding security benefits at relatively low costs. Dogs have been well documented for having a keen sense of danger and can sense an intruder up to 250 yards away. Their hearing is many times more sensitive than humans, with frequency ranges twice those of humans; and their sense of smell is much more developed, having been measured at 100 times greater than humans. Also, while a dog's senses of touch and sight are not as well developed as a human's, they are more sensitized to movement and therefore more cognizant of human presence, giving dogs the ability to quickly differentiate between a familiar human and strangers. This is why dogs are still one of the best home, workplace, or specialized security assets.

In the Special Forces, guard dogs are still considered one of the hardest security challenges to defeat. They take away the element of surprise before most intruders even know they are there. Some breeds or combinations of breeds make better security dogs than others, and specialized training, such as drug sniffing or explosive detection, further enhance their utility in increasing security and awareness. However, any dog that is going to be used for security purposes must be trained by a reputable training school and properly cared for by professionals.

AESTHETICS IN SECURITY DESIGN

Additional security measures, if properly configured, can in fact be reflected positively in marketing strategies and in insurance considerations. However, aesthetics are an increasingly important consideration in most security barrier decisions. From a business perspective, it is just as important to provide a sense of safety and security to employees and customers as it is to make it obvious to the criminal element that you are prepared to stop them.

In terms of basic environmental design, the most important areas of consideration are visibility and lighting. Making high-risk areas more visible and installing good external lighting can decrease the risk of workplace assaults as well as other nefarious activities. However, consideration should also be given to more complex issues, such as modifying angles of approach, access to and control of loading docks, and means of verifying the authenticity of various suppliers who come to your workspace or facility.

External Lighting

Perhaps the single most effective issue you can address for your workplace security is exterior lighting. All avenues of approach to enter into a workplace facility should have sufficient lighting to ensure that the receptionist, security guard, and CCTV monitors can distinguish human features. Good security lighting will also help identify the color and type of clothing an individual is wearing, and any objects such as a briefcase, backpack, or package the suspect may be carrying. The point is to see what is coming and stay ahead of an attacker.

First, survey your present nighttime lighting to identify those areas that are not well served by your current lights. You want to ensure your facility does not have any dark areas around any of the approach routes, including ones that are not routinely used. The goal is to avoid dark or concealed areas where someone with nefarious intentions could hide or preposition equipment for future theft or attack. Therefore, make sure the areas and employees and customer-approach routes are brightly lit. If addressing a large facility, you can check with your power company or hire a consultant to design a lighting diagram to help you select the most appropriate size, number, and location of lights.

Moderate to highly powerful lights pointed outward cause glare and make it difficult to see and photograph when doing surveillance of a facility. If your facility has sensitive or valuable materials, government offices, or other recognizable assets that would invite industrial espionage or terrorist surveillance, your exterior lighting should be positioned outward. Additionally, strong exterior lights have the benefit of lighting up the areas beyond the facility's perimeter, further enhancing your ability to capture important images through your own surveillance equipment. Remember, however, that it is critically important to institute procedures for regularly maintaining and replacing lightbulbs, sensors, and starter boards, as well as installing a secure and uninterruptible power supply.

Parking Lots

Parking areas have become a very important area of concern for security. Security problems and incidents of criminal activity in parking lots and garages run the gamut, including everything from petty theft to carjacking, assault, rape, and murder. In recent years there have been multiple reports of children being kidnapped and of increased gang violence and shootings. Remember, too, that the first attack on the World Trade Center in 1993 was carried out with a truck bomb, in and under the parking lot, as was the 1995 Oklahoma City bombing. It is all too likely that we'll see such attacks in the Unites States again.

Ideally, parking lots will be located 150 feet from all buildings with high concentrations of people and should have elevated ground in the form of green areas like gardens, lawns, trees, and even fountains. At a minimum, these provide aesthetically attractive standoff distances and natural barriers for protection from explosions. They also keep the concentration of people away from the incoming and outgoing traffic, helping to avoid all-too-common pedestrian-related traffic accidents. Parking areas within a facility's perimeter walls should be restricted to employees and well marked. It is best to establish visitor parking in an area that allows your security surveillance good coverage and ample lead time to notice anomalies before the person or persons enter the facility.

Whenever possible, parking areas should not be located directly adjacent to or underneath any building with a high concentration of people or valuable assets. If underground parking is necessary, it requires security checkpoints at all entrances and clearly posted height limitations for truck traffic, including delivery vehicles, which should not be allowed into the underground parking area. Mirrors also should be positioned so as to reflect the view of openings outside any garage elevators or doorways, as well as to show around corners and blind spots or tight curves.

All parking should be well lit and designed so that even at night there are no areas of concealment or dark recesses. It is equally important to have very good video surveillance of the entire parking area. When trouble occurs in the parking area, you want to see it coming to give your security personnel time to respond as well as to have a video record for law enforcement to facilitate any arrests and prosecutions that may result. With good video you also have an example to teach or remind your security of what to look for in the future.

Fencing and Gates

Fences generally serve a dual purpose: they define the property lines of your installation, facility, or home and are your outermost line of security. For many situations an eight- to twelve-foot chain-link security fence with concertina (barbed) or razor wire along the top will provide a reasonable amount of security. It is also important to anchor the base of the chain-link fence into the ground and add additional vertical posts of galvanized pipe, which is anchored in a concrete footing where the ground is uneven and leaves gaps between the bottom of the fencing and the earth below it. The barbed or razor wire serves as an additional and dangerous obstacle for an intending intruder but often is most useful as a psychological deterrent for petty criminals or vandals who might attempt to penetrate your property. Ensuring that the fence is properly secured to the ground further deters many would-be intruders. Of course, you must inspect the fencing regularly for vandalism and general-maintenance issues such as ground erosion. Note that any intruder more ambitious than a petty thief will likely repair his point of entry through a fence to cover his tracks. By early identification of penetration points through maintenance inspections you will greatly enhance the efforts of your security personnel or the law-enforcement officials following up on the incident.

As always, be careful to randomly vary the time of day of the inspection to preclude surveillance by anyone trying to determine large windows of vulnerability. Also be sure to provide a clear path or internal roadway to allow for these inspections and for additional patrolling, as necessary. Consider installing an employee gate with an automatic keypad or a remote

---

PARKING AREA BEST PRACTICES

- Install digital CCTV cameras capable of recording throughout the entire parking lot or facility with feed directly into the security control center.
- Lighting must be adequate to support the video cameras and illuminate the entire parking lot or facility.
- Install emergency communication systems, such as telephones or intercoms, and ensure that they are easily identifiable and in working order.
- Locate visitor parking within areas that allow security surveillance prior to the visitors entering the building.
- Underground parking should have security checkpoints at all entrances and clearly posted height limitations.
- Parking ideally is located 150 feet from buildings with high concentrations of people. These standoff distances should contain natural elevated barriers such as gardens, lawns, and trees for protection from ballistic effects.

---

control, and if public utility companies regularly visit the facility you can place a phone at the gate that connects with the gate operator. You should also post signs notifying passersby that all vehicles and persons are subject to search, and fluorescent lettered signs that read KEEP OUT or ONLY AUTHORIZED PERSONS ALLOWED ON THE PREMISES, every fifty feet on each side of the perimeter fence and on each gate.

Closed-Circuit Television (CCTV) and Thermal Imaging

Some businesses may find it appropriate to install a closed-circuit television surveillance system. CCTV should not be used as a primary means of detection because it is a passive system that requires human interaction for detection. It should be utilized as a tool to assess alarms triggered by motion detectors or other more active forms of detection such as microwave, radar, infrared, or fiber-optic intrusion sensors. The important issues here are to use only high-quality systems with excellent nighttime performance and cameras coupled with motion sensors that automatically direct the camera to the point of intrusion and alert attendants to activity in the area. Also keep in mind that studies prove attentive monitoring time is only about two hours, so employees must be regularly relieved or their attention will lapse.

Thermal imagers such as those used by the military key-in on heat, rather than light, and use contrasts in thermal readings to produce visible images. Unlike other night-vision or infrared devices, which amplify ambient light, these systems work in zero-light conditions and can be used to determine such facts as whether a vehicle's engine has recently been running, or the heat signatures of people or animals hiding in the dark. Recently such items have been crafted into compact, lightweight devices that can be coupled with television cameras or other sensors to provide true day/night surveillance.

Vehicle Inspection

If you have a large facility or especially sensitive areas to protect, you must consider establishing a guard gate with a barrier, where you can have trained security guards inspect all vehicles, including those of your employees. Vehicle inspections can be difficult and costly in terms of time and effort. However, there are some simple techniques that can cover the basics, and just by having a vehicle-inspection station you will deter some of those with malicious intent.

First, you should set up the vehicle-inspection area in a safe zone a minimum of 150 feet from any critical facilities. In designing your screening area be sure that vehicles that have not yet been cleared are unable to approach any critical buildings or utility areas and also that you have a pull-off area for conducting any comprehensive inspections that may be warranted without having to shut down your entire vehicle-access lanes. *Be sure that your security screening has a minimum effect on traffic flow, as improper planning creates long traffic backups resulting in large concentrations of people that then become targets while waiting to enter your facility!* Finally, certain industries require vehicle-loading inspections and have paperwork and packing seals to verify compliance with those requirements. Any security personnel conducting vehicle inspections must be trained in the industry requirements as well as the more generic vehicle security sweeps designed to detect weapons, unusual cargo, or packages or bombs hidden in vehicles.

Security Barriers[3]

Security barriers are useful in a variety of safety and security scenarios. Whether a car has swerved to avoid a pedestrian or a suicide bomber is trying to hop the curb to deliver a payload into a hotel lobby, well-placed and properly constructed barriers will prevent the vehicle from getting to the areas where people could be injured. Use of properly placed vegetation, hedges, and garden planters in planned security zones also channel pedestrians and vehicles into areas where security personnel and surveillance equipment can more easily identify them and conduct an initial threat assessment.

There are also many new aesthetically pleasing barriers commercially available, such as box planters with flowers or trees and concrete-reinforced sculptures and fountains. Careful planning must be used when designing security barrier options for permanent installation or medium- to high-threat situations, to ensure that people are protected while waiting to process through the barrier systems. An additional consideration is the environment in which a particular barrier system will operate. For instance, hydraulic systems must be kept relatively clean and therefore should not be used in dusty and windy areas, while other mechanical systems require higher maintenance in colder environments and freezing temperatures. Additionally, protective equipment may be necessary around the electrical or hydraulic equipment of the barrier systems in medium- and high-threat environment to keep the equipment in working order.

- *Active barriers*: Active barriers are those that require action by security personnel or equipment to permit entry into the facility. Some examples of active barriers are systems that move horizontal beams, gates, and tire shredders. These are a good idea when a facility has an increased threat posture and resources are limited.

[3]Portions of the following are adapted from the Federal Emergency Management Agency, "Reference Manual to Mitigate Potential Terrorist Attacks Against Buildings," at www.fema.gov/pdf/fima/426/fema426.pdf.

- *Passive barriers*: Passive barriers are those that rely on their mass and do not have moving parts. Typical passive barriers are the large concrete blocks called Jersey barriers, typically used along interstate highways. Large pilings and guard rails are also types of passive barriers.
- *Fixed barriers*: Fixed barriers are a system permanently installed by heavy equipment and require dismantlement to be removed. Examples of these would be hydraulically operated rotation or retracting barrier walls or steel plates over a trench. Fixed barriers can be both active and passive systems.
- *Movable barriers*: Movable barriers are barriers that can be moved from place to place. They may require heavy equipment or additional personnel for assembly after transfer. Highway medians, sand bags, sand barrels, or planters are just some of the more typical movable barriers.
- *Expedient Barriers*: Expedient barriers are articles or vehicles normally used for other purposes. Busses, trucks, and cargo containers are some of the more common examples of expedient barriers.

PERSONNEL ISSUES

Given what is at risk to individuals and businesses, it is little wonder that so many are taking much greater interest in the background and character of the people they employ. Employers should contact three references for each applicant and subject them, where permissible and appropriate, to drug and alcohol testing, both random and for cause (an accident or similar incident). You can screen applicants by requiring a minimum of two interviews, as well as verifying their application against their school records. All employees should be verified through the I-9 process to ensure that they are authorized to work in the United States of America (whether they are citizens or otherwise legally in this country).

Background investigations are another excellent tool for determining useful and relevant information about employees, contractors, and subcontractors, though it is very important to use a reputable and well-documented firm with all the correct professional certifications to avoid any potential liability or impropriety. Employers should set acceptance guidelines for background investigations based on the type of jobs performed, including department of transportation background checks for all drivers,[4] credit checks on employees who will have access to large sums of cash, and also consider recurrent credit checks for key employees (periodically, every three or five years).

Behavioral Strategies Training

The National Institute for Occupational Safety and Health (NIOSH) notes that training employees in nonviolent response and conflict resolution is a means of reducing the risk that volatile situations will escalate to physical violence. It is also important to emphasize training that addresses hazards associated with specific tasks and site-specific hazard-prevention strategies. Training should emphasize the appropriate use and maintenance of protective equipment, adherence to administrative controls, and increased knowledge and awareness of the risk of workplace violence. However, such behavioral training alone is never the whole prevention strategy but rather only a component in a comprehensive approach to reducing both the likelihood and the severity of any future episodes of workplace violence.

Emergency Response Planning[5]

Proper emergency planning can help your employees and your business survive and recover from catastrophic events. No matter how well you imple-

---

[4]Note: You must have the person's authorization to obtain the Department of Transportation document. Visit the DOT Web site: http://www.fmcsa.dot.gov for more information.

[5]Portions of the following section are adapted from the comprehensive South Carolina's *Workplace Security Guide,* Updated February 1, 2003, available at www.llr.state.sc.us/workplace/fullreport.pdf.

ment the above recommendations unexpected events can still occur, and pre-event emergency response planning is a key factor in improving the likelihood of survival for yourself, your employees, and your business or community. A recent South Carolina survey of businesses found one-in-four businesses with less than 250 employees and one in five with less than 500 had no formal emergency response plan. While all larger companies had written plans, there were still some deficiencies in the plans (see box). During a crisis, however, is the worst time to be making the decisions that may affect the health and safety of the employees and the company as a whole. The major elements of an Emergency Action Plan are:

TOP 10 ERRORS IN EMERGENCY RESPONSE PLANS*

1. No upper management support for the plan.
2. Lack of employee buy-in.
3. Poor or no training of employees on the plan.
4. Lack of practice with the plan.
5. No designated leader in the event of an emergency.
6. Failure to keep the plan up to date.
7. No method of communication to alert employees to an emergency event.
8. OSHA regulations are not part of the plan.
9. No procedures for shutting down critical equipment.
10. Employees are not told what actions to take in the event of an emergency.

- Alarm or notification systems.
- Established escape routes.
- Designated rallying points/safe areas.
- Means to account for all employees.
- Training employees in the proper response.

Employers should also develop specific detailed procedures for employees selected and trained to remain behind (until evacuation becomes absolutely necessary) to care for essential plant operation. Such plant operations may include monitoring power supplies, water supplies, and other essential services whose functions cannot be shut down for every emergency alarm. Essential plant operations may also include chemical or manufacturing processes that can only be shut down in stages, and in which certain employees must be present to assure that safe shut-down procedures are completed.

Alarm/Emergency Notification

You should begin by installing a communication or buzzer system at the reception desk and in isolated work areas so that individuals can always access an alarm trigger. You also should have several points with panic alarms installed that ring in adjacent areas. Develop policies for responding to the buzzer, including times to accomplish certain tasks and a phone tree for who will notify the authorities of the need for assistance. As part of this plan you will need to establish a chain of command for crisis communications among key personnel and security providers, involving intercoms, telephones, duress alarms, and other concealed means of communication. The employer should also develop and explain in detail what rescue and medical first-aid duties are to be performed and by whom. It is important to establish separate alarms for security and fire, as fire may call for immediate evacuation while other contingencies will not. By the sound of the alarm employees should know what type of evacuation is necessary and what their role is in carrying out the emergency action plan.

Escape Routes and Evacuation Wardens

Use clearly marked exits with luminescent strips placed along the floorboards to ensure they remain visible in the event of smoke or other obscurants affecting visibility. In larger facilities color-coding routes and floors further aids employees in determining their current position and best available escape route. Be sure to include floor plans and schematics that clearly show emergency escape routes in the emergency action plan binder that can be used for coordination with emergency responders. In the event of the most serious of emergencies, total and immediate evacuation of all employees is necessary; while in other emergencies a partial evacuation of nonessential employees with a delayed evacuation of others may be necessary for continual plant operations. Further, in some cases only those employees in the immediate area of the emergency may be expected to evacuate or move to a safe area, such as when localized fire-suppression systems (such as over-head water sprinklers) are activated.

Employers also should ensure that adequate numbers of employees are available during work hours to act as "evacuation wardens" so that employees can be swiftly moved from the danger location to the safe areas. As a rule of thumb, one warden for each twenty employees is sufficient to provide adequate guidance and instructions at the time of the emergency. Evacuation wardens should be taken on a tour of the entire facility and made familiar with the complete workplace layout, including various alternate escape routes and especially hazardous areas to be avoided during emergencies. Wardens can also serve to ensure that any customers, visitors, or vendors delivering supplies to their area are properly and safely escorted out of harm's way. All wardens and fellow employees also should take extra care in planning for employees with disabilities who may need extra assistance. Before leaving their assigned areas, wardens should check rooms and other enclosed spaces in the work area for employees who may be trapped or otherwise unable to evacuate. Finally, wardens will also play an important role in accounting for all personnel at the safe area/rally points.

New technologies and businesses specifically dedicated to securing the homeland and preparing for attacks have greatly increased the number of options available to employers and federal or state agencies looking at large-scale evacuation planning, specific-evacuation modeling. Industry specialists such as Maryland-based Regal Decision Systems can assist by collecting data, determining how the evacuation of a massive port or other facility would actually occur, and modeling the event graphically to allow you to determine and counteract evacuation bottlenecks in advance of an actual emergency.

Safe Areas/Rally Points

Safe areas should be identified and clearly designated as rally points where employees and others can regroup following an event. In a building divided into fire zones by firewalls, the refuge area may still be within the same building but in a different zone from where the emergency occurs. Exterior refuge or safe areas may include parking lots, open fields, or streets that are located away from the site of the emergency and that provide sufficient space to accommodate the employees. Employees should be instructed to move away from the exit doors of the building and to avoid congregating close to the building where they may hamper emergency operations. Additionally, as New Yorkers learned on 9/11, it is not enough to have only localized "across the street" or "in the parking lot" rally points. In the modern era hazardous events may require much greater separation between you and the scene of the incident, and therefore it is important to have predetermined redundant rally points at varying distances from the facility.

Shared Buildings and Business Parks

Employers need to coordinate their plans with the other employers in shared buildings and business parks in order to prevent conflicting emergency response actions that could endanger all involved. In buildings with multiple tenants, a building-wide or standardized plan for the whole building is acceptable if each employer ensures proper training for their respective employees. When multiemployer building-wide or business park—wide plans are not feasible, employers should coordinate their plans with neighboring businesses to assure conflicts and confusion are avoided during times of emergencies and that emergency responder activities are unhampered.

Training

Employees must be sure that they know what is expected of them in all likely emergencies in order to ensure their own safety. Common training issues include personal safety and security measures, the types of incidents to report to law enforcement, reactions to armed aggression and angry customers/clients/employees, and information to note during telephone harassment or bomb threats. Additional training can include security/law-enforcement response measures, handling of suspicious packages, and best practices for hostage situations. However simple or complex individual training is, each employee and manager must know what actions they are to take in the event of a disaster, as well as what part they play in emergency response. Training should provide the background to achieve this end, and tests, drills, and exercises provide the practical experience to identify gaps in understanding or planning and information as to the readiness of the company for various contingencies.

Four groups of actors are important to include when creating emergency-response plans and designing training exercises: employees, response team leaders, customers, and local emergency responders.

- Employees should be trained on specific reactions for scenarios including fire, contamination, and civil disorder. It is important to focus on the principles of orderly evacuation as well as quarantine and shelter-in-place, as discussed more fully in Part III of this book. In particular, employees should be encouraged (or required) to provide for themselves such items as food, water, and a change of clothes, as well as being encouraged to learn life-saving skills such as basic first aid, fire safety, and cardiopulmonary resuscitation (CPR).

- Response Team Leaders are key employees (often department heads or safety and security managers) whose duties need to include additional considerations for emergency preparedness. These obligations include ensuring maintenance of sprinkler systems, power supplies, and other utilities. They also work to ensure that everyone is accounted for during an emergency, that internal communications and response efforts are effectively addressing collective security needs, and that appropriate local, state, and/or federal agencies are contacted for support as soon as possible. Additionally, recognizing that a chain is only as strong as its weakest link, the role of the response team leaders is to ensure that all due attention is paid to preparedness on the part of fellow employees.

- Customers present a more difficult challenge because they often cannot be trained directly and firms are generally reluctant to impose security or other restrictions on their clients. However, certain industries, such as airlines and cruise ships, do provide their customers safety familiarization briefs. Even if overt training is not feasible, it is important to think about issues such as proper emergency lighting, effective, low-light visible signage, and ensuring employees know how and what to communicate to customers who may be involved in an emergency on the premises.

■ Of all the outreach activities one can undertake, involving local (or in select cases, internal) emergency responders is perhaps the most important. Be the scenario fire, flood, armed attack, or a hazardous chemical accident, the level of training and facility familiarization of emergency-response personnel can often make the difference between a small event and a significant tragedy. Accordingly, it is important to engage these individuals in various training exercises and to document and ensure emergency-responder awareness of any significant recent alterations or changes in weapons, chemicals, or other significant storage locations and procedures.

Emergency Exercises

Decades of experience have taught both the military and the corporate business world that exercises and simulations are invaluable tools for improving an organization's ability to execute required objectives effectively during crises. It is important to routinely test these procedures because only realistic simulations can identify shortfalls in equipment, communications, planning, or redundancy of critical operational functions. In general, according to the Department of Defense, the Red Cross, and other government and emergency response agencies, exercises fall into three categories: tabletop, partial, or full-scale.

The least intrusive, and therefore most common, form of emergency and disaster preparedness exercise is called a "tabletop" exercise. Tabletops are facilitated discussions that follow a certain simulated event script, compressing timelines and relying on the exercise designers to determine approximate actions and reactions based on the scenario being tested. While physical inventories are not moved and actual people are not dislocated during a tabletop, these actions are simulated in order to identify current capability gaps. Of note, recent technological advances have greatly improved the ability to simulate various aspects of a crisis and, as a result, tabletop exercises are becoming seen as a cost-effective means to test ones' response capabilities with minimal disturbance.

A partial exercise, as the name implies, is more aggressive and widespread than a tabletop exercise and usually involves a limited mobilization of people and equipment. They often test coordination for certain specific tasks such as evacuation of a hospital or distribution of medicine, but do not require participants to actually go through the full-event profile in a realistic or sequential fashion.

Full-scale exercises, by contrast, comprehensively test all aspects of interaction and coordination in the emergency-planning program. They are more expensive and disruptive than the lesser-intensive forms of exercises, but they also provide the most accurate representation of how an emergency response effort would unfold. Such exercises also often involve external agencies, including a variety of first responders and simulated contamination or evacuation drills.

In order to extract value from an exercise, senior management must be responsive to acting on the lessons learned from the exercise. For this reason perhaps the most important portion of any exercise is its debrief, usually referred to as a "hot-wash" because it comes on the heels of the event and captures participants' immediate reactions. All too often opportunities to address shortcomings and avert future crises are identified during exercises but the participants fail to act on them. If you have the chance to participate in exercises, be sure you work hard to capture and share all notable areas for improvement, as well as effective solutions that need to be shared in order to promote security and resiliency throughout your industry or community.

Three-Dimensional Simulations

One of the most interesting and useful recent training developments is the advent of user-friendly, relatively low-cost software applications that create three-dimensional (3-D) training environments. The U.S. military has been using these types of products for years to ensure pre-mission planning and mission rehearsals are as realistic as possible. Now the technology has migrated to the private sector through firms such as Digital Sandbox, Bridgeborn, and Intellipix, who input building schematics, blueprints, or photographs to create entirely virtual worlds that replicate existing structures. These lifelike environments enable tabletop simulations to be carried out at a fraction of the cost of actually running full-blown exercises and yet retain the verisimilitude that is needed to obtain results relevant to the real world. In addition, firms such as Regal Decision can take the environments created above and match them against actual event-simulation data to demonstrate the benefits of various courses of action and/or structural modifications based on traffic flow, emergency response needs, and evacuation modeling. Together, such tools make exercises and drills much more effective in a shorter period of time than was previously possible.

Postincident Follow-up

Immediately following any evacuation or significant event, you should conduct a head count to ensure everyone is accounted for. If applicable, you then need to evaluate the medical condition of any affected individuals; you may be aided in this by identifying people in your employee pool who are certified in first aid or CPR. Next, survey the scene to identify specific roles for security-and-safety personnel, and, when the immediate concern has abated, gather all relevant data to provide to the responding officials who may be investigating the incident.

You should plan to hold a "defusing" session led by someone trained in Critical Incident Stress Management in order to begin to assist employees with the after effects of trauma, and also a debriefing twenty-four to forty-eight hours after the incident. Since experience is often the best master, it is important to not only plan for the immediate response and recovery efforts but also to have a system in place by which to evaluate the effectiveness of your response and to draw lessons for improving future response efforts. In this critiquing session you will gather managers, supervisors, and employees together and review how the situation was managed, addressing issues such as:

- How was the incident handled?
- Who responded?
- How could it have gone better?
- How could it have been prevented?
- How effective were the defusing and debriefing sessions?
- Is there a need for policies to manage similar incidents?
- Do safety procedures and work-flow procedures exist? Were they followed? Did they work?

By addressing these and related issues you can best ensure that you have responded to the emotional and other stress that can be created by events of grievous harm that affect individuals in powerful ways.

SEVEN

▼

Defensive Landscaping and Antiterrorism Architecture

Retrofitting facilities and sites to improve security has proved
challenging, especially in addressing threats associated with
blast mitigation and perimeter security issues. In some cases
the response has resulted in the closure of streets, the creation of
checkpoints, and the hasty erecting of barriers, and
has affected the aesthetics of our urban landscape,
creating a fortress-like environment of fear.

ROBERT CIZMADIA, IN *HIDING SECURITY IN PLAIN SIGHT*

The increased threat of domestic terrorism gives new impetus to the imperative to insulate one's home and place of work from security risks. The goal of this section is to provide an overview of relevant antiterrorism security measures in order to familiarize individuals, business owners, and community leaders with some of the alternatives and trade-offs available to them. Many of these measures are also useful in lessening the effects of natural hazards. A comprehensive risk-based security approach to landscape architecture, land use, and site planning will necessarily involve balancing the facility's imperatives for risk reduction, aesthetics, and the support of normative business practices. It also will involve such issues as hardening

TALES OF TERROR: THE OKLAHOMA CITY BOMBING*

On April 17, 1995, Timothy McVeigh rented a Ryder truck that he and accomplice Terry Nichols then loaded with approximately five thousand pounds of ammonium nitrate fertilizer laced with fuel oil (AMFO). Two days later, on the morning of April 19, McVeigh drove the Ryder truck to the parking lot of the Murrah Federal Building. He parked, set the bomb's fuse, locked the keys inside the truck, and walked to a nearby alley and began to jog away. Most employees of the Murrah Federal Building had already arrived at work and numerous children had been dropped off at the daycare center when the huge explosion tore through the building at 9:02 A.M. Nearly the entire north face of the nine-story building was pulverized into dust and rubble. It took weeks of sorting through debris to find the victims. In all, 169 people were killed in the explosion, which included 19 children.*

*Adapted from "McVeigh Chronology" by Public Broadcast Service's *Frontline,* available at www.pbs.org/wgbh/pages/frontline/documents/mcveigh.

physical structures beyond the minimums imposed by building codes and regulations, maximizing the use of nonstructural systems, and deliberately incorporating room for implementing future security solutions.

Numerous custom and ready-made alternatives have been developed in recent years to enable anyone to design simple and often low-cost security solutions for new or existing buildings and private homes. You may have noticed the increase in large concrete planters or raised stone or concrete gardens at higher-end downtown hotels and many government buildings. These objects provide protective standoff distances between primary points of entry and the building itself by blocking main avenues of approach. Even beyond the direct protection they provide by preventing explosive-laden vehicles from getting close enough to harm the people inside, such measures clearly also deter attacks at those particular sites. Many similarly practical solutions are in use by defense and state departments worldwide, who have well documented procedures including guard posts, fences, and other structures with obvious surveillance or security roles, and these standards can be used as guidelines in the civilian world here at home as well.

In the business and home security environment, however, the goal is often to increase security unobtrusively so the general public and visitors are adequately protected without creating an omnipresent and overwhelming sense of being at risk. Indeed, one of the fastest-growing sectors in the security-preparedness market is "environmental security design," where experts find clever, aesthetically pleasing means to design and install modern security monitors, barricades, and the like. Additionally, simple and inexpensive lighting techniques for your home and business will deter most criminal activity, especially if neighboring properties can see your home. Properly placing shrubbery, fences, and gates will limit the vulnerability of your property to foot and vehicle traffic.

The goal here is to make your business or residential neighborhood less likely to be victimized by random or deliberate crime, including terrorism, because the target becomes "hardened" relative to similar areas. Likewise, if there is only one way in and out of your property, and you can install a drainage ditch narrowing the entrance to a single lane with a security gate, you have limited accessibility so that it becomes more difficult for criminals to try to exploit your home or to bring a large truck in to haul away your valuables. Another option is to form an aggressive neighborhood watch committee to promote community security.

Local law enforcement offers extensive resources and recommendations on forming such an organization, and this can be an efficient and very effective means of heightening your personal and residential security.

BASIC SITE-LAYOUT CONSIDERATIONS[1]

Some of the key issues in land use include selection of a particular build site, orientation of your buildings with respect to neighbors and physical land features, and the integration of vehicle access, control points, physical barriers, landscaping, parking, and protection of utilities and other critical systems. Such decisions are ultimately least costly when they are incorporated early in the design and planning process, although many of the solutions described here can be retrofitted to existing buildings.

Preliminary factors to consider include the building's footprint relative

---

[1]Portions of this section adapted from the Federal Emergency Management Agency's "Reference Manual to Mitigate Potential Terrorist Attacks Against Buildings," at www.fema.gov/pdf/fima/426/fema426.pdf.

to the total amount of available land; access routes for foot, road, rail, and air travel; and current and planned infrastructure systems such as tunnels, pipes, easements, and transportation corridors. Physical factors such as water features, type, density of vegetation, and terrain characteristics should also be evaluated. Each of these affect perimeter-security considerations, just as adjacent facilities or entities, which may themselves be targets of disruptive attack, affect overall security and threat assessments.

The second set of considerations involve the overall design of a structure. For more rural facilities there is often a security trade-off between collocating assets, which makes for easier security and surveillance, and dispersal of buildings, which reduces the risk that a single event or attack will destroy multiple high-value assets. The best solution in this case is to consolidate assets with similar threat profiles, thereby enabling you to create moderate security throughout the facility and develop specific "enclaves" with heightened security for sensitive areas. Similarly, in an urban area where the per-foot price of property generally dictates high-density buildings, simple solutions such as designating certain floors as restricted access will enable efficient and targeted security procedures.

Vehicle and Pedestrian Access

Once the building design and orientation are determined, the next step is to design appropriate vehicle and pedestrian access routes. The primary security objective in terms of vehicular control is to keep car and truck bombs as far away as possible from the exterior of the building because, as explained earlier, the velocity of the explosion from a truck bomb dissipates with distance. Accordingly, a bomb that could be devastating to a building's foundation and cause partial or total collapse if detonated in an underground garage or adjacent to the main entrance may cause exponentially less damage at a stand-off distance of as little as fifty yards.

The most common security risk in vehicle-access routes is the use of straight-on avenues of approach to buildings and other critical facilities. While the most economic and simplest road design is a straight line, roads or pathways that create perpendicular building approaches may enable vehicles to gather sufficient speed to penetrate security barricades. Roadways that curve or "snake," on the other hand, inherently restrict the speed of travel and, in turn, lessen the likelihood the vehicle will penetrate protective barriers outside the building. Accordingly, perpendicular approaches to buildings or to gated access roads should be avoided, including of course secondary access points and service roads as well. Similarly, whenever possible, place the ground-floor elevation of a building four feet above grade in order to preclude a vehicle from ramming into the ground floor of the building.

Traffic-calming solutions such as raised crosswalks, speed bumps, and traffic circles, all of which create areas where vehicle speed must decrease, also can be implemented in new structures or retrofitted into existing ones. Another solution is to use decorative but defensive flowerpots or smaller and somewhat innocuous-looking security bollards to keep vehicles at a safe distance from a building. Similarly, you can install a combination of hardened versions of more common items such as light poles, large planters, sturdy trees, and water fountains or heavy-duty benches that serve a security function as well. While the specific effectiveness for each of these objects in a given scenario will be determined by both the size and speed of the oncoming vehicle, as a general rule, the vehicle blocking arrangement should be capable of restraining light commercial vehicles (7.5 tons) traveling at thirty miles per hour. Properly installed barriers and bollards can stop a variety of sizable cars and trucks, especially if they are traveling at such speeds as this.[2]

A related concern is that of parking lots, which for convenience or for economic reasons have in recent decades often been built underneath buildings where the cost of the space is relatively minimal. As with the 1993 World Trade Center bombing, however, underground parking garages offer easy access to the structural support areas of a building, while the Oklahoma City bombing demonstrates the dangers of unsecured adjacent parking lots. If publicly accessible lots are provided, they require at a minimum secure access gates with manned security details at all their entrances and exits.

Just as the traffic-calming and parking solutions listed above relate to

[2]"Risk of Terrorism: Advice for British Businesses," Foreign & Commonwealth Office, UK, at www.fco.gov.uk/servlet/Front?pagename=OpenMarket/Xcelerate/ShowPage&c=Page&cid=1099137407013.

vehicles, a variety of features can also be use to restrict or control the flow of pedestrians and cyclists. These include decorative elements such as flagpoles, gardens, and decorative fountains, as well as other aesthetic elements. Their proper placement will slow movement but not unduly impede the normal flow of legitimate commerce or imperil the efforts of emergency workers and others who may be responding if and when an incident occurs. Perhaps the best strategy in terms of dissuading enemy surveillance and actions against your particular facility is ensuring that you create open sight lines for increased surveillance. Through these, and similar, subtle measures you can readily create an unobtrusive but protective environment, in which your security and other personnel are aware of their surroundings. In turn, potential attackers will see that your facility will be a relatively hard target to penetrate.

Single-point Infrastructure Vulnerabilities

The military's special operations community has a saying that "two is one, one is none," which refers to the seemingly inevitable fact that when you really need something to work, like a radio battery, and you only have one, it usually doesn't. There is a parallel concern in defensive design and antiterrorism architecture, where identifying and eliminating "single points of failure" for your facility's critical infrastructure can literally mean the difference between life and death for you, your employees, and the company as a whole. For example, if your facility relies upon a single source of power or water, or if your facility is serviced by a single bridge or road, then you have significant operational risk of an attack or other event causing your

UTILITIES TO SAFEGUARD

- Emergency generators, including fuel systems, fire sprinklers, and water supply.
- Fuel and petroleum, oil and lubricants storage.
- Telephone distribution and main switchgear.
- Fire pumps.
- Building control centers.
- Uninterruptible power supply (UPS) systems for critical building functions.
- Primary refrigeration systems, if critical.
- Elevator machinery and controls.
- Stair, elevator, and utility shafts.
- Distribution points for emergency power.

operations to cease. In such instances you could arrange for alternate power supplies or back-up generators, construct a water reservoir, or connect yourself to another access road. Caution: Be careful not to make the common mistake of placing your primary and secondary utility sources side-by-side or connecting them through a common control room, as any event affecting one will likely damage or destroy the other as well; instead, in order to promote true redundancy, the two systems need to separated as much as possible.

PROTECTING ESSENTIAL EQUIPMENT

Among the most important factors to keep in mind when creating security zones is that truly critical assets are often also among the most mundane. Anyone can reason that their company's secretive research and development laboratory needs extra security, but having done so, many of these companies fail to protect the utilities that enable and protect the use of these labs and related facilities. There are many companies that have spent tremendous amounts of money to design and build state-of-the-art secured bio-research laboratories, complete with "floating" ceilings and shockproof floors and redundant air-circulation systems. All told, depending on the size of the facility, these security precautions added construction costs in the tens if not hundreds of thousands of dollars. These companies then placed all their critical power-, water-, and fire-control centers in unprotected areas adjacent to completely unprotected loading docks. What's more, while using cameras for perimeter security, the facilities often lacked even a basic fence to restrict large delivery trucks from pulling right into their loading dock. Accordingly, while a security guard could potentially watch as the rented truck laden with explosives drove right up to the loading area and destroyed all the utilities that ran and maintained the facility, he wouldn't be able to do anything to prevent the act. The "secured" labs would be rocked by the explosion, lose their air and other specialized containment seals, and in the confusion of scientists and workers fleeing the labs surely many a dangerous substance would be leaked into the outside world. All because the obvious was extremely well protected while the functional but critical was ignored.

LANDSCAPE DESIGN

Security implications for landscape design include everything from selection of tree and vegetation species to working with existing or building new landforms, water features, and environmental drainage infrastructure. One of the primary considerations is the trade-off between using heavy, thick, nearly impenetrable vegetation that at the same time will offer an enemy numerous places to hide. If you will have limited security personnel, then making the perimeter as unaccessible as possible through dense and thorny bushes is probably the best strategy. On the other hand, if you anticipate having an active and robust guard force coupled with technological surveillance systems, then you would generally prefer a more open space because you will have the resources to control the area and the enemy will have fewer means of concealment.

Placing earthen mounds or other organic shielding between the parking lot and a building also may serve to absorb some of the blast affect and resultant blast fragments from an explosion, although you are better served using large soil beds for plantings rather than smaller pots, which themselves may break into shards and create additional dangerous fragments. The proper mix of absorptive material and clearing for the sake of security surveillance will vary by site, threat, and security posture. It is important to ensure that any shielding measures are not counterproductive in terms of clouding security forces' lines of sight relative to building and perimeter security.

UNDERSTANDING BLAST EFFECTS

When a high-order explosion is initiated it creates a rapid exothermic chemical reaction, which in turn converts the solid or liquid explosive material into very hot, dense, and high-pressure gas. Because there is a now violent imbalance in air pressure, the explosive products expand outward at high velocities in order to reestablish equilibrium. This is known as the "shock wave" because the highly compressed air traveling outward at supersonic velocities creates a palpable disturbance that, depending on the size of the explosion, can literally crush everything in its path. As dramatized in the movies and on television, this shock wave bowls outward like an invisible bubble of air that continues to expand until equilibrium is reached.

To put the power of a vehicle-borne explosive into context, the intensity and pressures released on the targeted building will often be several orders of magnitude greater than in the typical natural disaster, such as an earthquake, flood, or severe wind storm. Even though the period of incidence will be measured in thousandths of a second, the fact that the pressure is so great, even for an instant, can crack and damage the foundation of even modern buildings, which can lead to progressive structural collapse. This gives rise to effects such as those seen at Khobar Towers in Saudi Arabia or the Oklahoma City bombing. It should be noted as well that in an urban setting the sound and air waves can reverberate back and forth and cause extended damage to a greater area by prolonging the effects of the wave before the air returns to normal pressurization.

Standoff Distances

Standoff distance is defined as the distance between an asset and the threat or event. Variables such as the size and type of the bomb, building construction and positioning, and even weather conditions will affect defining the optimal standoff distance for any specific event, but it is a sure bet that more distance is always better than less. This is because, as explained above, the explosive effect of a blast wave is a function of explosive power created by overpressurization, the effects of which decline exponentially over distance as the overpressurized air dissipates and pressures return to normal.

The U.S. government has spent several decades modeling the protection levels it believes are adequate for protecting its workforce. The assigned risk-mitigation categories are based on such factors as sensitivity of the work being done and its value to the nation, the number of people at the site, and the likelihood of that site being targeted. For their planning and design purposes the government uses the following scale:

MEANS OF DELIVERY	POUNDS OF TNT EQUIVALENT
Pipe Bomb	5
Briefcase Bomb	50
Van/Sedan Bomb	500 to 4,000
Large Truck Bomb	10,000+

COLOCATING KEY ASSETS

Many security professionals encourage the building of certain similarly critical assets into enclaves where they can be commonly monitored. This creates a smaller, inner circle area that needs to be at heightened security status, in turn allowing you to practice economy of force by not protecting all areas to the maximum degree and also to maintain reasonably open work in less sensitive areas. In a facility plan you might, for instance, keep maintenance and administrative functions in the relative open while placing research or key-production facilities inside a more tightly regulated and defined perimeter. The objective here is to establish standoff distances for your most critical elements by creating concentric rings of protection. The outermost ring, referred to as the "perimeter zone," is where you establish entry-control procedures, and incorporate vehicle barriers such as fences, planters, bollards, and traffic-calming measures. The edge of this zone blends into the "nonexclusive zone," which increases traffic control and maintains a public right-of-way but implements procedures to slow and control both vehicle and pedestrian traffic. Finally you have the "exclusive zone," which is where you use guards and keypad locks to control access. This can be a useful approach in certain instances, although concentrating all your resources in such a manner further heightens the relative importance of specially securing them, as now a single incident that does penetrate to the core will have an even more disastrous effect.

BUILDING DESIGN

Historically, the greatest loss of life from terrorist attacks against buildings has come from structural collapse; although of those who survive the initial event, fire is the leading cause of death. Given what we know about the enemy's intent and capabilities in terms of chemical, biological, radiological, or nuclear weapons, however, it is clear consideration must be given to protection against these threats as well. In addition to the facility-protection measures discussed above, specific measures can be taken to better protect the buildings where your employees and customers conduct their business. These include hardening the exterior of the building, updating fire-suppression systems, properly using guard and other security forces, and securing access to heating, ventilation, and air-conditioning (HVAC) systems.

SECURITY IN PRACTICE

The Pentagon has instituted this security-in-depth process by burrowing deeper underground and increasing security-access measures for the offices of many of its more critical assets. As those in the building often joke, however, they are not sure that being so invaluable is a great honor because if there is an incident, they have the farthest to go and therefore the least likelihood of getting out!

At the building exterior your focus shifts from deterring and preventing an attack primarily to lessening the effects of any attack that does take place. Accordingly, in hardening your building's exterior your goal is to minimize the number of objects that are likely to fragment upon an explosive blast. This in turn will minimize the amount of flying debris that can injure and even immobilize those who survive the initial blast.

Window Specifications

Window design is the primary consideration in the hardening of your exterior because when windows shatter the shards of glass often become deadly projectiles. While few designs can withstand the pressures caused by a large truck bomb detonated adjacent to or inside a building, blast-mitigation window designs can be very effective for lower-pressure events such as when a package

DESCRIPTION OF DOD MINIMUM ANTITERRORISM STANDARDS FOR BUILDINGS*

DOD PROTECTION LEVEL	POTENTIAL FOR STRUCTURAL DAMAGE	HAZARDS	POTENTIAL INJURY
Below Standards	Severely damaged; frame collapse; massivedestruction; cannot be repaired	Doors and windows fail and become lethal hazards	Majority of personnel will suffer fatalities.
Very Low	Heavily damaged; some structural collapse; major deformation; cannot be repaired	Glazing breaks and glass is likely propelled into the building, causing serious damage and injury	Majority of personnel suffer serious injuries. Likely to be 10–25 percent fatalities.
Low	Major deformation; cannot be repaired	Glazing will break but fall within one meter of window	Majority of personnel suffer significant injuries. Less than 10 percent fatalities.
Medium	Damaged, but should be repairable	Glazing will break but remain in the window frame; doors damaged and not reusable	Some minor injuries, but fatalities are unlikely.
High	Superficial damage only	Glazing will not break and doors will be reusable	Only superficial injuries are likely.

*Adapted from DoD "Unified Facilities Criteria," UFC-4-010-01, July 31, 2002.

bomb goes off or a truck bomb detonates a block or more away. The first consideration is the type of glass to use, common types of which range from basic plate glass to heat-strengthened or fully thermally tempered. Plate glass is the most common but least safe type of glass, for its tensile strength is quite low and in a blast event it can cause great injury. For this reason most modern building codes require the use of thermally tempered glass in areas where the public has open access, such as in building lobbies. However, for high-threat zones additional measures may be called for, including laminated glass, which has multiple glass layers and a pliable interlayer material.

Installing windows and window frames to a greater depth than is typical for commercial construction also is important because the window is less likely to come loose if it is better seated into the frame; and the better seated the frame, the less likely it will come loose from the wall. Another increasingly popular option (in part because it can easily be retrofitted into existing structures) is to adhere fragment-retention film to the interior surface of the window. It is a polyester film that reduces the dispersal pattern of glass if it shatters. Many businesses, from hotels to office buildings to factories, have discovered that having relatively inexpensive film placed on windows is an effective means to protect against all manner of causes that might shatter a particular panel of glass.

HVAC Systems

The next major consideration for building safety is HVAC systems, which in most instances can be all too easily used to introduce a chemical, biological, or other contamination source into a building's air supply. The threat here includes terrorist attack, but for most people the more likely scenario is that of malicious acts by a disgruntled employee or a single-issue extremist. Fortunately, some basic precautionary techniques can greatly reduce your HVAC vulnerabilities. These include raising and protecting fresh-air intakes so that external contamination is made more difficult and securing access to utility areas. Similarly, in new construction you can ensure that you have the capability to rapidly isolate certain floors or areas in order to prevent cross contamination and also to aid in the protection of shelter-in-place "safe rooms," as described elsewhere in this book.

Electrical Systems

The primary security function of an emergency power system is to maintain power to essential building services, especially those required for safety and evacuation, as well as support for critical emergency communications. This is a different mission from the normal power supply, which is used for a wider variety of purposes. Given this distinction in purpose it is easy to see that emergency power supplies must be separate from your primary supply, or else the risk is too great that whatever adversely affects the primary system is likely to also disable the backup system. All too often, however, people collocate their primary and emergency systems, and as a result unnecessarily increase their risk. For the same reason these functions should be separate from the loading docks, mailrooms, and other at-risk areas discussed above. Additional considerations include installing conduits and lines for external trailer-mounted generators that can be attached in a prolonged recovery situation. Fuel tanks that serve the emergency generators should be protected as well.

- Least cost.
- Least effort.
- Least protection.

- Ensure emergency exit doors prevent outside entry.
- Secure all roof access hatches.
- Train HVAC staff.
- Avoid mounting plumbing, electrical fixtures, or utility lines on the inside of exterior walls.
- Establish emergency plans, policies, and procedures, including evacuation and shelter-in-place.
- Illuminate building access points.
- Lock all utility access openings.
- Have emergency power for emergency lights.

- Most cost.
- Most effort.
- Most protection.

- Install internal public address system.
- Offset interior and exterior doors.
- Use badge ID system for building access.
- Install electronic security alarm system and/or CCTV.
- Isolate lobbies, mailrooms, loading docks, and storage areas.
- Elevate HVAC fresh-air intakes.

- Install blast-resistant doors.
- Use structural design to resist progressive collapse and harden exterior walls.
- Ensure fire system is protected from single-point failure in case of blast event.
- Install a back-up Emergency Control Center.

EIGHT

▼

Executive Security and Hostage Survival/Recovery

Although unprecedented global integration has created
tremendous business opportunities for corporations, it is
tempered by unprecedented increases in crime, including
kidnapping and extortion. According to experts, two new
kidnappings occur somewhere in the world every hour. Likewise,
multinational corporations report—far too frequently—threats
against employees from political terrorists and other groups.
Corporate security directors are revisiting as never before the level
of physical security they provide in the United States.

BROCHURE FROM THE CHUBB INSURANCE GROUP'S EXECUTIVE PROTECTION PRACTICE

In today's world executives face a particularly increasing risk of being personally involved in violent crime or other high-risk security scenarios.
This fact has led many companies to consider alternatives ranging from
holding special kidnap-recovery insurance coverage to physical and mental
security and survival training for their executives and enhanced collabora-
tion with public law-enforcement agencies. Additionally, more and more

executives are hiring private-sector, executive-security protection services, and private companies are emerging to fill this need. What follows is a review of certain executive-security-related services and executive-security alternatives drawn from U.S. and UK advisory documents for overseas businesses.

THE THREAT

Conducting international business in today's global marketplace includes managing executive-security risks that go well beyond those typically found in the United States, including risk of murder, kidnapping, extortion, and theft. For example, in 1996 an American executive from a major hotel chain was murdered at a train station in Moscow. That same year a Japanese executive was kidnapped from his car as he left a company baseball game in Tijuana, Mexico. He was later released after nine days of captivity and after Mexican authorities delivered a $2 million ransom. While the risks are significant, it is important to remember that they are not omnipresent or insurmountable and are determined primarily by a failure to calibrate your security measures commensurate with the country that is involved and your length of stay.

Monitoring International Risk

The U.S. State Department and other intelligence agencies consistently monitor the changing level of risk associated with traveling to various foreign countries. The State Department then issues travel warnings based on a combination of their own internal analyses and classified and unclassified intelligence, such as the CIA's Foreign Broadcast Information Service (FBIS), which translates the open press of foreign language newspapers and other public information. In addition, when a travel warning is not warranted but risks are nonetheless elevated, the State Department issues a notice of an "Area of Instability," and both of these documents are available on their Web site. For deeper analysis one can also research demographic, political, economic, and other country-by-country data provided annually in the CIA's unclassified World Fact Book.

The international business community has in recent years determined that it needs more timely and predictive analysis than the government provides, giving rise to an entire industry of risk and threat analysis. Some of these firms are strictly finance- or economic- centric and tend to measure the long-term likelihood of a military coup or political instability (so-called "political risk") in order to help Wall Street and others to hedge their international portfolio predictions. Other companies specialize in monitoring broader security threats and offering timely predictive analyses of ongoing and future events. This information is then made available in a variety of formats, mostly by targeted daily or weekly e-mails focusing on a particular industry, country, or region. These reports tend to include local and regional perspectives on political instability, local conflicts, and religious or ethnic tensions.

Four additional sources of reliable information also bear mention, the first being *The Economist,* the British-run newsweekly that offers excellent periodical "Surveys" of regions, industries, and countries. Another British source of high caliber is *Jane's,* which offers everything from weekly defense and military analysis to industry-specific detailed military-and-risk analysis available for corporate purchase. Stratfor, which stands for Strategic Forecasts, is an American-owned risk-and-intelligence analysis provider run by several former CIA agents and analysts, which digs deeply into the local language for often accurate and unconventional warnings and indications of the changing nature of events. Finally, a firm named Intellibridge offers analysis and review of global and industry-specific, open-source material; and although their prices tend to be a bit lower, it is because their analysts generally have less experience than those at *The Economist, Jane's,* and Stratfor.

Outsourced Risk Solutions

Some firms are finding that they prefer to outsource their risk-assessment and international concerns whole cloth. One of the better-known alternatives for executive risk solutions is The Ackerman Group, which is a well-established firm that works for many of the major insurance firms as the subject matter experts for carrying out the Kidnap & Ransom Insurance policies. In addition, several other leading international firms offer political and security-risk analysis, confidential investigations, security consulting, crisis management and response, and investigations of incidents. Another potentially useful resource is iJet corporate travel risk management, which offers real-time intelligence and risk-management services, including means to use GPS to track people, assets, and, if desired, customers, and software to store and retrieve response plans and crisis-management tools.

Reducing Your Risk

It is clear from the disparate numbers and types of incidents that occur around the globe that no single set of determinants can predict who will or will not become a target. In some cases it seems that having even minimal security is enough to deter common thieves, but may in turn make you more likely to be the target of more deliberate crime, under the criminals' logical deduction that anyone who warrants security must be important or wealthy enough to merit consideration for exploitation or attack. Still, all things being equal, there are a number of indicators that executives clearly should do their best to avoid, especially those who choose to forego hiring private security.

The first red flag for personal security is ostentatious displays of wealth, either personally or through your selection of limousines, extravagant restaurants, and hotel suites. In a high-risk environment executives working for big American or international companies that appear capable of paying dearly are more tempting to kidnappers and extortionists, and in many cases low-wage hotel and restaurant employees provide information to criminals on who is in town and who might be of interest to them.

OTHER TRICKS OF THE EXECUTIVE PROTECTION TRADE[1]
Personal Security Details

In addition to the basic deterrent effect of having personal security, executives also stand to gain from having dedicated experts attending to such details as vehicle security systems, route selection, and emergency medical supplies and training.

Proper planning and sound advance work are the key elements in all successful protective details. Generally, executives will find themselves with at most one- to three-person teams, depending on threat, location, and cost. However, by properly harnessing technology, even small teams can provide extremely effective protection in many situations, including ones that directly threaten their protectees' lives.

Executive Transport: GPS Security Monitoring Systems

The recent combination of satellite-based geo-location services, such as global positioning systems (GPS) with near ubiquitous cellular phone coverage, has enabled a new era in remote executive security monitoring. Commercial systems like OnStar offer certain safety advantages over just using cell phones, including the ability to remotely control automobile locks, offer directions, and direct police or emergency services directly to your vehicle. OnStar and its clones have limitations, however, such as obvious external communications gear that can be disabled, limited

---

[1]See chapter 5, "Personal Security," for additional driving tips. For details on site or installation security procedures, please see chapter 6, "Securing Your Workplace," and chapter 7, "Defensive Landscaping and Antiterrorism Architecture."

kidnapping or other robbery response training for their control-center operators, and an inability to discreetly communicate with victims during an attack.

Nonetheless, the basic geo-location, communication, and call-center elements of such systems do offer distinct security advantages, ones that can be maximized through dedicated executive alert systems. These systems cost between $8,000 and $10,000, depending on options, and typically conceal both the system's key communications components and one or more "panic" buttons to enable discrete activation. Such systems also offer other safety features like remote disabling of the engine to preclude high-speed chases and back-up batteries so the system will function even if the car's primary battery is inoperable, and are coupled with twenty-four-hour call centers and a trained staff better prepared to interact with police or other authorities.

Emergency Medical Equipment

A protective security detail must be capable of providing basic and intermediate medical attention in order to be properly prepared for any eventuality. Heart attacks and other ailments are common in both the population at large and especially with older protectees, and a good team not only will know how to administer CPR but will also have on hand the newly portable automatic external defibrillators (AEDs), such as you may have noticed recently in airports and other large gathering places. In addition, the U.S. military has recently acquired two types of high-tech, fast-clotting bandages. The first was developed jointly by army researchers and the American Red Cross and involves a bandage coated with fibrinogen and thrombin, two clotting factors found naturally in human blood. As soon as the bandage is applied to the wound the two clotting factors combine to form fibrin, the major component of a blood clot. These bandages are rumored to cost approximately $1,000 apiece, but the prices should go down as they become more widely available. The second new clotting bandage was developed by scientists at the Oregon Medical

Laser Center and is based on chitosan, a sugary molecule that helps bind the outer shells of shrimp and other crustaceans, but also seems to promote the formation of blood clots. These can be found for as little as $99 apiece.[2]

Additional items of use for a security-detail emergency medical kit will include:

- Portable emergency oxygen tanks and masks.
- Protective face shield.
- Sterile gauze pads and rolled gauze for wrapping.
- Latex gloves and bandage supplies, including butterfly bandages.
- Adhesive tape.
- Cotton balls (sterile).
- Blunt-ended scissors.
- Tweezers.
- Space foil blanket or a fleece blanket.
- Thermometer.
- Flashlight with extra batteries.
- Candle and matches.
- Bottled water.
- Fire extinguisher.

Basic medicines that should be carried include:

- Antibiotic cream or ointment.
- Antiseptic spray with anesthetic.
- Sterile saline solution.
- Antiseptic wipes (individually packaged).
- Aspirin and nonaspirin pain relievers, such as Tylenol® and Advil.

NOTE: If you are putting together an emergency medical kit, make sure all

[2]David Hamilton, "Battlefield Medical Advances May Save Wounded Soldiers," *The Wall Street Journal*, March 20, 2003.

medications you store with your medical kit are sealed and have similar ex-
piration dates.

Route Planning and Advance Reconnaissance

The now commonplace use of Palm Pilots or similar handheld computers
coupled with GPS and cellular phone service makes the older methods of
using a map and pencil for all premovement route planning seem elementary. However, as with most issues, the technological solutions are only as
good as those who use the information, which can now be gathered and organized more easily. Caution: remember that the enemy can access the same
data just as easily as you. Accordingly, executive-protection details must
still adhere to strict guidelines in developing primary and alternate routes
and conduct thorough advance reconnaissance to account for any alterations
that have occurred since the last update to the maps and other data that are
remotely accessible.

Another particularly useful new tool that has traditionally been re-
served for the exclusive use of the military is the recent civilian advent of
high-grade commercial satellite imagery and aerial photography. In particular, Keyhole, TerraServer, and Intellipix offer excellent satellite and
other imagery services. Similarly, Digital Sandbox offers data-overlay
solutions and advanced graphics solutions for pre- and postevent emergency planning.

Secure Communications

World-class executive protection must also provide guidance and implementation on issues such as industrial espionage as well as kidnapping and
terrorist threats. The extensive use of cell phones has dramatically increased
the speed of business, but at the same time has increased the speed of business espionage, inadvertent disclosures, and leaking of travel and security
details, especially as it relates to intercepted communications. Fortunately
the marketplace has developed any number of solutions for these problems,

ranging from encryption and password protection to special window coverings that can refract and trap sound vibrations. Motorola and others are now producing civilianized versions of previously military-only encryption and related technologies, though in some cases, because of licensing restrictions and technology transfer concerns, European encryption systems can offer much better protection than that which is commercially available in the United States. When you consider the potential cumulative costs of the unauthorized disclosure of proprietary information, such as proposal details, labor costs, expansion and development plans, salary, and other cost data, reasonable security efforts can be seen to be a real bargain.

Emergent Wireless Technology

Wireless technology has transformed the way travel- and mobile-security details operate to extend well beyond just cellular communications. Portable wireless security systems are now affordable for almost any conceivable use, including to create temporary security perimeters in conjunction with motion detectors and closed-circuit television equipment. Significantly, this can reduce the long-term cost of security services, because individuals properly equipped with wireless and other cutting-edge technologies can now do so much more. Several retailers are available online and through catalogs for the procurement of emergent surveillance and related communications equipment. However, rather than spend your money on less reliable items or those that may be unsuited to your particular needs, it is always advisable to seek guidance from a reputable security professional, discuss your needs in detail, and then develop an appropriate executive protection strategy.

Hostage Incidents

Much of this book has been written to give individuals and companies the benefits of the authors' many years spent working to stop terrorism and ensure personal security. As such it has focused on the active measures you can take to avoid becoming just another statistic. The many precautions provided here will serve you well in your efforts to maximize your own preparedness and to minimize your chances of being harmed. Sadly, nevertheless, for many Americans and especially businessmen and -women who live or travel overseas, the risk of being taken hostage is all too real. As has been stated repeatedly, the most important thing you can do to prepare yourself is to plan appropriately and account for all conceivable risks. This chapter explores various hostage-insurance alternatives and provides advice on how to deal with such an eventuality should it come to pass.

Where you are and who your assailants are make a tremendous difference in determining the likelihood that you will survive the ordeal intact. Historically, kidnappers in such places as Europe, Central Asia, and South America have sought out Westerners as symbols of wealth or for purposes of class warfare and usually have wanted money or publicity from their crime. Tragically, beginning with reporter Daniel Pearl in Karachi, Pakistan, in January 2002, and continuing in Iraq and Saudi Arabia, a trend of Islamic radicals beheading their captives in order to sensationalize their claims began changing the rules for potential kidnap victims. Just as the murderous acts of September 11, 2001, changed the standard reaction for a hijacked civilian airliner from compliance with demands and working to have passengers released to maximum resistance at the time of initial conflict, the increased likelihood of losing your life if kidnapped gives you all the more incentive to take all possible means (as opposed to only all reasonable means) to avoid capture. Accordingly, if you are in a part of the world, including Southeast Asia or certain former Soviet Union republics bordering on Chechnya, your best move is to resist at all costs. Nonetheless, for those who are kidnapped, the advice later in this chapter will help you increase your chances of coming home alive.

Know the Threat

The vast majority of worldwide kidnapping incidents are for ransom, not politics. Further, the annual number of incidents—be it of oil executives in the Caucasus, tourists in Latin America, or missionaries in Southeast Asia—indicates that this is a serious issue, albeit an underreported one in the public press because most companies and victims prefer to keep the story out of the newspapers. Individuals simply must be prepared to deal with such events, however unlikely they may seem. Preparations include various forms of survival training, learning how to play on the emotions of the captors, and means of communicating with the outside world. There are also arrangements that can be made in advance or after the fact with private-sector, executive-recovery specialists.

Insurance and Executive Recovery Specialists

Many companies that have executives who work or travel in high-risk areas of the globe recognize that the delicate details of hostage negotiations and specialized recovery services will exceed the capabilities and specialties of their in-house security departments. Significantly, it is not, as commonly believed, a duty of the U.S. Embassy, directly or militarily, to assist American victims of kidnapping, and the efforts and capabilities of the local governments vary widely. Accordingly many companies will seek the assistance of a security-consulting firm or work with their insurance carrier to arrange for a kidnapping and ransom (K&R) policy. The insurance companies, in turn, have their own approved security firms that they keep on retainer to handle such incidents.

The costs of obtaining K&R policies vary greatly based on the country your employees travel to or live in, the size of your company, and your ability to provide appropriate security. As with most insurance policies, however, if you need it even once it will more than pay for decades of having it. The typical corporate kidnap-and-ransom insurance policy will include bringing in a team of experts to handle everything from negotiating with the kidnappers to delivering ransom payments and even lost wages or business disruptions caused by the event. Most major insurance providers can offer this type of coverage as an addition to your existing policy.

Preparing for the Worst: Hostage Survival[3]

The goal for any hostage victim is to be returned to their loved ones having survived the ordeal with dignity and self-respect. Because kidnappings and hostage takings affect family members as well as the victim this section also provides several helpful tips for family members of those who are abducted.

At the first sign of danger you have to make a calculation as to whether you will attempt to resist, flee, or surrender to your assailants. This decision will be driven by many factors, including whether and how you and your assailants are armed, if your family or others are with you, and, as noted above, if the country you are in makes it more or less likely that this is a for-profit rather than Islamic radical kidnapping. Another realistic consideration is your own skill level in terms of survival versus resistance skills. The specific circumstances of the kidnapping or hostage seizure (at night while you are sleeping, when you are alone, isolated, and unarmed; after an evening on the town when your guard is down, etc.) may dictate that the matter is well beyond your control, but it is important to think about what you would do if faced with the problem because you will likely have only a moment to make that choice.

The most dangerous moments to victims of kidnapping or hostage taking occur at the very onset of the episode. This is because during the chaos of such a disruptive physical event, the kidnappers or hijackers are at their most intense emotional peak at just exactly the moment the potential victims must make the critical decision to resist, flee, or surrender. Accordingly, you need to resist the urge to panic and try to remain calm. Regain your composure as quickly as possible after capture and prepare to deal with the mental challenges that lie ahead, accepting that for the most part your fate is now out of your control, unless or until an opportunity for action presents itself. If you are taken hostage and decide not to resist, assure

[3]The U.S. military has given considerable consideration to all aspects of kidnapping and hostage survival and collected many lessons learned in the Chairman of the Joint Chiefs of Staff's CJCS Guide 5260, *Antiterrorism Personal Protection Guide,* and the Department of Defense Directive 0-2000, 12-H, chapter 14, on which much of this chapter is based.

your captors of your intention to cooperate, especially during the abduction phase.

After the initial shock of capture wears off, both the kidnappers and the victims will stabilize their emotions and begin to plan for the future. The terrorists may divulge information about themselves, their organization, their goals, and objectives. They may share their demands, and they may even begin to discuss roles and responsibilities the victim or victims will have in the future. Those taken hostage also should begin to make an emotional transition from being a "victim" to being a "survivor." Several discrete actions will help in this process, such as taking mental note of the direction, time in transit, noise, and other environmental factors that may help you identify your location; noting numbers, names, physical characteristics, accents, personal habits, and rank structure of your captors; beginning to consider the requirements for an escape attempt and the tools you have at your disposal.

Surviving Detention

Being held hostage is one of the most stressful and difficult circumstances conceivable. Several factors make this situation especially difficult for many victims, beginning with the lack of human interaction. Kidnap victims and hostages are usually isolated from all outside contact. While they may have access to radios and televisions, they are never allowed to call their families, friends, or colleagues. Even if seized in large groups, victims are often separated and held individually or in small groups. In some circumstances, separation from the group can compound anxiety and fear, especially if the victims are separated from their children, elderly parents, or spouses. Also, hostages tend to try and make sense out of the situation that has unfolded and can have a difficult time imagining or understanding why anyone would want to kidnap them or hold them hostage. Third, kidnappings and hostage-taking events occur as ugly surprises, totally disrupting plans and activities for an unknown period of time. Surprise is often very stressful; for those individuals who take special pride in making and fulfilling commitments, such events can be emotionally shattering. These individuals are easily rattled when thrown off schedule or when their daily, weekly, or monthly plans are upset.

Being kidnapped is the ultimate disruptive event—no one can know or predict how or when the episode will end. For victims, but especially those who are schedule conscious, the stress level in and of itself can be a major obstacle.

Perhaps most important, victims must come to grips with an incredible host of intangibles and unknowns. Once the trauma of initial capture has subsided and the victims have adjusted to the total loss of freedom and being placed in a position of complete dependence on their captors, other uncertainties begin to manifest themselves in the victims' behavior and demeanor. Victims wonder who knows of their predicament, what is being done to bring the episode to a close, who will take care of "things" in their absence, and what is going to happen next. Kidnappers will frequently undertake certain actions to increase the degree to which victims become dependent upon them, including small issues like confiscating wristwatches, calendars, and even eyeglasses. These actions are all part of a concerted plan by terrorists to exacerbate the psychological hazards associated with being kidnapped or taken hostage: claustrophobia, loss of sense of time, and isolation from society. Previous victims also report they were often placed in dark, confined surroundings for prolonged periods. The victim must be able to compensate for feelings of depression, adjust to living alone, and offset the demoralizing realization that human contacts they may have for the foreseeable future are likely to be quite hostile.

In order to maintain a sense of order, personal dignity, and personal functionality, each victim or hostage should try to prepare himself mentally and avoid speculation about what lies ahead in terms of this ordeal and concentrate instead on longer-term goals and issues such as building elaborate plans for the future upon release. For example, Americans held hostage in Lebanon during the 1980s taught each other collegiate-level courses from memory, designed plans for a dairy farm down to the smallest detail, played chess on a self-made board with self-crafted pieces, and studied one another's religion. You should also try to remain calm during captivity because if you do, it is easier for terrorists also to remain calm. If you treat yourself, your fellow hostages, and your captors with respect, you can often expect similar treatment from your captors, though don't think they are your friends or expect any substantive assistance from them. Still, you should identify those captors with whom you can communicate and attempt to establish a relationship with one or more of them. Do not debate or argue about things where you disagree but instead search for common ground. This may come in handy in the future if you decide and are able to attempt an escape.

Physical and Mental Health

Eat whatever food is offered to you to maintain your strength. Kidnap victims rarely gain weight during their captivity. However, eating enough to maintain body weight and sustain proper functioning of the immune system is important, and if you lose too much weight by not eating available rations you can become seriously ill and develop medical conditions that exceed the medical resources of your captors. If allowed you should also exercise daily, a key technique that prisoners of war and long-term hostages emphasize to not only strengthen physical durability but also give added mental strength as well. Exercise and good physical conditioning also increase resistance to disease, which may be a by-product of dietary changes or inadequate food, poor living conditions, and general emotional deprivation associated with victim status. And while the library available to kidnapping victims may be quite limited, reading is still an excellent activity to keep one's mind active while maintaining vigilance, offering no overt acts of opposition, but no overt acts of cooperation with captors either.

Being aware of your surroundings will remain an important determinant in whether or not you recognize an opportunity for escape or an attempted rescue that may occur. Listen for unusual sounds that seem out of place or inconsistent with usual activities; such sounds might include helicopter blades beating in the air, high-performance aircraft overhead, or diesel-engine sounds in the neighboring street. Watch for unexplained changes in guard behavior, unexplained increases or decreases in civilian traffic observable from one's place of detention, or other signs of unusual activity on the part of the terrorists.

There are also actions to avoid because they generally increase the risk of physical violence to the victim without increasing opportunities for escape. This includes aggravating your abductors, especially the guards who watch over you. They will be low-level operatives at best and unable to make decisions that would really assist you, such as to release you, but their ill will can create an even worse situation out of what is already sure to be dire enough. For this reason you should avoid political or ideological discussions with your captors. Also, in many instances you will not be their only captive, and no matter how satisfying it may be to provoke an outburst of anger from your enemy such provocative behavior can increase the risk of violence to all captives.

Similarly, do not refuse favors offered by the terrorists if doing so will aggravate them or cause further harm to the health and safety of all hostages; do not, however, accept favorable treatment at the expense of others, as this will weaken your collective strength and begin a downward spiral where the few people who are truly on your side may become hostile to you. During informal conversations with terrorists and captors, victims can sometimes develop human relationships by conversing with their captors and responding to personal questions that do not require discussion of the victims' positions, responsibilities, and purposes of travel.

Conduct During Interrogation

Depending upon the personality of the terrorists holding the victims hostage, their purpose in seizing hostages, and the prominence or position of the hostages, the terrorists may elect to interrogate victims. Be aware that you likely have very little to offer the captors in terms of valuable information and choose to tell the truth by taking simple positions that you feel comfortable with and will be able to maintain.

Rescue/Release

Episodes of kidnapping and hostage taking do end and it is almost surprising how often they do so with no loss of life or physical injury to the victims. The psychological casualties suffered by kidnapping victims are difficult to assess, as are the casualties incurred by victims' families, friends, and colleagues. Nevertheless, hostage and kidnapping episodes can end as a result of terrorism counteraction, successful negotiations, or fatigue on the part of the terrorists, and the manner by which an episode comes to an end will have considerable bearing on how you need to behave at the conclusion of the event. If you are freed following successful negotiations or because the terrorists decided to release you, simply follow the instructions of your captors until you reach safety. In the event of an armed rescue attempt, however, keep in mind the following:

- Do not run, because the terrorists may shoot you or rescue forces may mistake you for the enemy. Even if you can, do not pick up a gun to assist rescue forces; they are trained professionals with a plan and special skills and your period of captivity may have hindered your physical capabilities more than you know.
- Drop to the floor and remain still. During the rescue attempt, both the hostage and the rescue force are in extreme danger. If the facility confining victims is breached by rescue forces, drop to the floor immediately, and lie as flat as possible. Remain still and do not move until told to do so.
- After order has been restored by rescue forces, there may be some moments when the victims may be handled roughly or ordered up against the wall. Victims may be handcuffed, searched, and even gagged until the rescue forces have positively identified all persons. This procedure is common to special-response teams and hostage-rescue teams and is employed for their safety as well as the safety of hostages upon release.

Family Roles and Responsibilities

You can help victims' families deal with the trauma of kidnapping and hostage taking by preparing them for what might happen in advance of the event. Such preparations include implementing protective security measures, explaining to them the risks you feel you face, and creating specific family-security contingency plans. These plans should be used by every

PERSONAL INFORMATION SHEET

- Name.
- Nickname.
- Place and date of birth.
- Address of principal residence and telephone number.
- Address of secondary residence and telephone number.
- Precise physical description (e.g., height, weight, scars, tattoos, prostheses, dentures, etc.).
- Other identifying characteristics (e.g., birthmarks, physical handicaps, etc.)
- Prescription for eyeglasses, if used.
- Chronic illnesses.
- Special medicines and instructions for their use.
- Pharmacies regularly used.
- Vehicles (types and license).
- School (type, class, address, names of teachers).
- Recent information on educational qualifications, specialization's, hobbies, etc.
- Information about friends residing in diverse localities, including their telephone numbers.

family and include simple means for communicating that one member of the family is under duress. For example, notes from parents to children should include a code phrase, word, or set of innocent-looking alphanumeric characters that can be understood by the children as authenticating the message, with one code used to indicate everything is OK and another that indicates danger or duress. Telephone conversations should begin or end with similar codes so that parents and children know whether or not the discussion is voluntary or is occurring under duress. Practical matters should also be attended to in advance to ease the stress family members feel during an actual crisis. All family members should assemble a personal history and/or information sheet (see accompanying box), preferably in their own handwriting, which can be used as an aid to law-enforcement and intelligence officials in the event of an incident, as well as strands of hair for DNA cataloguing. Having each family member record this information orally on a cassette could also be helpful by providing a sample of the family member's voice that can be used to help identify voices on recordings mailed to the authorities or media outlets in the event of a kidnapping.

You should also update family legal documents such as wills and powers of attorney at least annually and keep copies at home and the originals in a secure place like a bank safety deposit box. Also discuss with your family what they should do in the event of your abduction, especially if you are residing overseas. Make a packet containing instructions, money, airline tickets, credit cards, insurance policies, and the name of a company contact to get in touch with for survivor assistance. Be sure to discuss what should be done if those kidnapped are parents, including issues such as the continuation of education for the children, if and where the family might relocate, and the disposition of family property. Holding these discussions and undertaking these preparations will ease worries about family matters during captivity in the event you are taken hostage or are kidnapped.

Dealing with the Media

No matter how the episode comes to an end, it also is likely that sooner or later the victim(s) will have to face the media, even if the families of kidnapping or hostage situations would prefer otherwise. As survivors of difficult ordeals, the victims will be encouraged to speak out on their experiences. Just as the terrorists stripped away virtually all privacy and dignity during the victims' captivity, so too will some members of the press seek out answers to the most demeaning, humiliating, or private questions conceivable. In the past many victims wanted to share their stories but have been shocked, angered, and even humiliated by their treatment at the hands of the press. Therefore, victims need to recognize that press interviews can be very difficult, and survivors may be able to return to normal life more easily by minimizing their interaction with the press. If you feel compelled or forced to issue a statement, a good general response to all press inquiries is to note the simple joys of freedom and that given a choice between being free and being a hostage, being free is far superior.

NINE

▼

Conclusions

The threat of Terrorism gives us a choice:
we can be afraid or we can be ready. Get Ready!

TOM RIDGE, FIRST SECRETARY OF

THE DEPARTMENT OF HOMELAND SECURITY

This book has explored the myriad of ways in which the terrorist threat continues to grow and to shape the amount of risk we face in our everyday lives. The theme of this book is that preparedness is a way of life, and that vigilance is ever more necessary in modern times. The sad reality is that life *did* change forever on September 11, 2001, because that was when we learned all too clearly that our oceans no longer protect us from foreign aggression. We each must take responsibility for properly measuring risk, defending ourselves, and taking appropriate actions.

Threats to individual security and well-being come in many forms, including theft, terrorism, kidnapping, and murder. Even terrorism itself is mutable, adjusting to our every action with a new and insidious means of harming the innocent to give voice to perceived social, political, and religious wrongs. We are likely to see attacks in the future that make 9/11 pale in comparison, hideous attacks of unspeakable evil that change the very fabric of our society and confront us with questions about quarantine, contamination, and long-term care for thousands of victims. We are also likely to encounter a new threat stream as yet unknown in America—a rash of shooting sprees and suicide bombings that do not kill great numbers but nonetheless disrupt our lives and affect our sense of what is right and how to protect ourselves.

But the threats we face go beyond terrorism. Routine mechanical failures can wreak great havoc on entire sectors of the national energy grid, foot-and-mouth or avian flu can attack our livestock and affect our trade, or the next global flu pandemic may strike and decimate a large segment of even the relatively healthy population.

If the worst does happen, and you are caught up in a specific scenario such as one of those described in this book, then you will be glad to have thought through your options in advance, to have made the necessary arrangements for your own survivability, and to know how best to respond. The first step on the path of preparedness is to arm yourself with the knowledge to avoid threatening scenarios and to properly provision yourself for evacuation or shelter-in-place, as appropriate.

From a personal level, each of us needs to look into ourselves and determine how we want to approach the future, how willing we are to join community response efforts and to seek out CPR and other medical training. We have to decide if we are willing to carry supplies in our cars at all times and have plans for emergency communications with loved ones. We need to set a plan for response and ensure that our children, our parents, our loved ones, and our friends understand what we plan to do and how best to respond themselves.

From a business perspective, too, it must be understood that the risk equation has changed. If the efficiencies associated with "just-in-time" manufacturing and delivery were the business imperative of the 1990s, then the imperative of 9/11 was that supply-chain continuity is a risky proposition and redundancy and contingency planning are key for long-term survival. No longer can the "status quo" be expected to rule because the risk of disruption has just increased dramatically. Failing to plan can lead to failure of the business, and the plans that are developed must be comprehensive, up-to-date, and practiced on a regular basis.

The only reasonable response to today's uncertainty is to study your business, your industry, and your alternatives to fully understand how any events might adversely affect you. With a more fully informed approach you can do everything reasonable to understand the risk you face, decide what risks to address and which to accept, and then be better situated to respond to events as they occur. Just as no one would try to operate a business without adjusting to technological or process-manufacturing changes, terrorism is the new reality and the heightened risk of adverse events is the new norm.

One major stumbling block in creating comprehensive security is related to a theorem in economics known as the "tragedy of the commons," which relates to how certain commonly beneficial actions will not be undertaken because expenses borne by the few will benefit others, so-called "free-riders," who did not share in paying the costs. In homeland security the parallel concern arises when an entire industry can be viewed as at risk, as opposed to individual companies per se. Each firm can decide that it does not have an incentive to secure itself if its industry partners do not for two very clear reasons: first, their costs of business will increase relative to their competitors, which is bad for business; and second, even if they individually are better protected their industry is not, opening the door to industry-wide failure or government regulation. As a result the response must not be just individual security improvements, but industry-wide, and indeed nationwide.

So you must learn how to examine your relative risks and how to drive your business forward, at the same time influencing and bringing along major industry players. There is tremendous uncertainty about how the Department of Homeland Security will fare in the long run—will it even survive, or will it fade away like the Transportation Security Administration (TSA) sometimes appears ready to do? Most likely it will always exist, though certain key functions will migrate out and reestablish their independence. How effective it will be at implementing sustainable increased preparedness is the real issue, and so far the indicators are not good. First responders have equipment, but no one has studied the cascading effects of events that create indirect effects.

The military has long studied this—how do you create a desired effect, such as winning on the battlefield? Whenever possible the best answer is to preclude the enemy from engaging you—turn out their lights, disrupt their communications, and create disorder in their chain of command. With our deep reliance on technology, all this and more is likely to happen at all levels—massive disruptions of personal lives, communities, companies, and industries, and even the national defense establishment.

The good news is that the actions outlined in this book will be relevant for reducing your risks from a whole host of threats, not just terrorism. Statistically the greater risk comes from our daily lives than from terrorism, although again the spiraling and cascading economic effects of an attack will have a tremendous effect on all aspects of our lives.

It is important to understand that technology has fostered the *empowerment of the weak,* beyond historical norms and beyond the tolerable threshold for a civil society. As a result of technology and communications, even a small cell of militants can put many individuals at risk, and indeed could potentially cripple our entire economic system. The civil liberties and freedoms we could once afford based on a relatively low threshold of potential damage are now at direct risk, not from the government, but from the terrorists. They aim to use our strengths—an open and free society, acceptance of others, respect of privacy—against us.

Understand that the genie is out of the bottle. Just as decades ago front doors didn't need to be locked and your identity was not something someone could steal, times are changing. Take the measures outlined in this book to improve your personal preparedness, to determine how and why you are at risk, and to determine what actions would be appropriate for you in weighing prudent risk mitigation versus reasonable risk acceptance. Most of all, prepare yourself for the risk of darker times ahead when the threat has changed, the enemy again comes to our shores, and their methods of attack place the burden of preparedness on you, the individual, the business, and the community.

To paraphrase former secretary of Homeland Security, Tom Ridge, you have a choice: "Be afraid, or be ready." By following the recommendations, checklists, and procedures described in these pages, you have chosen to be ready.

Get Ready.

Fight Back

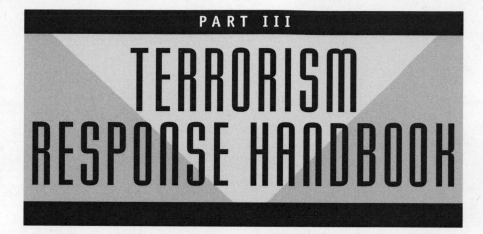

PART III

TERRORISM RESPONSE HANDBOOK

A Personal Preparedness Guide for
Responding to Terrorism

DR. JOEL D. SELANIKIO, M.D.

TEN

▼

General Preparation

Go-Bags

Q: What's a Go-Bag?

A: A go-bag is a collection of essentials to keep in your home or office in case you need to quickly move to another location (i.e., evacuate). It contains some food, water, clothing, and other essentials to increase the chance that you make it to your destination.

Suggested Go-Bag Items

Breathing
- N95 mask:
  Available at any hardware store. Does not protect against smoke inhalation; "N95" means that it can block even small particles, including anthrax spores. Look for "NIOSH N95" on the package.

Communication
- Radio—battery powered or hand crank:
  If battery powered is chosen, make sure you have extra sets of batteries.
- Cell phone and extra battery
- Whistle:
  Extremely useful to catch someone's attention from a distance or in a crowd.

Lighting
- Waterproof flashlight:
  Battery-powered, hand crank, or "shake powered" (powered by magnetic induction).
- Headlamp:
  Very useful to keep hands free while providing light for work or movement.
- Chemical light sticks
- Chemical hand warmers

Medical and Hygiene
- Basic first-aid kit
- At least three-day supply of prescription medicines
- Potassium iodide (KI):
  See "Potassium Iodide" section on page 223.
- Household bleach (unscented):
  Household bleach can be used to decontaminate the skin or personal items (such as eyeglasses) after exposure to certain harmful chemicals. The bleach should only contain 4–6 percent hypoclorite. It should not contain any soaps or fragrances.
- Non-aspirin pain and fever reducer:
  Such as Tylenol® (acetaminophen) or Motrin® (ibuprofen).
- Antidiarrheal:
  Such as Imodium® (operamide).
- Extra pair of glasses in a hard case
- For women tampons (and Ziploc® plastic bags for disposal).

Miscellaneous
- Multitool:
  Make sure it has a can opener if you have canned food!
- Antibacterial wipes
- Toilet tissue two-pack
- Duct tape
- Plastic bags

Mobility
- Compass and laminated area map:
  Many camping stores have a combined whistle and compass.

Nutrition
- Water-purification tabs:
  Often called "iodine tablets," but don't always contain iodine. Useful if you're not sure about the safety of your water source. Two tablets kill most bacteria in one quart of water (about one liter).
- Household bleach (unscented):
  Household bleach can be used instead of water-purification tablets to kill bacteria in water. The bleach should only contain 4–6 percent hypochlorite. It should not contain any soaps or fragrances. See the "Nutrition" section on page 214.
- Water boxes—*at least* 25-oz worth:
  Similar to the popular children's "juice boxes." Several brands are available that will last for five years if unopened. Very useful to stock your shelter-in-place room, too.
- Water carrier (2.5 gallon):
  Every person will require a gallon of water (3.75 L) each day.

Note: See the "Nutrition" section (page 214) for more information about food and water requirements.

Shelter and Clothing
- Plastic poncho or waterproof jacket
- "Space" blanket:
  Inexpensive and lightweight Mylar® blanket.
- Fleece jacket:
  Fleece is better than wool or cotton because it retains warmth even
  if it becomes wet.
- Change of pants, shirt, underwear, socks
- A pair of sturdy, comfortable shoes

GO-BAG PLANNING CHECKLIST

Individual Three-Day Go-Bag Checklist

The following checklist will help you plan to make a set of go-bags for an individual, or a collection of individuals, who may or may not stay together as a group. An example of the latter would be coworkers in an office, who might initially be together but would then separate to rejoin their families. For such a situation, each person would need his own first-aid kit, radio, etc.

A Note on Water and Food for Go-Bags

Water: Our standard recommendation is to stock a go-bag with nine water boxes. That is about 0.6 gallons, not even a one-day supply. Unfortunately, since each day's supply of water (about one gallon in an emergency situation) weighs about eight pounds, it can be difficult to carry a full three-day supply. Our strategy is to use the go-bag to carry a minimum amount of water, and then obtain more water on arrival in a safe resting spot.

Bottom line: If you can easily fit and carry more than our recommended amount of water in your go-bag, you should do so!

INDIVIDUAL THREE-DAY GO-BAG CHECKLIST

CATEGORY	ITEM	# ITEMS/ PERSON	# OF PEOPLE	TOTAL ITEMS	COMPLETE?
Breathing	N95 mask	2			
Communication	Radio	1			
	Set of radio batteries, if needed	2			
	Whistle	1			
Lighting	Waterproof flashlight	1			
	Sets headlamp batteries, if needed	2			
	Headlamp	1			
	Set of headlamp batteries, if needed	2			
	Chemical lightsticks	2			
Shelter & Clothing	Plastic poncho	1			
	Space blanket	1			
	Fleece jacket	1			
	Change of clothes	1			
Mobility	Compass	1			
	Laminated map	1			
Medical	First-aid kit	1			
	3-days Rx meds	1			
	Potassium iodide (KI)	1 dose			
	Pain and fever reducer (like Tylenol®)	3-day supply			
	Antidiarrheal (like Loperamide®)	3-day supply			
	Extra eyeglasses	1			
	Thermometer	1			
	Tampons & plastic bags for disposal	3-day supply			
Nutrition	Water-purification tablets	1 bottle			
	Water boxes (8.45 fl oz)	9			
	PowerBars®	48			
Misc.	Backpack	1			
	Multitool	1			
	Antibacterial wipes packet	1			
	Toilet tissue 1 roll	1			
	Duct tape 1 roll	1			
	Plastic garbage bags	1 box			
Optional Items	SCBA evacuation hood	1			
	Smoke filtration mask	1			

Food: Our standard food recommendation is to stock a go-bag with forty-eight PowerBars®, which is about a three-day supply in a high-stress situation. That three-day supply weighs about 6.8 lbs (3.1 kg), which is a manageable weight when combined with the other items in the go-bag. We recommend carrying fewer days' worth of water than food simply because of the weight issue: one day's water weighs four times more than one day's food!

Many people have asked why we use PowerBars® as the standard food for our go-bags. We do this because they are lightweight, high calorie, and require no preparation, so it's easy to carry a three-day supply. If you want to use other foods, by all means do so! This is especially true if you are stocking a shelter-in-place room, where weight is not a consideration: you could have a good variety of canned and other foods. Remember that unlike in your daily life, in an emergency you want lots of energy (that is, lots of calories) in as small a package as possible.

Some good high-energy (that is, high-calorie) foods for stocking a go-bag or shelter-in-place room:

- Dried fruit or nuts
- Peanut butter
- Crackers
- Chocolate bars
- Nonperishable pasteurized milk
- Potato chips or nacho chips: The fried kind, not the baked kind (more calories)

Shelter-in-Place Supplies

You can use the "Individual Three-Day Go-Bag Checklist" in the section preceding this one to plan for groups that will be staying together; for example, coworkers in an office that are sheltering-in-place for several days or a family in a basement safe room.

For items that can be shared, such as radios, you probably don't need to include one for every person in the group. It would be reasonable to have two radios, keeping one of the two as a spare.

See the beginning of the "Go-Bag Planning Checklist" section, on page 208, for a discussion of food and water requirements for go-bags.

Special Foods: Infants and Pets

Make sure that if you have infants or pets you store the appropriate foods. This also applies, of course, to anyone with special dietary requirements.

SHELTERING-IN-PLACE

What Is a Safe Room, and When Do I Need to Use One?

In many instances, you will want to remain where you are until conditions are safe to go out. This is called "sheltering-in place." There are two basic situations for which you would want to shelter-in-place:

1. If there is an infectious disease epidemic, such as would result from a smallpox attack. In this case, since the disease is contagious, you need to minimize your contact with other people. You can do this just by remaining in your home or office without sealing the doors and windows. We call this "standard shelter-in-place."

2. If there is something harmful in the air, such as a chemical released from a plane. In this case you need to minimize your contact with the outside air. You can do this by remaining, not only indoors (for example, in your home), but by remaining in a room that is sealed to the outside air. This kind of room is called a "safe room," and we call this activity "safe room shelter-in-place."

It is *highly* recommended that you set up and stock a safe room in your home and one at your place of work *in advance.* The supplies you put in the safe room will be useful to you even if you just need to shelter-in-place without sealing up a safe room.

How Do I Pick My Safe Room? Should It Be Above- or Below-ground?

If possible, you should choose a room with few or no windows or heating/air vents. For this reason, people often choose a basement room as a safe room and that is usually fine. **Exception:** In a chemical or biological attack, an **above-ground** room is preferable because most chemicals or biological agents are heavier than air and so will tend to seep into basements.

Keep your safe room provisions stored in several easy-to-carry bags or backpacks. Then you can easily move them into whichever room in your home or office is most appropriate when an attack occurs.

What Do I Put In My Safe Room?

In addition to supplies listed in the section above on go-bags, suggested supplies for a safe room include the following:

- Bedding
- A large plastic bucket with sealable lid (in case toilet facilities are not working or not available)
- Matches or a lighter, candles and a candleholder
- Duct tape and plastic sheeting to seal cracks in doors, windows, and vents

It is probably a good idea to have a few distractions in your safe room, such as board games, in case you need to spend more than a few hours there.

Sealing a Safe Room

In several kinds of terrorist attack, or other emergencies (such as an accidental chemical release), there could be harmful substances in the air. Examples could include botulinum toxin, anthrax spores, or chlorine gas. Under those circumstances, you will want to keep your safe room as sealed as possible from the outside air.

Your prestocked safe room should include duct tape and plastic sheeting to seal windows and doors. If you have no duct tape or plastic, you can use cloth, crumpled paper, or other materials to try to seal cracks around doors and windows.

How Long Can I Remain In My Sealed Safe Room?

Sometimes people wonder if they will run out of air while in their sealed safe room. This is unlikely, since most shelter-in-place situations will only last a few hours (that's how long it would take most chemicals in the air to dissipate).

As a general rule, though, DHS recommends that you allow ten square feet of floor space per person in order to provide sufficient air for up to five hours. This means, of course, that a sealed 4 × 10-foot room (40 square feet) would be large enough to let a family of four shelter for five hours.

What Kind of Duct Tape Is Best?

The Federal Emergency Management Agency (FEMA) recommends using duct tape with a minimum thickness of ten millimeters (0.01 in).

What Kind of Plastic Sheeting Is Best?

FEMA recommends using plastic sheeting with a thickness of ten millimeters (0.01 in). Keep in mind, though, that *any* plastic sheeting is better than nothing.

ELEVEN

▼

Nutrition

REQUIREMENTS PER PERSON PER DAY

Stress, illness, hyperventilation, exercise, wounds (especially burns), and blood loss increase water and nutritional needs. The estimates given below are for the average healthy unstressed person, and so should be considered minimum figures for nutrition in emergency situations. As an estimate, we multiplied our normal numbers by 1.5 to provide extra water and nutrition for high-stress situations.

Things that increase water and nutritional needs:

- Stress
- Exercise/exertion
- Pregnancy
- Hot or cold environment
- Illness
- Wounds and burns
- Blood loss
- Being tall or thin or young

All figures below are estimates and are calculated for the "average" person weighing about 154 lbs (70 kg).

Water

Normal requirement equals two to three gallons of water per day, which is the same thing as 2.5 L or 85 fl. oz.

Emergency requirement equals three to four and a half gallons per person per day, which is the same thing as 3.75 L or 128 fl. oz.

How Do I Purify Water?

There are several ways to kill harmful bacteria or other organisms in water:

- **Boiling:** If you have access to a heat source, you can boil water for ten minutes to kill bacteria.
- **Water purification tablets:** Add two of these standard tablets per quart (or per liter) of water. Allow to sit for thirty minutes if possible. It is normal for the water to have a slight chemical taste.
- **Household bleach:** Add eight drops of 4–6 percent household bleach per gallon of water. Allow to sit for thirty minutes if possible. It is normal for the water to have a slight chemical taste. The bleach should not contain perfumes or soaps.

Food

A normal requirement equals 2,500 Kcal per day, which is about eleven PowerBars®.

Emergency requirement equals 3,750 Kcal per day, which is about sixteen PowerBars®.

Q: Why are your nutritional requirements given in PowerBars®? Is that a very healthy diet?

A: A balanced diet is important, but not in the immediate aftermath of an emergency. PowerBars® are high-calorie and highly portable foods that require no preparation. If you can provide a better selection of foods then by all means do so! This is especially true if you're stocking a shelter-in-place room, where the food's weight is not an issue. Note also that "breakfast bars" such as Nutri-Grain® have many fewer calories per bar (140) than standard PowerBars® (230), so keep this in mind if choosing other products. Unlike in your daily life, in an emergency you want **lots of calories** in as small a package as possible.

TWELVE

▼

Responding to Emergencies

GENERAL RESPONSE INFORMATION

In any emergency, specific information will help you to decide what to do. In the initial stages of an emergency, however, there may be little specific information available. By following these general suggestions, you will minimize your risk of injury:

1. **Stay calm:** Though this can be easier said than done, you will be more useful to yourself and others if you stay calm.
2. **Cover up:** Try to protect your breathing, eyes, and skin. Wear a mask or piece of cloth over your mouth and nose. Wear eye protection, if available. Leave as little skin exposed as possible.
3. **Move away:** If you think there may be dangerous substances in the air, and you think you know where they are coming from, move away from their source. Remember to move *uphill* and *upwind* of the source if possible. If you cannot move, get inside and shelter-in-place to minimize contact with the contaminated air.
4. **Wash up:** If you think you have been exposed to dangerous substances in the air, remove your clothing, *wash thoroughly with soap and water* if possible, and put on new clothing.

5. **Get more info:** Try to get to a television or radio for more information. Adjust your actions as you learn more about the situation.

SHOULD I STAY OR SHOULD I GO?

The sections below explain how to respond to specific emergencies. In almost every instance, however, you will need to make a very important decision: *Should I evacuate or "shelter-in-place"?*

For many of us, the only experience with emergencies is the "fire drill," which teaches us how to evacuate a building in case of fire. In a fire it is the burning building itself that poses a danger to us.

Similarly, in some terrorist scenarios the danger lies in the building. Certainly that was true for the tragedy at the World Trade Center on 9/11.

In other likely scenarios, though, the danger lies outside the building. In those cases the building you are in, whether it is your home or your office, offers the best protection, and you should "shelter-in-place" or remain in the building.

The information below can explain to you which situations require evacuation and which require you to shelter-in-place.

EXPLOSIONS
What to Do in an Explosion

Probably the highest terrorist risk is for the use of conventional (that is, nonnuclear) explosives. If there is an explosion, you should initially:

1. Get inside a building and away from the windows. This is to avoid falling debris.
2. Get under a desk, or a table, if you have one.
3. Wear a mask or piece of cloth over your mouth and nose to avoid breathing in any dust in the air.
4. Notify authorities if possible.

Once it seems safe to get up and go outside:

5. Grab your go-bag if possible.
6. Exit the building and get to a safer spot, such as your pre-arranged rendezvous point.
7. If you have your go-bag, use the radio to find out more information.

If you are trapped by debris:

1. Wear a mask or piece of cloth over your mouth to avoid breathing in any dust in the air.
2. Communicate to rescuers by
   ▪ cell phone
   ▪ whistle
   ▪ tapping or banging
   ▪ shouting—this is the worst option if you are trapped in an enclosed space because it will use up the most oxygen.

More Information

▪ National Terror Alert Web site:
http://www.nationalterroralert.com/readyguide/explosive
attack.html.
▪ Ready.gov:
http://www.ready.gov/explosions.html.

FIRE

What to Do in a Fire

The danger from fire and smoke include the risk of burns, of course, but also the risk that the fire will consume so much oxygen that you will be breathing more smoke (and the harmful gases in smoke) than oxygen.

Simple ways to protect yourself and your respiratory (breathing) system in these situations include:

1. Stay close to the ground. Smoke tends to rise, so the air near the ground will be clearer.
2. Put a wet cloth over your face to shield your breathing from both the smoke and the heat. If you have a fire-evacuation hood or a mask, use it (see "Safety Equipment" section below).
3. Block smoke from coming under doors by putting newspaper, clothes, or other materials in the cracks around the doors.
4. Touch doors before opening them to see if they are hot.
5. Never use elevators in a fire.
6. If you catch on fire, do not run. Stop-drop-and-roll to put out the fire.

Safety Equipment

In addition to the simple methods of respiratory protection listed above, fire-evacuation hoods can also help. There are two basic kinds:

WITH "CANNED AIR"
This kind is called a self-contained breathing apparatus (SCBA) and is commonly used by firefighters. These devices will give you ten minutes or more clean air to breath, depending on the model. The main disadvantage to using these is the expense, which can be close to one thousand dollars, depending on the model. In addition, these masks may require special training and may need to be fitted individually to each person.

WITHOUT "CANNED AIR"
These devices usually consist of a plastic hood that goes over your whole face and a built-in filter that stops you from breathing harmful gases in the smoke. In intense fire/smoke these may not be as useful as a SCBA because there may not be enough oxygen in the air to allow you to breathe.

More information

U.S. Fire Administration (USFA):
http://www.usfa.fema.gov/public/index.shtm.

RADIATION EVENT

General Information

If there is a nuclear detonation, a "dirty bomb" detonation, or an explosion at a nuclear facility in your vicinity, the risks to your health and survival include:

- the explosive force
- fire and smoke
- radiation.

See the "Explosion" and "Fire" sections above for more information in dealing with the first two risks.

The effects of radiation are minimized by three strategies: maximizing distance, maximizing shielding, and minimizing the time spent in contact with radiation.

How you use these strategies depends on what information is available at the time. This is particularly important to decide if you should try to evacuate the area or shelter-in-place.

What to Do in a Radiation Event

If you think there may be radiation involved in an explosion, the best thing to do is to shield yourself from the explosion either be moving away (that is, evacuate) to a safer distance or by sheltering in an underground location.

Listen to the radio and follow instructions from the authorities.

If you do not have any information about whether to evacuate or to shelter-in-place:

1. Cover your nose, mouth, and eyes if possible, and quickly get inside, away from possibly contaminated air.
2. Shelter-in-place in a safe-room that is sealed from the outside air. If possible choose an underground room with thick walls and no windows. It is much better to have a shelter-in-place room chosen and stocked *before* there is a problem.
3. Use plastic sheeting and duct tape to seal any doors and windows to prevent radioactive particles in the air from entering. Turn off any air-conditioning or ventilation systems.
4. If you think you have been exposed to radioactive dust in the air, remove your clothing, wash thoroughly with soap and water if possible, and put on new clothing.
5. If you must travel, try to protect your breathing, eyes, and skin: wear a mask or piece of cloth over your mouth and nose. Wear eye protection if available. Leave as little skin exposed as possible.
6. Get more information from radio, television, or other source.
7. If instructed, take your dose of potassium iodide (see below).

The Difference Between a "Nuclear Bomb" and a "Dirty Bomb"

The terms "nuclear bomb," "hydrogen bomb," and "atomic bomb" all refer to bombs that produce an explosion by the process of nuclear fission or "splitting atoms." This was the kind of bomb used at Hiroshima. These bombs produce their damaging effects both through their powerful explosive force (a "nuclear explosion" or "nuclear detonation") and also through the effects of the radioactive particles they produce, which linger in the environment and can produce both short-term and long-term illness. These lingering radioactive particles are called "fallout." In addition, the tremendous heat produced by a nuclear bomb often causes enormous fires in the area surrounding the blast. These are sometimes called "firestorms."

A "dirty bomb" (also called an "RDD" or "radiological dispersion device") is a conventional explosive, like dynamite, that is packed with some kind of radioactive material. When the bomb explodes, it scatters some of that material and contaminates the area affected by the explosion and the areas downwind. But the explosion and the radioactive contamination from a dirty bomb are much smaller than those produced by a nuclear bomb.

Potassium Iodide (KI)

Certain kinds of nuclear explosions or dirty bombs could release radioactive iodine. That radioactive iodine can be absorbed by your thyroid gland, an important gland in your neck that helps to regulate your metabolism. This increases the risk of thyroid cancer and other problems. The younger you are, the more at risk for thyroid cancer you would be if exposed to radioactive iodine.

Potassium iodide, also known by its chemical initials KI (pronounced "kay-eye"), protects the thyroid gland by filling it up with nonradioactive iodine. Then, if you are exposed to radioactive iodine, your thyroid gland is "full" and won't absorb the radioactive iodine.

The appropriate dosage of KI should be in your go-bag or in your shelter-in-place room.

WHEN TO TAKE KI

In the event of an emergency, it will be important to get more information from authorities by radio or other means. Public officials may advise you to take your KI, so keep it on hand, but only take it if instructed to do so.

PROBLEMS WITH KI

- It only protects the thyroid gland, not the rest of the body.
- It only works against radioactive iodine, so if there are other kinds of radioactive particles in the environment, KI won't help.

Who Should Take KI (If Directed by Authorities)?

- Infants, children, and adults under the age of forty.
- Pregnant and breast-feeding women.

Who Should *Not* Take KI?

- Adults who are forty or older.
- People who have ever had thyroid disease (including hyperthyroidism, thyroid nodules, or goiter).
- People who are allergic to iodine (people who are allergic to shellfish may also be affected).
- People who have certain skin problems (including dermatitis herpetiformis or urticaria vasculitis).

What Is the Correct Dose of KI?

- Adults (and any children who weigh more than 150 lbs (68 kg) should take one 130-mg tablet.
- Children between three and eighteen years of age should take one-half of a 130-mg tablet (65 mg).
- Children between one month and three years of age should take one-fourth of a 130-mg tablet (32 mg).
- Infants from birth to one month should be given one-eighth of a 130-mg tablet (16 mg).
- If a woman is breast-feeding, she should take her dose and then give the appropriate dose to the infant.

Where Can I Find More Information About KI?

The FDA recommendations for KI can be found at their Web site: http://www.fda.gov/cder/guidance/4825fnl.htm.

Other Drugs for Radiation Emergencies

There are other drugs that can be of use in a nuclear/radiation emergency, including diethylenetriaminepentaacetate (DTPA), Neupogen, and Prussian blue. All of these must be taken under the supervision of a doctor. In the case of DTPA and Prussian blue, they must be taken under the guidance of the Radiation Emergency Assistance Center/Training Site (REAC/TS) of the Oak Ridge Institute. **Note:** Prussian blue medication is *not* the same thing as the Prussian blue dye used by artists.

More information about these and other medications for radiation exposure can be found at the REAC/TS Web site: http://www.orau.gov/reacts/resources.htm

More Information

- Ready.gov: http://www.ready.gov/radiation.html.
- CDC radiation page: http://www.bt.cdc.gov/radiation/index.asp.

CHEMICAL EVENT

General Information

The most likely terrorist use of harmful chemicals would involve releasing them into the air. The chemicals would cause harm through contact with the skin or eyes or by being breathed into the lungs. In the event of a release of harmful chemicals into the air, you should protect your skin, eyes, and mouth.

Symptoms of a Chemical Event

In a release of toxic chemicals, certain symptoms are likely to develop quickly:

- Small pupils (the pupil is the dark circle in the center of your eye)
- Cough, shortness of breath, or cessation of breathing
- Sweating, hypersalivating/drooling
- Nausea and vomiting
- Seizures, blackout
- Skin redness and/or blisters

These symptoms should be considered extremely suspicious if they would develop in a number of people at the same time.

Types of Chemical Agents

There are many different types of harmful chemical "agents" of potential terrorist use. All of these chemicals can kill or produce long-term damage. They include many common industrial chemicals, chemical weapons developed for military use, and others. The main categories of chemical agents are:

- **Nerve agents:** These are "organophosphate" chemicals that include the military nerve agents VX or sarin, among others. They can cause seizures and death, in addition to the symptoms listed above. Industrial pesticides, which are chemically similar, can produce the same symptoms in a sufficiently high dose.
- **Blood agents:** These "chemical asphyxiates" prevent your blood from properly carrying oxygen from the lungs to the body, and so lead to death by asphyxiation (suffocation). This category includes hydrogen cyanide and hydrogen sulfide.

- **Choking agents:** Also known as "respiratory irritants," these chemicals include chlorine gas and anhydrous ammonia, and cause severe coughing, shortness of breath, and gagging.
- **Blister agents:** Also known as "vesicants" (vesicle means blister), these agents, including mustard gas, produce severe blistering on all body surfaces, leading to burning, pain, eye irritation, and trouble breathing.

What to Do in a Chemical Event

Chemical agents would most likely be released as a liquid or vapor into the air. Your response to a chemical exposure would depend on the symptoms. **Note:** In many cases treatment for chemical exposure requires specialized medicines or supplies only found in a hospital or other health-care facility. If you think you have been exposed and are experiencing severe symptoms, get to a hospital as soon as possible.

If you learn that chemical agents been put into the air, whether by aerial spraying or by introducing it into your building's ventilation system, you must minimize your contact with the contaminated air.

If you learn that chemical agents have been introduced into the food or water system, you must minimize the possibility of ingesting contaminated food or water.

CHEMICAL AGENTS IN THE OUTSIDE AIR

If you learn that chemical agents have been spread in the outside air (for example, by spraying from a plane):

1. Cover your nose, mouth, and eyes if possible and quickly get inside, away from possibly contaminated air.
2. In most circumstances, you should shelter-in-place in a safe room. It is much better to have a shelter-in-place room chosen and stocked *before* there is a problem.
3. Use plastic sheeting and duct tape to seal any doors and windows or

cloth/paper stuffed under doors to prevent chemicals in the air from entering. Turn off any air-conditioning or ventilation systems.

4. If you think you have been exposed to chemicals in the air, remove your clothing, wash thoroughly with soap and water if possible, and put on new clothing.

   If you do not have soap and water use the "brush and blot" method:

   - Brush off any visible droplets of chemical using a blunt object (a credit card works well). Do *not* use your bare hands. Be careful not to break or scratch your skin.
   - Blot up remaining liquid with absorbent materials like flour, dirt, or soap powder.

5. If you travel, try to protect your breathing, eyes, and skin: wear a mask or piece of cloth over your mouth and nose. Wear eye protection if available. Leave as little skin exposed as possible.

6. Get more information from radio, television, or other sources.

7. Do not take antibiotics: antibiotics do not work against chemical agents! If you are experiencing difficulty breathing, eye irritation, or sudden blistering or skin irritation, contact a doctor immediately.

CHEMICAL AGENTS IN THE AIR INSIDE A BUILDING

If you believe that chemical agents have been spread in the air inside your building (for example, in the ventilation system):

1. Cover your nose, mouth, and eyes if possible, and quickly go outside, away from possibly contaminated air.

2. If you think you have been exposed to chemical agents in the air, remove your clothing, wash thoroughly with soap and water if possible, and put on new clothing. If you do not have soap and water, use the "brush and blot" method:

   - Brush off any visible droplets of chemical using a blunt object (a credit card works well). Do *not* use your bare hands. Be careful not to break or scratch the skin.

- Blot up remaining liquid with absorbent materials like flour, dirt, or soap powder.

3. Get more information from radio, television, or other sources.
4. Do not take antibiotics: antibiotics do not work against chemical agents! If you are experiencing difficulty breathing, eye irritation, or sudden blistering or skin irritation, contact a doctor immediately.

More Information

CDC's chemical agent page: http://www.bt.cdc.gov/agent/agentlistchem.asp.

BIOLOGICAL EVENT

General Information

There are numerous biological "agents" that might be used for a bioterrorism attack. These include:

- **Bacteria:** Living organisms that can multiply within a human being, causing disease, or outside the body (for example, in food or water). Examples of bacteria that might be used for bioterrorism include anthrax *(Bacillus anthracis)* and plague *(Yersinia pestis).*
- **Viruses:** Organisms that can only reproduce by "hijacking" the mechanisms inside human cells. Examples of viruses that might be used for bioterrorism include smallpox *(variola major)* and Ebola virus (Filoviridae/Ebola).
- **Toxins:** Chemical substances produced by living organisms that can cause disease in humans. An example of a dangerous biological toxin is botulinum toxin, which causes botulism (and is produced by *clostridium botulinum* bacteria).

Class-A Agents

CDC divided potential biological weapons into several classes. The Class-A agents, which are thought to pose the greatest threat, are:

AGENT	DISEASE
Smallpox virus *(variola major)*	Smallpox
Anthrax bacteria *(Bacillus anthracis)*	Anthrax
Plague bacteria *(Yersinia pestis)*	Plague
Botulinum toxin (produce by *Clostridium botulinum* bacteria)	Botulism
Francisella bacteria *(Francisella tularensis)*	Tularemia
Filoviruses and arenaviruses (including Ebola and Marburg viruses)	Viral hemorrhagic fevers

Smallpox

BACKGROUND

Smallpox is estimated to have caused 300 million deaths in the twentieth century alone, far more than any wars. It killed roughly one-third of those who were infected, and the survivors often were left with terrible scarring or blindness.

The last case in the United States was in 1949. The smallpox eradication program, lasting from roughly 1960 to 1979 eliminated naturally occurring smallpox, and the last natural case was in Somalia in 1977.

Since then, the only known cases were caused by a laboratory accident in 1978 in Birmingham, England, which killed one person and caused a limited outbreak. Smallpox was officially declared eradicated in 1979.

The United States stopped vaccinating the general population in 1972 and the military in 1990.

Though the smallpox virus no longer exists in nature, at least two countries are known to have stores of the virus (the United States and Russia),

STAGE (duration)		CHARACTERISTICS
Incubation (1–2 weeks)	Symptoms: Contagious:	None No
Prodrome (2–4 days)	Symptoms: Contagious:	Fever over 101° aches, vomiting Sometimes
Early rash (4 days)	Symptoms: Contagious:	mouth sores, then body rash, fever on and off VERY
Pustules (pus-filled sores) (5 days)	Symptoms: Contagious:	Hard, "BB"-like sores on body Yes
Scabs (10 days)	Symptoms: Contagious:	Crusting of rash, then scabs Yes
Resolution	Symptoms: Contagious:	Scabs all gone No

while numerous others are strongly suspected of having them (North Korea, for example). This means that there is a real possibility that groups hostile to the United States could obtain smallpox virus.

DISEASE

If a person is infected with smallpox, they typically go through the series of stages (described in box above), after which they will either recover or die. Our best information shows that about one-third of infected people will die.

Photos of the stages of smallpox can be found at: http://www.idph .state.il.us/Bioterrorism/smallpoxposter.htm.

How Good Is Our Information About Smallpox?

It's important to remember that all of our information about smallpox is quite old (since it doesn't occur naturally anymore), and often inexact. In addition, our population has changed and now includes many more people with impaired immune systems: HIV/AIDS patients, transplant patients, cancer patients, and others. No one is sure how this might affect a smallpox outbreak in the United States today.

PREVENTION: VACCINATION

People have been protecting themselves against smallpox for thousands of years, long before they understood about viruses. In the late 1700s, Edward Jenner noticed that people who got cowpox, an illness related to smallpox but much less lethal, were immune to smallpox. He began the process of vaccinating or exposing people to cowpox to prevent smallpox.

In the twentieth-century eradication program, and today, we use a vaccine developed from the cowpox, or vaccinia, virus to make us immune to smallpox (caused by variola virus).

Important Points About Vaccination

- Smallpox vaccine does *not* contain smallpox virus.
- You *cannot* get smallpox from the vaccine.
- Your risk of dying from smallpox vaccination is roughly one in one million.

The United States now has sufficient smallpox vaccine and special needles to vaccinate the entire population of the country.

Because there are almost three hundred million people in the United States, it is expected that several hundred people may die if the entire population is vaccinated.

Because of this, there are currently no plans to vaccinate the entire population *unless* there was an actual smallpox attack, and most people cannot get vaccinated at present, even if they agree to accept the risks.

TREATMENT

There is no "cure" or specific treatment for smallpox. The best treatment for smallpox is prevention—getting vaccinated before you get infected.

There are a number of experimental drugs, including Cidofovir, that might be used to treat patients in a smallpox attack. These drugs are only available in limited supply right now.

What to Do in a Smallpox Attack

Smallpox is contagious: it spreads from person-to-person by contact with respiratory secretions of an infected person or small droplets of body fluid breathed or coughed into the air by the sick person.

IMPORTANT: In *any* smallpox epidemic, to minimize your chance of getting the disease, you must minimize your contact with other people. If you learn that smallpox has been put into the air, whether by aerial spraying, or by introducing it into your building's ventilation system, you must minimize your contact with smallpox-infected air.

Smallpox in the Outside Air

If you learn that smallpox has been spread in the outside air (for example, by spraying from a plane):

1. Cover your nose, mouth, and eyes if possible and quickly get inside, away from possibly contaminated air.
2. In most circumstances you should get inside and shelter-in-place in a safe room. It is much better to have a shelter-in-place room chosen and stocked *before* there is a problem.
3. Use plastic sheeting and duct tape to seal any doors and windows or cloth/paper stuffed under doors to prevent smallpox germs in the air from entering. Turn off any air-conditioning or ventilation systems.
4. If you think you have been exposed to smallpox in the air, remove your clothing, wash thoroughly with soap and water if possible, and put on fresh clothing.
5. If you must travel or expose yourself to others during an aerial smallpox attack, wear a mask or piece of cloth over your mouth and nose. Wearing gloves and eye protection may also be a good idea.
6. Get more information from the radio, television, or other sources.
7. Do not take antibiotics: antibiotics do not work against

smallpox! If you are experiencing high fever (more than 102°), rash, or sudden fatigue contact a doctor immediately.

Smallpox in the Air Inside a Building
If you learn that smallpox has been spread in the air inside your building (for example, in the ventilation system):

1. Cover your nose, mouth, and eyes if possible and quickly go outside, away from possibly contaminated air.
2. If you think you have been exposed to smallpox in the air, remove your clothing, wash thoroughly with soap and water if possible, and put on new clothing.
3. Get more information from radio, television, or other sources.
4. Do not take antibiotics: antibiotics do not work against smallpox! If you are experiencing high fever (more than 102°), rash, or sudden fatigue, contact a doctor immediately.

MORE INFORMATION
- CDC's smallpox page:
  http://www.bt.cdc.gov/agent/smallpox/.
- *MedlinePlus Medical Encyclopedia:*
  http://www.nlm.nih.gov/medlineplus/ency/article/
  001356.htm.

Anthrax

BACKGROUND
Anthrax (Bacillus anthracis) was the first germ ever determined to cause disease, and in 1881 the first vaccine ever made was created to prevent anthrax.

Anthrax is still a common disease in poorer countries and the germ is still present even in many wealthier countries, including the United States. Natural infections are usually the result of handling animals or animal products.

Anthrax is a kind of bacteria and can be found in "spore" form. A spore is something like a seed: a very hardy, dehydration-resistant form of the organism that lasts a very long time. When the spore comes into contact with moisture it can then invade body tissues. The spore form of anthrax is the one that was used in the biological weapons programs of the United States and the USSR, and in the anthrax letter attacks in 2001.

From 1945 to 1994, 235 cases of anthrax were reported in the United States, including 235 cases of "cutaneous" anthrax (anthrax acquired through the skin) and 11 of "inhalational" anthrax (anthrax acquired through breathing in spores).

DISEASE
Anthrax can cause three types of diseases:

1. **Inhalational:** disease centered in the lungs.
2. **Cutaneous:** disease on the skin.
3. **Gastrointestinal:** disease in the digestive tract.

The most likely kinds of anthrax from a terrorist attack are inhalational and cutaneous.

Inhalational Anthrax
Inhalational anthrax is the most deadly form. All of the 5 deaths in the 2001 anthrax letter attacks were from inhalational anthrax from breathing in the spores.

When anthrax spores are breathed in, they lodge in the lungs and germinate. The affected person can feel fine, sometimes for nearly a week, before symptoms occur.

Anthrax symptoms can include:

- cough
- fatigue
- fever over 102°

Once the person begins to show these symptoms, the disease can progress very rapidly if untreated.

Cutaneous Anthrax

Anthrax skin infections usually produce a blackened ulcer on the skin. If treated with antibiotics, death or long-term effects are very unusual. Even if antibiotics are not given, about 80 percent will recover without complications.

VACCINATION

There is an anthrax vaccine that is used to vaccinate people at high risk of occupational exposure to anthrax (for example, veterinarians) and also military personnel. The anthrax vaccine is not available to the general public.

TREATMENT

Treatment for anthrax consists of antibiotics as soon as possible. With inhalational anthrax, if antibiotics are *not* given the death rate is very high. The antibiotics that usually work against anthrax include:

- penicillin
- doxycycline
- ciprofloxacin

WHAT TO DO IN AN ANTHRAX ATTACK

Anthrax is not contagious: it does not spread from person-to-person under most circumstances. To reduce your risk of anthrax you should minimize your contact with anthrax spores. How to do this depends on how the anthrax has been delivered in an attack.

If you learn that anthrax has been put into the air, whether by aerial spraying, or by introducing it into your building's ventilation system, you must minimize your contact with anthrax-infected air.

If you believe that a piece of mail may contain anthrax, you must minimize your contact with that piece of mail.

Anthrax in the Mail

In 2001 anthrax spores were sent to some prominent people by mail. Some people handling those letters got cutaneous anthrax and others breathed in the spores and got inhalational anthrax.

If you receive a letter or package that seems suspicious, do not open it! Whether you have opened it or not:

1. Put the letter or package into a plastic bag or other container and seal it as best you can. Keep this for the police.
2. Don't try to clean up any powder or liquid from the letter or package.
3. Leave that room and keep anyone from entering the room if possible. If others were with you in the room, write down their contact information.
4. Wash your hands thoroughly with soap and water. Then wash them again!
5. Call the police to tell them what happened.
6. Remove all your clothing and put it into a plastic bag or other container and seal it as best you can. Keep this for the police.
7. Shower thoroughly with soap and water as soon as possible. Do not use bleach or disinfectants on your skin.
8. Wait for the police.
9. Do not start taking antibiotics unless instructed by a doctor. If you are experiencing high fever (more than 102°), cough, or sudden fatigue, contact a doctor immediately.

Anthrax in the Outside Air

If you learn that anthrax has been spread in the outside air (for example, by spraying from a plane):

1. Cover your nose, mouth, and eyes if possible and quickly get inside, away from possibly contaminated air.
2. In most circumstances, you should shelter-in-place in a safe room.
3. Use plastic sheeting and duct tape to seal any doors and windows or cloth/paper stuffed under doors to prevent anthrax spores in the air from entering. Turn off any air-conditioning or ventilation systems.

4. If you think you have been exposed to anthrax in the air, remove your clothing, wash thoroughly with soap and water if possible, and put on fresh clothing.

5. If you must travel or expose yourself to others during an anthrax attack, wear a mask or piece of cloth over your mouth and nose. Wearing gloves and eye protection may also be a good idea.

6. Get more information from the radio, television, or other source.

7. Do not start taking antibiotics unless instructed by a doctor. If you are experiencing high fever (more than 102°), cough, or sudden fatigue, contact a doctor immediately.

Anthrax in the Air Inside a Building

If you learn that anthrax has been spread in the air inside your building (for example, in the ventilation system):

1. Cover your nose, mouth, and eyes if possible and quickly go outside, away from possibly contaminated air.

2. If you think you have been exposed to anthrax in the air, remove your clothing, wash thoroughly with soap and water if possible, and put on fresh clothing.

3. Get more information from the radio, television, or other sources.

4. Do not start taking antibiotics unless instructed by a doctor. If you are experiencing high fever (more than 102°), cough, or sudden fatigue, contact a doctor immediately.

MORE INFORMATION

- CDC's anthrax page: http//www.bt.cdc.gov/agent/anthrax/.
- *MedlinePlus Medical Encyclopedia:* http://www.nlm.nih.gov/medlineplus/ency/article/001325.htm

Plague

BACKGROUND

The plague bacteria (*Yersinia pestis*) has caused human disease for centuries. It is estimated to have killed about one-third of the European population in the Middle Ages, and an even larger portion of the Asian population. In nature the fleas on various animals, including rats, carry plague, but the bacteria could also be spread by aerial spraying. It is not unusual for people in the Southwest United States to get infected with plague from the bite of an infected flea.

DISEASE

There are two main types of plague disease:

1. **Bubonic:** The kind you get if bitten by an infected flea.
2. **Pneumonic:** The kind you get if you breathe in plague bacteria.

Pneumonic plague is the most likely to be used in a terrorist attack, possibly by spreading plague bacteria from a plane. Symptoms of pneumonic plague usually appear one to four days after exposure to the bacteria and can include:

- Severe cough
- Frothy, bloody sputum (phlegm)
- Difficulty breathing
- High fever, chills, headache

PREVENTION

There is a vaccine against plague, but it is currently only recommended for use for those people with a high risk of being exposed to plague through their jobs (for example, laboratory workers doing experiments with the plague bacteria).

Besides the vaccine, the only way to prevent plague is to avoid contact with infected fleas or infected people.

TREATMENT

If plague is treated with antibiotics, death or long-term effects are very un-usual. If antibiotics are not given, however, 95 percent of plague victims will die. Antibiotics that usually work against plague include:

- streptomycin
- tetracycline (not usually used in children because it can discolor the teeth)
- chloramphenicol

WHAT TO DO IN A PLAGUE ATTACK

Pneumonic plague is contagious: it can spread from person-to-person by contact with respiratory secretions of an infected person or small droplets of body fluid breathed or coughed into the air by the sick person.

IMPORTANT: In *any* plague epidemic, to minimize your chance of getting the disease, you must minimize your contact with other people. If you learn that plague has been put into the air, whether by aerial spraying or by introducing it into your building's ventilation system, you must min-imize your contact with plague-infected air.

Plague in the Outside Air

If you learn that plague has been spread in the outside air (for example, by spraying from a plane):

1. Cover your nose, mouth, and eyes if possible and quickly get in-side, away from possibly contaminated air.
2. In most circumstances you should get inside and shelter-in-place in a safe room.
3. Use plastic sheeting and duct tape to seal any doors and windows or cloth/paper stuffed under doors to prevent plague germs in the air from entering. Turn off any air-conditioning or ventila-tion systems.
4. If you think you have been exposed to plague in the air, remove your clothing, wash thoroughly with soap and water if possible, and put on fresh clothing.

5. If you must travel or expose yourself to others during an aerial plague attack, wear a mask or piece of cloth over your mouth and nose. Wearing gloves and eye protection may also be a good idea.
6. Get more information from the radio, television, or other sources.
7. Do not start taking antibiotics unless instructed by a doctor. If you are experiencing cough (especially if you are coughing up bloody or frothy sputum) or have difficulty breathing, contact a doctor immediately.

Plague in the Air Inside a Building
If you learn that plague has been spread in the air inside your building (for example, in the ventilation system):

1. Cover your nose, mouth, and eyes if possible and quickly go outside, away from possibly contaminated air.
2. If you think you have been exposed to plague in the air, remove your clothing, wash thoroughly with soap and water if possible, and put on fresh clothing.
3. Get more information from the radio, television, or other sources.
4. Do not start taking antibiotics unless instructed by a doctor. If you are experiencing cough (especially if you are coughing up bloody or frothy sputum) or have difficulty breathing, contact a doctor immediately.

MORE INFORMATION
- CDC's plague page:
  http://www.bt.cdc.gov/agent/plague/.
- *MedlinePlus Medical Encyclopedia:*
  http://www.nlm.nih.gov/medlineplus/ency/article/000596.htm.

Botulism

BACKGROUND
The disease called botulism is caused by exposure to a "toxin" or toxic chemical produced by the *Clostridium botulinum* bacteria. The toxin, called

"botulinum toxin" or Botox, prevents muscles from working (including the diaphragm muscle that powers the lungs).

Like anthrax, the *Clostridium* bacteria are able to produce hardy spores that last a long time in dry environments and then "germinate" once conditions are moister. In natural botulism, the disease occurs when the bacteria or spores are eaten or when they contaminate a wound. When used as a biological weapon, the toxin can be sprayed in the air or possibly added to the food supply. Botulinum toxin was part of the biological weapons programs of the United States and the USSR. The Aum Shinrikyo cult tried unsuccessfully to use it against the Japanese civilian population.

Botulinum toxin is also used cosmetically to paralyze wrinkle-producing muscles in the face or by neurologists to treat certain neurological diseases.

DISEASE

Symptoms of botulism usually appear twelve to thirty-six hours after exposure to the toxin. Symptoms can include:

- double vision
- difficulty swallowing
- difficulty breathing

Symptoms do *not* usually include fever, and the ability to think clearly is not usually affected.

PREVENTION

There are several experimental vaccines for botulism, but none are widely available.

TREATMENT

Treatment for botulism can include the use of an antitoxin that can block the effect of the botulinum toxin (antitoxin *cannot* reverse any paralysis that has already occurred, however). If breathing is affected a "respirator" (breathing machine) is also necessary until the affected people can breathe for themselves again. Recovery can take weeks or months.

If a large population were exposed to botulinum toxin, it would be difficult to obtain enough respirators, and technicians trained in their use, to support that population.

WHAT TO DO IN A BOTULINUM TOXIN ATTACK

Botulism is not contagious: it does not spread from person-to-person. To reduce your risk of botulism you should minimize your contact with botulinum toxin. How to do this depends on how the toxin has been delivered in an attack.

If you learn that botulinum toxin has been put into the air, whether by aerial spraying or by introducing it into your building's ventilation system, you must minimize your contact with botulinum toxin in the air.

If you learn that botulinum toxin has been introduced into the food or water system, you must minimize the possibility of ingesting same.

Botulinum Toxin in the Outside Air

If you learn that botulinum toxin has been spread in the outside air (for example, by spraying from a plane):

1. Cover your nose, mouth, and eyes if possible and quickly get inside, away from possibly contaminated air.
2. In most circumstances, you should shelter-in-place in a safe room.
3. Use plastic sheeting and duct tape to seal any doors and windows or cloth/paper stuffed under doors to prevent botulinum toxin in the air from entering. Turn off any air-conditioning or ventilation systems.
4. If you think you have been exposed to botulinum toxin in the air, remove your clothing, wash thoroughly with soap and water if possible, and put on fresh clothing.
5. If you must travel, or expose yourself to others during a botulinum toxin attack, wear eye protection and a mask or piece of cloth over your mouth and nose. If you have any open cuts or other wounds, you must cover them completely.

6. Get more information from the radio, television, or other sources.

7. Do not take antibiotics: antibiotics do not work against botulism! If you are experiencing double vision, difficulty swallowing, or difficulty breathing, contact a doctor immediately.

Botulinum Toxin in the Air Inside a Building

If you believe that botulinum toxin has been spread in the air inside your building (for example, in the ventilation system):

1. Cover your nose, mouth, and eyes if possible and quickly go outside, away from possibly contaminated air.

2. If you think you have been exposed to botulinum toxin in the air, remove your clothing, wash thoroughly with soap and water if possible, and put on fresh clothing.

3. Get more information from the radio, television, or other sources.

4. Do not take antibiotics: antibiotics do not work against botulism! If you are experiencing double vision, difficulty swallowing, or difficulty breathing, contact a doctor immediately.

Botulinum Toxin Attack by Food or Water

Bioterrorism experts believe that a botulinum toxin attack by contaminating the water supply is unlikely, both because normal water treatment inactivates the toxin and because a very large amount of toxin would be needed.

If you learn that botulinum toxin has been put into foods:

1. Eat only sealed foods if possible.

2. If you have to eat unsealed foods, be sure to properly cook any unsealed food, as heat will inactivate the toxin.

3. Get more information from the radio, television, or other sources.

4. Do not take antibiotics: antibiotics do not work against botulism! If you are experiencing double vision, difficulty swallowing, or difficulty breathing, contact a doctor immediately.

More information

- CDC's botulism page:
  http://www.bt.cdc.gov/agent/botulism/.
- *MedlinePlus Medical Encyclopedia:*
  http://www.nlm.nih.gov/medlineplus/botulism.html.

Tularemia

Background

Tularemia, or "rabbit fever," is caused by *Francisella tularensis* bacteria, which are very common in squirrels and other animals in North America. People can be infected if bitten by those animals or if bitten by ticks from those animals. Ingesting contaminated food or water can also cause infection.

Tularemia was developed for use as a biological weapon, with the idea that it would be spread in the air.

Disease

Symptoms of tularemia usually appear three to five days after exposure to the bacteria. Symptoms usually include:

- A red spot on the skin that gradually becomes an open sore
- Enlarged lymph nodes ("glands") in the groin or armpits
- Headache, muscle pains, joint stiffness
- Shortness of breath
- Red, swollen eyes
- Fever, chills, sweating

Prevention

There is an experimental vaccine against tularemia, but it is very limited in supply.

Treatment

If tularemia is treated with antibiotics, death or long-term effects are very unusual. Even if antibiotics are not given, 95 percent of tularemia victims will survive. Antibiotics that usually work against tularemia include:

- streptomycin
- tetracycline (not usually used in children because it can discolor the teeth).

What to Do in a Tularemia Attack

Tularemia is not contagious: it does not spread from person-to-person under most circumstances. To reduce your risk of tularemia, you should minimize your contact with the bacteria. In a bioterrorist attack, the bacteria are most likely to be spread in the air.

If you learn that tularemia has been put into the air, whether by aerial spraying or by introducing it into your building's ventilation system, you must minimize your contact with tularemia-containing air.

Tularemia in the Outside Air

If you learn that tularemia has been spread in the outside air (for example, by spraying from a plane):

1. Cover your nose, mouth, and eyes if possible and quickly get inside, away from possibly contaminated air.
2. In most circumstances you should get inside and shelter-in-place in a safe room.
3. Use plastic sheeting and duct tape to seal any doors and windows or cloth/paper stuffed under doors to prevent tularemia germs in the air from entering. Turn off any air-conditioning or ventilation systems.
4. If you think you have been exposed to tularemia in the air, remove your clothing, wash thoroughly with soap and water if possible, and put on fresh clothing.
5. If you must travel or expose yourself to others during an aerial tularemia attack, wear a mask or piece of cloth over your mouth and nose. Wearing gloves and eye protection may also be a good idea.
6. Get more information from the radio, television, or other sources.
7. Do not start taking antibiotics unless instructed by a doctor. If you are experiencing high fever (more than 102°), new sores on

the skin, or other symptoms listed above, contact a doctor immediately.

Tularemia in the Air Inside a Building

If you believe that tularemia has been spread in the air inside your building (for example, in the ventilation system):

1. Cover your nose, mouth, and eyes if possible and quickly go outside, away from possibly contaminated air.
2. If you think you have been exposed to tularemia in the air, remove your clothing, wash thoroughly with soap and water if possible, and put on fresh clothing.
3. Get more information from the radio, television, or other sources.
4. Do not start taking antibiotics unless instructed by a doctor. If you are experiencing high fever (more than 102°), new sores on the skin, or other symptoms listed above, contact a doctor immediately.

MORE INFORMATION
- CDC's tularemia page:
  http://www.bt.cdc.gov/agent/tularemia/.
- *MedlinePlus Medical Encyclopedia:*
  http://www.nlm.nih.gov/medlineplus/ency/article/000856.htm.

Viral Hemorrhagic Fevers (VHFs)

BACKGROUND

There are many different kinds of viral hemorrhagic fever (VHF), with Ebola being the best-known due to well-publicized outbreaks in Africa. The VHFs are very, very easy to spread from person to person and very lethal. Luckily, while this makes them especially frightening, it also makes them difficult to develop and use as weapons. Other VHFs include Marburg, Lassa fever, and Rift Valley fever. West Nile virus is *not* one of the VHFs.

DISEASE

Different kinds of VHF can have different symptoms, but the most common symptoms include:

- high fever
- fatigue and dizziness
- muscle aches and loss of strength
- bleeding from the mouth, eyes, and ears

VACCINATION

Vaccines have been developed for only two of the VHFs: yellow fever and Argentine hemorrhagic fever.

TREATMENT

There are no antibiotics or other specific treatments for most VHFs.

WHAT TO DO IN A VHF ATTACK

VHFs are contagious: they spread from person-to-person by close contact with infected people, particularly with respiratory secretions: small droplets of bodily fluid breathed or coughed into the air by the sick person.

IMPORTANT: In *any* VHF epidemic, to minimize your chance of getting the disease, you must minimize your contact with other people.

If you learn that VHF have been put into the air, whether by aerial spraying or by introducing it into your building's ventilation system, you must minimize your contact with the contaminated.

VHF *in the Outside Air*

If you learn that VHF have been spread in the outside air (for example, by spraying from a plane):

1. Cover your nose, mouth, and eyes if possible and quickly get inside, away from possibly contaminated air.
2. In most circumstances, you should shelter-in-place.
3. Use plastic sheeting and duct tape to seal any doors and windows or cloth/paper stuffed under doors to prevent virus in the

air from entering. Turn off any air-conditioning or ventilation systems.

4. If you think you have been exposed to VHF in the air, remove your clothing, wash thoroughly with soap and water if possible, and put on fresh clothing.

5. If you must travel, or expose yourself to others during a VHF epidemic, wear eye protection and a mask or piece of cloth over your mouth and nose. Gloves are also a good idea. Avoid close contact with others.

6. Get more Information from the radio, television, or other sources.

7. Do *not* take antibiotics: antibiotics do not work against VHF! If you are experiencing high fever (more than 102°), bleeding from the mouth, nose, or ears, or other symptoms noted above, contact a doctor immediately.

VHF in the Air Inside a Building

If you learn that VHF has been spread in the air inside your building (for example, in the ventilation system):

1. Cover your nose, mouth, and eyes if possible and quickly go outside, away from possibly contaminated air.

2. If you think you has been exposed to VHF in the air, remove your clothing, wash thoroughly with soap and water if possible, and put on fresh clothing.

3. Get more information from the radio, television, or other sources.

4. Do *not* take antibiotics: antibiotics do not work against VHF! If you are experiencing high fever (more than 102°), bleeding from the mouth, nose, or ears, or other symptoms noted above, contact a doctor immediately.

MORE INFORMATION

- CDC's VHF page:
  http://www.bt.cdc.gov/agent/vhf/
- *MedlinePlus Medical Encyclopedia:*
  http://www.nlm.nih.gov/medlineplus/ency/article/001339.htm.

Glossary and Abbreviations

CDC. The U.S. Centers for Disease Control and Prevention in Atlanta. www.cdc.gov

CONVENTIONAL. Usually used to contrast commonly used explosives from nuclear, chemical, or biological weapons.

DHS. The Department of Homeland Security. www.dhs.gov.

DIRTY BOMB. A conventional explosive device wrapped in radioactive material. Not the same as a nuclear bomb.

FEMA. The Federal Emergency Management Agency, now part of DHS. www.fema.gov

HHS. The Department of Health and Human Services, the parent department of CDC. www.hhs.gov.

GO-BAG. A backpack or other bag holding essential items for your evacuation plan.

KI. Potassium iodide, a medication that prevents some of the effects of certain kinds of radiation.

NUCLEAR BOMB. An explosive device that uses the power released when atoms are split (that is, nuclear fission). Much more powerful than a conventional explosive and produces much more radiation than a "dirty bomb."

REAC/TS. The Radiation Emergency Assistance Center/Training Site (REAC/TS) of the Oak Ridge Institute. REAC/TS specializes in response to radiation emergencies, including the various medications used to treat radiation exposure.

SAFE ROOM. A secure room that is sealed to the outside air to prevent harmful substances in the air from entering.

SCBA. Self-contained breathing apparatus. A device with a mask and air tank to allow breathing in low-oxygen environments (such as intense fire/smoke environment).

References

WEB SITES

CDC's emergency preparedness Web site: http://www.bt.cdc.gov.

DHS emergency preparedness Web site: http://www.ready.gov/.

MedlinePlus Web site: http://medlineplus.gov/.

BOOKS

Barry, Leonard. *Emergency Response to Terrorism: Job Aid.* FEMA, U.S. Fire Administration, National Fire Academy, U.S. Department of Justice, May 2000.

Bevelacqua Armando S. and R. Stilp. *Terrorism Handbook for Operational Responders.* 2002.

Index

About the Authors

G. GORDON LIDDY

Educated privately by Benedictine monks and Jesuit priests, Mr. Liddy earned a B.S. degree from Fordham College and an Ll.D. from Fordham Law School, graduating as a member of *The Fordham Law Review*. After two years of service as an army artillery officer during the Korean War, Mr. Liddy entered the FBI as a special agent and, after multiple commendations from the late J. Edgar Hoover, became, at age twenty-nine, the youngest Bureau supervisor at FBI national headquarters in Washington, D.C., where he served during the Kennedy administration.

After serving as a prosecutor and practicing international law in New York, Mr. Liddy joined the Nixon administration in 1969 as special assistant to the secretary of the treasury; was then appointed Treasury's enforcement legislative counsel, where he authored the Explosives Control Act; then was appointed staff assistant to the president of the United States, where he authored the memorandum that led to the creation of the Drug Enforcement Administration. In 1971 Mr. Liddy was appointed general counsel of the Committee to Re-elect the President and its Finance Committee, with additional duties as director of political intelligence. The rest is history.

Today, Mr. Liddy is one of the most listened to radio broadcasters in the nation, appears frequently on television, has authored four bestsellers as well as numerous magazine articles. After training and jumping with the elite Israeli Defense Force Parachute Regiment several times, Mr. Liddy was awarded IDF parachute wings by the Israeli government. He is a member of the Honor Legion of the New York City Police Department and a thirty-second-degree Scottish Rite Mason.

JAMES G. LIDDY, Commander, U.S. Navy, SEAL (Ret.)

In twenty years of active duty, Commander Liddy conducted five separate six-month deployments as an operational SEAL commando with special operations missions in thirty-seven countries. Most of his duties, responsibilities, and training remain classified.

Commander Liddy holds a B.S. degree from Fordham University, a M.A. degree in International Relations from the Johns Hopkins University School of Advanced International Studies (SAIS), and is a Ph.D. candidate in Complex Emergency and Disaster Management at Tulane University. Prior to his retirement from the navy, he served as the chief advisor for counterterrorism for the assistant secretary of defense for Special Operations and Low Intensity Conflict, and as the chief plans and policy officer for the U.S. Special Operations Command's Washington office. In these positions he planned and coordinated policy, operational plans and information, and strategic initiatives for the secretary of defense, the chairman of the Joint Chiefs of Staff, the military services, and other government agencies in support of the Global War on Terrorism.

Today Commander Liddy is president and CEO of Red Cell Associates Inc., a terrorism preparedness and risk mitigation firm focused on assessments, training, and solutions for securing critical infrastructure against the cascading effects of catastrophic events.

JOEL SELANIKIO, M.D.

Dr. Selanikio is a former senior health advisor within the Office of the Secretary of Health and Human Services. During his tenure he served as director of Emergency Response Coordination for the Office of Public Health Emergency Preparedness and chief of operations for the secretary's Emergency Command Center in the aftermath of the September 11 and anthrax attacks of 2001. The first chairman of the National Smallpox Vaccination Taskforce, Dr. Selanikio is a coauthor of the National Pre-Event Smallpox Vaccination Plan and served as medical director of the navy's Center of Excellence in Disaster Management and Humanitarian Assistance.

Dr. Selanikio is a graduate of the Brown University School of Medicine and maintains clinical competency as a staff physician at the National Medical Center and Georgetown University Hospital.

J. MICHAEL BARRETT

J. Michael Barrett served as a senior analyst for the Global War on Terrorism in the Special Operations Division of the Joint Chiefs of Staff, and as a counterterrorism intelligence officer for the Defense Intelligence Agency's Defense HUMINT Service (DHS), where he helped coordinate multiagency efforts to identify domestic and international terrorist cells. A University of Pennsylvania graduate, Mr. Barrett was selected as a Fulbright Scholar and holds an M.A. degree from the Johns Hopkins School of Advanced International Studies (SAIS), where he was named both the Phillip Merrill and Olin Foundation Fellow in Strategic Studies. His work has appeared in numerous scholarly publications, as well as *The Wall Street Journal* and *The Washington Times*.